HISTORY'S
WORST
CRIMES

HISTORY'S WORST CRIMES

AND THE PEOPLE WHO INVESTIGATED THEM

BILL PRICE

METRO BOOKS

NEW YORK

METRO BOOKS
New York

An Imprint of Sterling Publishing
1166 Avenue of the Americas
New York, NY 10036

METRO BOOKS and the distinctive Metro Books logo
are trademarks of Sterling Publishing Co., Inc.

© 2014 by Quid Publishing

Conceived, designed, and produced by
Quid Publishing
Level 4 Sheridan House
114 Western Road
Hove BN3 1DD
England

www.quidpublishing.com

ISBN: 978-1-4351-5344-8

For information about custom editions, special sales, and premium and corporate purchases, please contact Sterling Special Sales at 800-805-5489 or specialsales@sterlingpublishing.com.

Printed in Hong Kong

1 3 5 7 9 10 8 6 4 2

www.sterlingpublishing.com

To my brother, Jim Price, for keeping me on the straight and narrow.

CONTENTS

"Obviously crime pays, or there'd be no crime."

G. Gordon Liddy

INTRODUCTION

Statistics compiled by governments and crime agencies in many countries around the world over the past few decades show that crime rates have been steadily falling. The reasons for this are not entirely clear and most likely include complex social factors that make determining a single cause difficult. The use of increasingly sophisticated methods of crime prevention and detection will have contributed and it has been suggested that the declining use of tetraethyl lead as an additive to gasoline may have also played a part. At first sight, ascribing the reduction in crime to the fact that there is less lead in the environment may appear to be conflating two separate occurrences simply because of a coincidence in timing, but studies have shown that exposure to lead poisoning, particularly in young children, can cause an increase in dysfunctional and aggressive behavior because lead impairs the decision-making process in the brain.

If, on the other hand, crime rates were to be gauged solely according to the depiction of crime in the media, then the impression gained would be exactly opposite to that given by the statistics. Crime and the perpetrators of crime continue to make headlines in news reports and there has been an explosion of fictional crime in movies, TV shows, and books, from the ever-expanding CSI franchise to the proliferation of "Nordic Noir," as the apparently endless stream of crime novels coming out of Scandinavia is sometimes called. Anybody not familiar with Sweden, for instance, may come to the conclusion that the country is littered with dead bodies, when, in fact, it has the lowest murder rate of any country in Europe and one of the lowest in the world. But crime is an inherently dramatic subject and it sells, as TV executives and the authors of books on the subject, such as this one, are well aware. As long as it is not actually happening directly to us, then crime is a source of almost endless fascination and, even though we may be appalled and sometimes terrified by what criminals are capable of doing, we are also intrigued by those people who are prepared to live outside the constraints of the law and the moral codes of society.

This book aims to examine 50 of the most notorious crimes ever committed, together with the motivations of the criminals involved and the efforts made by the authorities to catch and punish them. The crimes are arranged chronologically to give a historical perspective and each has been chosen from one of eight categories to ensure that the book does not simply become a catalog of those crimes with the highest body count or the ones committed in the most depraved way. So, as well as murder and assassination, we have robbery, fraud, kidnapping, hijacking, and, finally, the related crimes of treason and espionage. All the chapters are concerned with examples of crimes committed by individuals or groups of individuals rather than those perpetrated by governments, armed forces, or terrorist organizations. This means that war crimes, genocide, crimes against humanity, and the atrocities committed in the name of a cause by terrorists, freedom fighters, guerillas, or whatever else they may be called, are not covered; this book is about crimes committed by people against other people for personal reasons rather than ideological ones, mostly for individual gain or gratification, or simply because the criminals involved think that they will get away with it.

One thing to emerge from this book is that crime has been a constant companion throughout our history, going back to the beginnings of civilization and no doubt beyond. The preponderance of examples discussed here that date from the mid-nineteenth century up until today simply reflects the development of mass communication and does not indicate that criminal activity is a particularly modern phenomenon. The book also demonstrates how the public perception of criminals has not changed all that much over the years, ranging as it does from the shock and revulsion felt at the depravity of the crimes committed by a few of the people depicted here, as in the cases of Ed Gein and the Moors Murderers, to the treatment of others as if they were folk heroes despite the nature of what they have done. Ned Kelly in Australia during the 1870s, John Dillinger in 1930s America, and Jacques Mesrine more recently in France were all, among other things, murderers, yet they captured the public imagination to the extent that they appeared to continue their criminal careers as much to play to their audiences as for any other reason, and long after it had become inevitable that they would be caught.

Between the extremes of revulsion and hero worship, the public has demonstrated a whole range of emotions in their reactions to crime: a certain admiration for the audacity and ingenuity shown by some robbers, jewel thieves, and fraudsters; anger when spies have betrayed their country; resignation when wealthy businessmen and bankers are shown to be crooks; grief and despair when public figures such as Mahatma Gandhi and Martin Luther King Jr. have been assassinated. Perhaps this emotional response goes some way to explaining our fascination with crime, together with the appeal of the larger-than-life characters and situations of heightened intensity that are also usually involved. Criminals behave as if they have no regard for the consequences of their actions, either to themselves or to others, and, while the rest of us may not want to emulate them, and certainly don't want to meet them, we do want to know about them in an effort to understand and explain what they have done. The 50 examples covered here cannot hope to cover the whole range of criminal behavior, but by taking infamous examples from across history this book provides a portrait of the world of crime and the criminals who inhabit it.

THE FIRST MURDER: CAIN AND ABEL

In Biblical times

Location: The lands of the Bible

Perpetrators: Cain

Outcome: The first murder, according to the Hebrew Bible

*And Cain talked with his brother: and it came
to pass, when they were in the field, that Cain
rose up against Abel his brother and slew him.*

*And the Lord said unto Cain, Where is Abel
thy brother? And he said, I know not:
Am I my brother's keeper?*

Genesis 4:8–9

Of the 50 crimes covered in this book, all but one are based on the available evidence. The exception comes in this first entry, the murder of Abel by his brother Cain. The only account we have of the crime is given in the Hebrew Bible, which some people accept as being the literal truth. For the others, however, no actual proof exists to show that any such crime really took place or even that the perpetrator and victim were real historical figures. Nevertheless, it is as good a place as any to start a book such as this one because it provides us with a demonstration of the ubiquitous nature of crime in the history of humanity and shows that it has been a central concern for us right from the beginning.

The fact that such a grievous offense as fratricide occurs so close to the start of the Bible can also be seen as a sign of the importance attached in the Jewish and Christian traditions to dealing with the implications of crime. It is an implicit acknowledgment of the potential in us all to commit such a dreadful act. These impulses, it could be argued, have been restrained by the vast majority of us because of our adherence to the moral codes of the societies in which we live. The murder occurs in chapter four of the book of Genesis, following immediately on from God's expulsion of Adam and Eve from the Garden of Eden after they have eaten the forbidden fruit from the Tree of Knowledge. This has been interpreted by theologians of some Christian denominations as being the moment when sin entered into the world, a consequence of Adam and Eve's act, while the punishment of the expulsion signifies humanity's fall from Grace.

THE FIRST CRIME

Cain and Abel were the first and second sons of Adam and Eve, born after the latter were expelled from Eden. The account given in the book of Genesis does not go into any great detail about their lives, other than to describe Cain as being a "tiller of the land" and Abel a "keeper of sheep." Both make offerings to the Lord of some of their produce, but, without any explanation, He favors the first-born lambs offered by Abel over the crops brought to him by Cain, who is angered by the favoritism shown to his younger brother. It is at this point that Cain murders Abel, again recounted in Genesis with little further detail and without giving an exact reason for the killing. Cain denies knowledge of the whereabouts of his brother in response to God's enquiry and, when the Lord discovers what has happened, He curses Cain, saying that the ground will no longer grow crops for him, and exiles him to a life of "wandering on the earth."

God may have cursed Cain, but he did not abandon him completely, providing him with protection from anybody who might try to attack him, putting a mark on him that singles him out "so that no one who came upon him would try to kill him." The nature of this mark, whether some sort of physical manifestation on his body visible to other people or whether another sort of sign by which it would be known that he was under God's protection, is not specified. This is perhaps because God had punished Cain himself so no human being had the right to exact further retribution. Genesis then goes on to say, "And Cain went out from the presence of the Lord, and dwelt in the land of Nod, on the east of Eden." It has been suggested that, rather than being a specific place, Nod refers to Cain living the life of a wanderer. However, Genesis goes on to relate how Cain founded a city that he named Enoch, for his first-born son, so it would appear that he spent at least some of his time living a settled life. The remainder of chapter four contains a list of the descendants of Cain, together with a passage in which Adam and Eve have another son, called Seth.

DIFFERING PERSPECTIVES

The book of Genesis, like much of the rest of the Hebrew Bible, is traditionally said to be the actual word of God as spoken to Moses. More recent research into its origins has concluded that it was compiled around the sixth century BCE from earlier, now lost, sources by various scribes, who brought multiple narratives together to form a continuous text. As with the story of Cain and Abel, much of this text does not provide comprehensive accounts of events, allowing for numerous different interpretations. It could be argued that this was the intention of the authors, reflecting the equivocal nature of life in which much of what we experience does not have a straightforward or easily understood explanation.

One interpretation of the Creation, for instance, suggests that, rather than being an account of how God formed the world from the beginning, it actually deals with the transition of human beings from a hunting and gathering lifestyle to one based on agriculture, a change expressed by the expulsion of Adam and Eve from the Garden of Eden, after which they had to provide for themselves by the sweat of their brows. Research has shown that, before the mechanization of agriculture, the time and effort required to provide sufficient sustenance through hunting and gathering was considerably less than it was by farming, giving hunters and gatherers more leisure time and what we might now think of as an easier life. Hunters and gatherers also tended to live longer and were generally healthier than farmers, being less prone to disease and less likely to suffer from the sorts of injuries caused by long periods of repetitive work. The adoption of farming may have led to an increase in food security, but at the cost of long hours of labor in the fields and a shorter life, leading some religious scholars to suggest that, by expelling Adam and Eve from the Garden of Eden, God was punishing them by forcing them to provide for themselves what had previously been given for free.

THE FIRST MURDER
The Body of Abel Found by Adam and Eve, ca. 1826, a tempera painting by William Blake now in Tate Britain, London.

The story of Cain and Abel has also been seen as a metaphor for the antagonism that has existed between the farmer and the herdsman as they compete with each other for the use of land. An alternative explanation is that of sibling rivalry, in which Cain becomes jealous of his younger brother because Abel's offering to God was accepted while, for no apparent reason, Cain's offering was rejected. The arbitrary nature of God's favoritism of Abel is the most puzzling aspect of the account, perhaps reflecting the possibility that the scribes who compiled the Hebrew Bible came from a background of nomadic pastoralism themselves and were intent on showing that shepherds such as themselves were closer to God than farmers.

If we assume that the motive for the murder was jealousy, leading to anger and then hatred, the meaning of the story becomes much more straightforward. In a world where we can suffer setbacks and injustice for no apparent reason, any of us can let our emotions get the better of our judgment so that we do things we later regret and that can have serious repercussions. The potential for evil, the story suggests, exists within us and, while the vast majority of us do not resort to the sort of murderous act committed by Cain, others are prepared to live beyond the constraints of society. As the following chapters in this book demonstrate, these people can commit crimes that are often as difficult for the rest of us to comprehend as the murder of one brother by another.

MOTIVATION

Murder

Assassination

Treason

Espionage

Robbery

Hijacking

Fraud

Kidnapping

THE ASSASSINATION OF JULIUS CAESAR
March 15, 44 BCE

Location: The Theater of Pompey in Rome

Perpetrators: Cassius, Brutus, and a group of about 60 other Roman senators

Outcome: Civil war and the eventual establishment of the Roman Empire

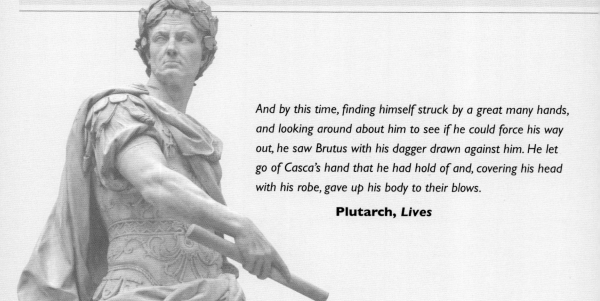

And by this time, finding himself struck by a great many hands, and looking around about him to see if he could force his way out, he saw Brutus with his dagger drawn against him. He let go of Casca's hand that he had hold of and, covering his head with his robe, gave up his body to their blows.

Plutarch, *Lives*

By 44 BCE, the Roman Republic had been in existence for almost 500 years and had expanded the territory it controlled far beyond Rome itself to encompass land around the Mediterranean Sea and in Northern Europe. In the previous few decades Julius Caesar had become the most powerful person in the republic, gaining huge popular support as a consequence of his military exploits in conquering Gaul and invading both Germany and Britain. Toward the end of January, 44 BCE, he had been appointed the Dictator in Perpetuity of Rome, having previously been awarded the position of dictator for an initial period of one year, later extended to ten years. It led to accusations from his political opponents that he intended to take supreme power, ruling as a tyrant and marginalizing the senate, the main governing body of the republic. It is not known for certain if there was any truth to these accusations because on the Ides of March, the 15th day of the month, Caesar was assassinated by a group of senators, stabbed 23 times as he attended a meeting of the senate.

The expansion of the Roman Republic had generated huge wealth, much of which was obtained by members of the aristocratic patrician class who dominated the senate and led the military campaigns of conquest. It led to some patrician families becoming very rich; they used their wealth to buy land, establishing huge estates worked for the most part by slaves. A consequence of this was the concentration of power in the hands of a few wealthy individuals, undermining the senate and the other Roman institutions of government. It also created a large class of landless people who had been displaced from the countryside around Rome and had moved to the city, leading to outbreaks of civil unrest and prompting the city's rulers to commit to providing sufficient food for the growing population.

Caesar's family were patricians, but they had not taken advantage of the opportunity to enrich themselves to the same extent as others. He appears to have judged that he could restore his family's fortunes by entering the political arena and so chose to use his considerable energy and talent as a military leader to become a senior commander in the Roman army. After the conquest of Gaul in 51 BCE, Caesar became the governor of the three Roman provinces to the north of Italia, the region around Rome governed directly by the senate. His military exploits had made him popular with the people of Rome as well as with the commander of four Roman legions and this power base was considered a threat by an influential group of senators

THE RISE

THE IDES OF MARCH
The Death of Caesar by
Jean-Léon Gérôme
(1824–1904), depicting
the assassins celebrating
while Caesar's body lies
prostrate on the ground.

known as the Optimates. One of the most powerful political and military leaders in Rome at the time, Gnaeus Pompeius Magnus, commonly known as Pompey, agreed with the Optimates. Pompey had previously been an ally of Caesar, forming what was known as the First Triumvirate, with him and Marcus Licinius Crassus, but he now viewed Caesar's power as a threat to his own position.

In 50 BCE, at the instigation of Pompey and the Optimates, the senate ordered Caesar to relinquish command of his legions and return to Rome. Had he done so, he would have been left defenseless against his political opponents and would potentially have faced a charge of treason. Rather than comply with the senate's command, in 49 BCE Caesar approached Rome with one of his legions, famously crossing the Rubicon, the river marking the border of Italia and, in doing so, breaking Roman law and initiating a civil war with Pompey. The fighting continued over the course of the next four years, with Caesar decisively defeating Pompey at the Battle of Pharsalus in Greece and then going on to defeat the remaining forces loyal to the Optimates. By that time, March, 45 BCE, Caesar was well established as the most powerful man in Rome, showing magnanimity in pardoning some of his political opponents, including Gaius Cassius Longinus and Marcus Junius Brutus, the two men who would lead the conspiracy against him the following year.

THE FALL

The appointment by the senate of a dictator in Rome was intended as an emergency measure, only undertaken during periods of crisis. After accepting the position of Dictator in Perpetuity, Caesar was accused by his political opponents of ruling the city as if he were king. Some of his actions were also interpreted as being signs of an increasing desire to take sole power for himself, including one occasion when he remained seated to receive a visit from a group of senators and another when his closest ally, Mark Antony, offered him a crown at a public event a month before the assassination, even though he had refused to wear it.

Whether it was his intention or not, the threat of Caesar assuming sole power in Rome prompted Cassius and Brutus to conspire against him. They resolved to act before Caesar left Rome toward the end of March to lead a military campaign against the Parthian Empire to the east. It is thought that as many as 60 senators were involved in the plot, many of whom had personal reasons to strike against Caesar beyond the wish to put an end to his ambitions to become king. Caesar's popularity among the people of Rome remained high, but he had made many enemies over the years in the senate. It would appear that some of the conspirators acted according to personal animosity rather than to principles or political ideals.

On the morning of the Ides of March, Caesar was warned by his wife Calpurnia not to attend the proposed meeting of the senate that day because she had had a premonition in a dream that he would be killed. He is also said to have also been warned by a soothsayer, but, after apparently initially agreeing to send word to the senate that he was unwell and could not attend, he changed his mind. As he was traveling to the meeting at the Theater of Pompey, at least according to Shakespeare's version of the story, he said to the soothsayer, "The Ides of March are come," to which the soothsayer replies, "Ay, Caesar; but not gone." Shakespeare based his account on those of the Roman historians Plutarch and Suetonius, both of whom were writing more than 100 years after the event, so it is impossible to know for certain how accurate their accounts were or if they were embroidering the known details.

As Caesar arrived at the meeting hall, Mark Antony, who is said to have learned some details of the plot the previous evening, was distracted outside the hall by one of the conspirators while a crowd of senators gathered around Caesar to present him with a petition. While Caesar was dealing with the petitioner, one of the senators struck Caesar from behind, stabbing him in the neck, prompting others in the crowd, including Brutus, to join in what must have been a frenzied attack, inflicting wounds on themselves as well as on Caesar. Both Plutarch and Suetonius do not record Caesar saying anything during the attack and those famous last words, "Et tu, Brute?" ("And you, Brutus?") were put into his mouth by Shakespeare.

The assassins dispersed quickly after the attack, leaving the dying Caesar in the hall. An autopsy was later carried out, the first ever recorded, in which it was established that only one of the 23 stab wounds he received was severe enough that it might alone prove fatal. Instead, he most probably died from a combination of blood loss and the accumulation of wounds. His body lay for a further three hours where it had fallen before being attended to. We can only speculate now whether, had he received immediate attention, he may possibly have survived the attack.

THE AFTERMATH

The conspirators, who called themselves "The Liberators," initially claimed that they had undertaken the assassination in order to free Rome from the danger of tyranny. They appear to have misjudged the mood of the people, who came out very much against them, forcing them to flee from the city. In his will, Caesar named his 18-year-old great-nephew Gaius Octavian as his heir, also posthumously adopting him as a son. Mark Antony may have been expecting to step straight into Caesar's shoes, becoming the prominent public figure in Rome, but the wealth and prestige suddenly conferred on Octavian despite his youth presented Antony with a serious rival.

At first Antony, Octavian, and other close associates of Caesar came together to fight a civil war against the forces loyal to Cassius, Brutus, and the other Liberators. Once these forces had been defeated, fighting continued between the former members of the alliance in a series of encounters that lasted for more than a decade. Octavian finally defeated Antony, together with his lover Cleopatra, the queen of Egypt, at the Battle of Actium in 31 BCE, opening up the way for him to become the sole ruler, under the name of Augustus Caesar, of what would become the Roman Empire. In this sense, the assassination of Julius Caesar had exactly the opposite outcome to what had been intended by the assassins. It resulted in an empire ruled by a single man and marked the end of the republic, with the descendants of Caesar holding the position of emperor for many of the following 100 years.

THE MURDER OF JULIA DRUSILLA

January 24, 41 CE

MOTIVATION

Murder
Assassination
Treason
Espionage
Robbery
Hijacking
Fraud
Kidnapping

Location: Rome

Perpetrators: Soldiers of the Praetorian Guard

Outcome: The death of Emperor Caligula's only child

Caligula's wife Caesonia was killed with him, being stabbed by a centurion; and his daughter had her brains knocked out against a wall.

Suetonius, *The Lives of the Twelve Caesars* (121 CE)

Julia Drusilla was the only child of the Roman emperor Caligula and his fourth wife, Milonia Caesonia. According to the historian Suetonius, writing approximately 80 years after the event, she and her mother were murdered by soldiers of the Praetorian Guard a few hours after Caligula had been assassinated in a conspiracy that involved senators and other units of the Roman army. In killing his immediate family as well as the emperor, the conspirators were ensuring that there could be no future claim of succession to the imperial throne of Rome by any direct descendants of Caligula. Suetonius also suggests that Drusilla was killed because she bit one of the soldiers involved in killing her mother, who then murdered her by smashing her head against a wall.

LITTLE BOOT

The emperor known as Caligula was actually named Gaius Julius Caesar and, although not a direct descendant, he was distantly related to his illustrious namesake and occupied a prominent position in what is sometimes known as the Julio-Claudian dynasty of Roman emperors. His father, Germanicus, was the nephew of Emperor Tiberius, the stepson of the first emperor, Augustus Caesar. Germanicus was a highly successful military leader and enjoyed widespread popularity among his legions and with the people of Rome. He took his young son with him on military campaigns, often dressing him in army uniform, including the *caligae* — marching boots that looked like sandals — worn by the soldiers. It led to the soldiers giving him the nickname Caligula, or Little Boot. The name has endured, in part because it distinguishes him from the other members of the dynasty who have similar names.

Germanicus died in 19 CE, when Caligula was five years old. Germanicus was rumored to have been poisoned on the orders of Tiberius because the emperor believed that his popularity among Roman citizens had become a threat. The rumors were never proven and Tiberius went on to adopt Caligula, together with his two older brothers and three sisters. Both older brothers were implicated in conspiracies against the emperor and died in exile, leaving Caligula to be named as joint heir-apparent to Tiberius along with his grandson Tiberius Gemellus. After Tiberius died in 37 CE, Caligula had the teenage Gemellus killed. It has been suggested that at this time Caligula suffered a serious illness that may have had a lasting effect on his mental health, a problem that would go on to manifest itself in his behavior after Gemellus had died and he had become sole emperor.

At first Caligula enjoyed widespread popularity in Rome, not least because he was succeeding Tiberius, whose reputation had never recovered from the suspicion that he had been involved in the death of Germanicus and because for the last five years of his reign he had hardly been seen in Rome, having largely withdrawn from public life to live on the island of Capri. The arrival in the city of the 24-year-old new emperor, the son of Germanicus, appeared to offer the opportunity of a fresh start. But Caligula's rule soon lost the support of both the populace and the ruling classes in the senate. His behavior was erratic and included ordering executions without trial. He was also financially profligate, which may have caused a shortage of food in the city. He is also said to have had incestuous affairs with all three of his sisters and was particularly close to Julia Drusilla, who died of a fever in 38 CE and after whom he would name his daughter.

THE MURDERS
One of a series of oil paintings by the Italian artist Lazzaro Baldi (1624–1703) showing scenes from the lives of Roman emperors.

The contemporary Roman writers Seneca the Younger and Philo of Alexandria both stated that Caligula was mad, citing among other actions his apparent desire to make his horse the Consul of Rome, the highest political office. He was also accused of numerous acts of sexual impropriety beyond incestuous relations with his sisters, conducting affairs with married women and turning his imperial palace into a brothel. Later authors, including Suetonius, concurred with this view of the emperor as being insane, but this has been challenged in recent years by certain Classical scholars, who have suggested that the claims were first made by Caligula's political opponents in an effort to diminish his reputation.

It is impossible to know now, some 2000 years later, the exact state of Caligula's mental health, but there can be little doubt that he deliberately set out to undermine the authority of the senate and to embarrass any senators who opposed his wishes. The rift between the emperor and the senate widened further in 40 CE when Caligula announced his intentions to leave Rome for Alexandria, where he had decided to move so that he could be worshipped as a living god in the manner of Egyptian pharaohs. Such an action would have reduced the senate's ability to influence the

THE CONSPIRACY

governance of the empire. In what would previously have been a very unlikely alliance, some senators began to conspire against the emperor with senior officers of the Praetorian Guard, whose positions in the Roman Army would also be much reduced in the event of Caligula leaving Rome.

The intentions of the conspiracy appear to have been confused, at least beyond the main goal of assassinating the emperor. Some senators wanted to bring the entire structure of the Roman Empire down, reinstating a republic in which the senate was its main governing body. For others, the removal of Caligula was the sole purpose of the plot. The Praetorian Guards involved in the conspiracy were similarly split and for a time, when a clear plan for the aftermath of the assassination could not be agreed, no action against the emperor was taken. An announcement that Caligula was to leave Rome for Alexandria on January 25, 41 CE, appears to have forced the conspirators into action.

On January 24, Caligula attended a series of games and theatrical performances on the Palatine Hill in Rome. As he was due to depart the following day, it represented the last opportunity for the conspirators to act. A group of Praetorian Guards led by the tribune Cassius Chaerea struck during a break in the theatrical performances. After Caligula had moved to a side room away from the main theater, he was, according to the account given by Suetonius, stabbed by Chaerea first and then by those other guards involved, receiving 30 wounds in total. Chaerea supported those senators who wanted to establish a republic, but also appears to have had his own personal reasons for killing Caligula, having been the butt of a number of the emperor's jokes. Such animosity may have also played a part in his order to a group of guards to find and kill Caesonia and Drusilla, who were discovered in a corridor underneath the imperial palace and brutally murdered.

Chaerea had probably also intended to kill Claudius, Caligula's uncle and the most likely candidate to follow him as emperor, but he failed. Claudius was discovered by a soldier of the Praetorian Guard hiding behind a curtain in a room of the imperial palace, having fled the theater after realizing that his own life was in danger. Fortunately for him, the Praetorian Guard who found him was not part of the conspiracy and, in the chaos that enveloped Rome in the aftermath of the assassination, he was taken out of the city to be protected and was later declared to be the new emperor.

THE THUGS

ca. 14th century–19th century

MOTIVATION

Murder

Assassination

Treason

Espionage

Robbery

Hijacking

Fraud

Kidnapping

Location: India

Perpetrators: Numerous groups of bandits across the subcontinent

Outcome: The murder of thousands of people until the Thugs were suppressed by the British

You have surmised from the listed callings followed by the victims of the Thugs that nobody could travel the Indian roads unprotected and live to get through; that the Thugs respected no quality, no vocation, no religion, nobody; that they killed every unarmed man that came in their way.

Mark Twain, *Following the Equator* (1897)

In the first few decades of the nineteenth century, reports began to emerge from the administration of the British East India Company, which then governed large parts of the Indian subcontinent, concerning groups of bandits who murdered their victims by strangling them with lengths of cloth. Banditry was by no means uncommon in India at that time; groups of robbers known as Dacoits regularly targeted travelers, but they rarely killed their victims. These newly uncovered groups also targeted travelers, employing a particular method of robbery that involved first ingratiating themselves into the group of travelers and then, once the usual suspicion of strangers had been overcome, murdering them and stealing their possessions. The bodies were then either buried or thrown down wells, while the Thugs, as they became known, returned home, which was usually many miles away from the scene of their crimes. As more details gradually came to light, it began to appear that the British had stumbled upon an extensive and organized cult devoted to the worship of Kali, the Hindu goddess of death and destruction, and that the killings were being carried out in a ritualized way.

THE BRITISH RESPONSE

The discovery and subsequent investigation of the phenomenon of the Thugs was largely the work of William Henry Sleeman, a captain in the Bengal army of the East India Company. He apprehended a man known as Feringhea who, under interrogation, revealed the location of a mass grave containing the bodies of at least 100 victims of his band of Thugs. As it became apparent that the problem extended much further than Bengal alone, the administration of the East India Company formed a new body to deal with it: the Thuggee and Dacoity Department. It was led from 1835 to 1839 by Sleeman. Over the course of its investigations thousands of people were arrested and interrogated. Some cooperated with the investigators, giving the names of numerous others who were involved and providing Sleeman and his colleagues with a detailed picture of the extent of Thuggee. One of the Thugs arrested was Behram Jemadar, the leader of a group who he said had strangled 931 victims. Before he was executed in 1840, he also claimed to have personally murdered 125 people, which if true would make him one of the world's most prolific serial killers.

Further investigations suggested that murders by numerous different groups of Thugs had occurred across the length and breadth of the Indian subcontinent and that the practice had been going on for hundreds of years. The earliest known written record of murders carried out using the methods of the Thugs, as opposed to more straightforward robberies of travelers, dated to the fourteenth century. One estimate, based on the extent of the crimes committed by Thugs during the 1830s and then extrapolated back over the centuries, suggested that they had been responsible for the deaths of over a million people across the subcontinent. More recent research has shown that this is probably a vast overestimate; while it is impossible to put an exact figure on the number of people killed, it appears more likely that there were in the region of 50,000 victims in total.

In 1839, the publication of a novel in Britain, *Confessions of a Thug* by Philip Meadows Taylor, caused a sensation. The book became a bestseller, read by Queen Victoria among many others, and was responsible for introducing the word "thug" into common usage in the English language to describe a person who used brutal and vicious methods to achieve their aims. Meadows Taylor had been involved in the investigations into the Thugs in India and his account in the novel was based on the details obtained from the interrogation of Feringhea. But, by the time the novel had brought the Thugs to the attention of the reading public, the measures taken by the British administration in India had already dramatically reduced the number of murders.

Between 1836 and 1848 a series of laws known collectively as the Thuggee and Dacoity Suppression Acts were passed. They gave the colonial administration the powers needed to effectively counter the Thugs. The combination of the necessary laws and a department dedicated to enforce them, which could coordinate British efforts and intelligence across India, resulted in numerous arrests. The subsequent prosecutions led to the execution of more than 400 people, while many more were either imprisoned in India or sent to penal colonies beyond the subcontinent. By the 1870s the British considered the threat posed by

THUGGEE
A photograph dating to ca. 1865 taken by Samuel Bourne in Peshawar and described as showing a group of Thugs.

the Thugs to have been eliminated. Since that time, no evidence has come to light of any further attacks carried out using the Thugs' singularly brutal methods.

**POST-
COLONIAL
THUGS**

More than 100 years later, in the late twentieth century, questions began to emerge about the accuracy of the British accounts of Thuggee. It was even suggested that it had been entirely the invention of the fevered colonial imaginations, intent on supplying the British public with stories of the exotic and mysterious East or, more cynically, as an attempt to demonstrate how British rule in India was necessary and desirable by eliminating a threat that, in reality, did not exist. More recent research in the extensive archives of the East India Company has shown that a huge amount of documentary evidence exists of the British investigation into the Thugs in India, giving details of the crimes and the people involved. This has been presented as proof that the Thugs really did exist in numerous groups across India and murdered travelers by strangling them with a length of cloth. What has not been found is any evidence that the Thugs constituted an organized cult or that there was a religious element in which victims were used as a sacrifice to the goddess Kali or to any other Hindu deity. In fact, many of the Thug groups were actually composed of Muslims, particularly those that operated in northern India, and those that were predominately Hindu do not appear to have any greater connection with a particular god or goddess than the majority of law-abiding people.

The idea of the Thugs that became prevalent in Britain and other Western countries, then, is most likely a product of imperial spin spiced up with a fantasy version of the mysterious "East." The reality may have been rather more mundane but it nevertheless involved a huge number of vicious murders, committed for personal gain rather than in the performance of a religious ritual of human sacrifice. Thugs in different parts of India employed the same method of targeting travelers and strangling them for the simple reason that it had proven to be successful. By eliminating all the potential witnesses, the crimes were initially unreported, before finally being discovered by the British, at which point counter-measures were put in place. After this, the number of these murders declined and eventually stopped completely. This version of the story of the Thugs may not be as exciting or mysterious as the older one, but it may be a little closer to the truth.

ELIZABETH BÁTHORY: THE BLOOD COUNTESS

ca. 1585–1610

MOTIVATION

Murder
Assassination
Treason
Espionage
Robbery
Hijacking
Fraud
Kidnapping

Location: Royal Hungary in the Habsburg Empire

Perpetrators: Countess Báthory and at least four of her servants

Outcome: After her crimes were discovered, Elizabeth Báthory was walled into a room in her castle for the remainder of her life

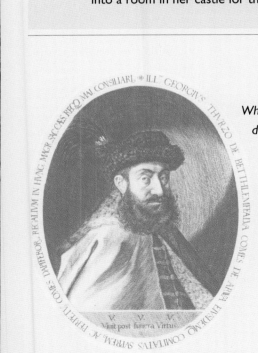

When my men entered Čachtice Castle, they found a girl dead in the house. Another followed in death as a result of many wounds and agonies. In addition to this there was also a wounded and tortured woman there. The other victims were kept hidden away where this damned woman prepared these future martyrs.

From a letter written by Count György Thurzó to his wife on December 30, 1610, the day he arrested Elizabeth Báthory

The ruins of Čachtice Castle stand on a ridge on the western edge of the Little Carpathians, a mountain range in what is now Slovakia, and overlooks the village of the same name. In the sixteenth and seventeenth centuries it lay within the territory of Royal Hungary, part of the Habsburg Empire, and is known today as the place where, during this period, Countess Elizabeth Báthory (or Báthory Erzsébet, as her name is written in Hungarian) tortured and murdered numerous girls and young women. It is also the place where she was arrested and where she was immured until she died.

ČACHTICE CASTLE
The ruins of the castle in Slovakia where Countess Elizabeth Báthory committed many of her crimes.

Ever since, stories about her have embroidered the verifiable details of the crimes she committed, blending fact and fiction. In some accounts, for instance, she is said to have killed 650 young women and bathed in the blood of virgins in order to restore her youth. Much in these accounts has been fabricated by authors intent on telling a Gothic horror story, presenting their own fantasy version of the Blood Countess, or Countess Dracula, as she has sometimes been called. But, despite the events having occurred more than 400 years ago, enough evidence remains for us to get at least some idea of what really happened in Čachtice Castle without having to rely on the imagination to fill in the gaps.

THE COUNTESS

Elizabeth Báthory was born in 1560 into a prominent and wealthy Hungarian aristocratic family. At the time, the nobility dominated what was essentially a feudal society, owning vast estates where they had the right to exercise absolute power over the lives of ordinary people. But it was also a period of great turmoil in which political, social, and religious upheavals were occurring, splitting apart the old order and leading to a high degree of instability. The medieval kingdom of Hungary had been divided between the Austrian Habsburg Empire and the expanding Ottoman Empire, which, after victory in the Battle of Mohács in 1526, established vassal states in the southern and eastern parts of Hungary, while the Habsburgs retained the western region. The borders between the two empires were in a constant state of flux and fighting occurred regularly over the course of the following centuries, a situation that was only finally resolved 400 years later with the dissolution of both empires in 1918 at the end of the First World War.

The constant conflict over territory was exacerbated by frequent occurrences of internal strife, including a number of peasant revolts against the harsh conditions imposed by feudal laws, which were brutally put down by the nobility. At the same time, the Protestant Reformation had spread through the region and had been followed by the subsequent Counter-Reformation. This had resulted in religious wars and inquisitions across much of the European continent, although it had a lesser impact in the Habsburg Empire, perhaps because Christians of all denominations were involved in the wars against the Islamic Ottomans rather than fighting each other. Nevertheless, divisions existed, not least between the Catholic Habsburg monarchs and those members of the aristocracy who had become Protestant, including the branch of the Báthory family to which Elizabeth belonged.

In 1571, the 11-year-old Elizabeth became engaged to Ferenc Nádasdy, who was 16 at the time and a member of another Hungarian aristocratic family, which was as least as wealthy as the Báthory family but whose name was not considered to be as prestigious. The engagement was arranged between the two families and, after the marriage five years later, the Nádasdy family gave the castle and estate at Čachtice, along with property in other parts of Hungary, to the couple. They became the Count and Countess Nádasdy, although Elizabeth appears to have continued to use her maiden name, perhaps reflecting the higher status it was perceived to carry. Over the course of their marriage, the count spent much of his time away from his wife, fighting in the almost continuous wars against the Ottomans and gaining a reputation as a formidable soldier who, even by the standards of the day, was known for showing no mercy to his enemies, having prisoners of war put to death by impaling them on stakes.

While Nádasdy was away with the Habsburg army, Elizabeth managed the estates. She was highly educated, writing in Latin and Greek as well as in Hungarian, and appears to have been well capable of looking after the family's affairs during her husband's long absences. She also had five children, three of whom survived into adulthood, but, if witness statements made at the subsequent trial of her servants are to be believed, by 1585 she had begun to engage in the shocking crimes for which she would become infamous.

THE BLOOD COUNTESS

Rumors about the countess had been in circulation for some years before any official investigation was instigated and they became particularly common after 1604, when her husband died. By 1610, the Habsburg authorities could no longer ignore them and, after witness statements had been collected concerning the conduct of the countess at Čachtice and other properties she owned, the Palatine of Hungary, György Thurzó, led a force of soldiers to the castle to investigate the matter personally. He arrived there on December 30, 1610, and, at least according to some accounts, caught the countess in the act of torturing a number of young girls. As Palatine of Hungary, Thurzó held the position of the chief minister at the court of the Habsburg monarch King Matthias II. The fact that he took charge of the investigation himself gives an indication of the seriousness with which such action against another member of the nobility was taken.

It was reported that Thurzó and his men found the body of one girl who had been tortured to death and another who was still alive but had suffered terrible injuries. Evidence of the torture of other victims was also found, resulting in four of Báthory's servants being taken away and the countess herself being placed under house arrest. The servants were put on trial almost immediately and their confessions, almost certainly extracted by torture, and statements made by witnesses form the bulk of what we now know about the crimes today. The accounts differ in many of the details given, particularly concerning the number of girls who were killed, but it is nevertheless possible to gain an impression of what is alleged to have happened. Girls from peasant families who lived on the estates owned by the countess were employed as servants in the castle and, once there, were subjected to severe beatings and other forms of torture. The torture appears to have been carried out by servants in the presence of the countess, who apparently participated on some occasions and, according to a number of the accounts, would bite the flesh of the girls. Others were held in iron cages where they were stabbed with spikes or were mutilated by other means. In some cases, the girls were said to be starved, taken out into the snow during the winter months, soaked with water and left to freeze to death.

One woman in particular, Anna Darvolya, was identified by a number of people as being instrumental in the crimes and as having perhaps some sort of hold over the countess that influenced her actions. Darvolya died a year or so before the trial and, without her testimony, it is impossible to know the extent of her involvement or if subsequent allegations that she had engaged in some sort of witchcraft had any basis in fact. The number of girls killed appears to have been somewhere between 30 and 80, either in the castle or at other properties owned by the countess, and their bodies were buried at night in graveyards or in unmarked graves in other locations. One witness described seeing a diary kept by the countess in which she had listed the names of 650 girls. However, because nobody else mentioned this diary and it does not appear to have been found in the castle, there is no way of knowing if there was any substance to this accusation.

THE COUNTESS
A copy of the only known contemporary portrait of Elizabeth Báthory, now lost, painted when she was about 25.

Whatever the truth of the matter, the four servants were found guilty of the charges, with three of them executed immediately and the fourth sentenced to life in prison because the court decided that she had been led by the others. The countess remained under house arrest and, in the end, did not face any trial herself, most likely because of her status in society and because of the influence of her family. Her punishment was to spend the rest of her life walled into a room in Čachtice Castle, from where she continued to protest her innocence until her death four years later. It has been suggested that she came under suspicion only after she began killing the daughters of minor aristocratic families as well as those from the peasants on her estates. However, there is no record of members of the nobility having enquired about any missing daughters so such claims cannot be substantiated.

An alternative explanation for why the Hungarian authorities decided to take action against the countess when they did is that King Matthias II was deeply in debt, having borrowed heavily from Ferenc Nádasdy before his death, and was intent on prosecuting Elizabeth Báthory as a means of avoiding paying her what he had owed her husband. It may also have been a political action aimed at damaging the powerful Báthory family as a whole, some of whom did not support the Habsburg monarchy. But even if the motivation to act against her had little to do with the actual crimes she was accused of committing, the weight of evidence against her, collected from hundreds of witnesses, must surely suggest that she had tortured and killed numerous young girls. More than 400 years after the events, it is impossible to know for certain the full extent of what happened, even if some of the myths that would later become attached to the countess can be discounted, but what we do know is horrific enough.

MOTIVATION

Murder

Assassination

Treason

Espionage

Robbery

Hijacking

Fraud

Kidnapping

THE BABINGTON PLOT

1586

Location: England

Perpetrators: Anthony Babington and Mary, Queen of Scots; Sir Francis Walsingham and numerous conspirators, spies, and double agents

Outcome: The executions of the conspirators and of Mary, Queen of Scots

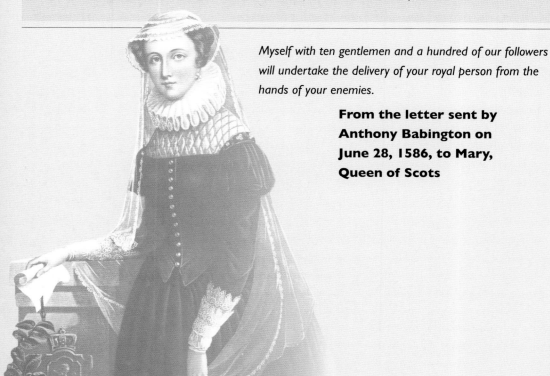

Myself with ten gentlemen and a hundred of our followers will undertake the delivery of your royal person from the hands of your enemies.

From the letter sent by Anthony Babington on June 28, 1586, to Mary, Queen of Scots

The 44-year reign of Queen Elizabeth I began in November 1558 and ended with her death in March 1603, at the age of 69, from natural causes. It is often described as having been a golden age in English history, a period when England began to emerge as a power in the world and that encompassed an extraordinary intellectual and artistic flowering. It was also a time of great religious and social turmoil that would see the monarchy face numerous threats from both internal and external forces, including the Spanish Armada, the invasion force sent to England in 1588 by King Philip II of Spain with the intention of deposing the Protestant Elizabeth and reestablishing Catholicism in the country. The armada was defeated by a combination of English defensive action and severe weather, but it was by no means the only attempt to get rid of Elizabeth. Two years previously a conspiracy known as the Babington Plot had much the same aims. It is named for one of its members, the young nobleman Anthony Babington, and is now remembered for how Elizabeth's spymaster, Sir Francis Walsingham, manipulated the events in order to implicate Elizabeth's rival, Mary, Queen of Scots, in treason.

QUEEN ELIZABETH
The so-called Phoenix Portrait of the queen, attributed to the court painter Nicholas Hilliard and dating ca. 1575.

THE BACKGROUND

The beginning of the Protestant Reformation is conventionally dated to the moment in 1517 when Martin Luther nailed a list of criticisms of the Catholic Church to the door of a church in the city of Wittenberg, Saxony. It would lead to the formation of several different Protestant denominations as groups broke away from the authority of the pope in Rome. It would also lead, between 1545 and 1563, to the development of the Catholic Counter-Reformation at the Council of Trent. In England, King Henry VIII split from Rome for political and personal reasons rather than religious ones. He wanted to annul his marriage to Catherine of Aragon in order to marry his mistress Anne Boleyn, in part because the only child to survive infancy from his first marriage was a daughter, Mary, and he wanted a male heir. The pope refused to annul the marriage, prompting the break with Rome. During the subsequent marriage to Anne, however, the only surviving child was also a daughter, who was named Elizabeth.

In 1553 Mary ascended to the throne of England after the death of King Edward VI, Henry's only surviving son, at the age of 15 and the removal of the successor named by Edward, his cousin Lady Jane Grey, after only nine days on the throne. Unlike both Henry and Edward, Mary was a committed Catholic, earning the soubriquet "Bloody Mary" because of the brutal nature of the repression of the Protestant faith she instigated during her reign. Elizabeth had been brought up as a Protestant and, as the pope did not recognize the annulment of her father's first marriage, was considered to be illegitimate by the Catholic Church. She was suspected of being involved in Protestant plots against Mary and was held prisoner for a time in the Tower of London, but no credible evidence against her was uncovered and she was recognized by the childless Mary as her heir.

After Elizabeth gained the throne in 1558, she reversed the anti-Protestant legislation introduced during Mary's reign, returning to the Protestant reforms begun by Henry and continued by Edward. One of the laws enacted at this time compelled people to attend Anglican services on Sunday, forcing English Catholics to decide between converting to the Church of England or breaking the law by continuing to attend Catholic masses. Those who chose to remain Catholic were known as recusants. Some of them worshipped in secret in England while others left the country, preferring a life of exile in a European Catholic country. The penalties imposed on Catholics in England were usually relatively minor for everybody except priests, who could be charged with the capital crime of high treason for celebrating the rites of the faith.

A group of Catholic exiles founded the English College in the seminary in Douai, a town in northern France, so that English Catholic clergymen could be trained in the expectation of a return to Catholicism in England at some point in the future. The college moved to the city of Rheims during the 1580s and became a center of Catholic opposition to Elizabeth, secretly sending priests to England with the intention of maintaining the faith in that country and of spreading opposition to her rule. A number of conspiracies developed involving both recusants in England and exiles in northern France aimed at overthrowing Elizabeth and replacing her with a Catholic monarch. The most obvious candidate was Mary, Queen of Scots, Elizabeth's cousin once removed and the granddaughter of Margaret Tudor, Henry VIII's sister.

Mary had succeeded her father, King James V, to the Scottish throne but had been forced to abdicate in 1567 in favor of her son, also called James, after her alleged involvement in the death of her husband, Lord Darnley, and subsequent marriage to the Earl of Bothwell, the man widely believed to have murdered Darnley. After the abdication, Mary fled from Scotland, seeking the protection of Elizabeth in England. It presented Elizabeth with a problem; Mary had made no secret of her claim to the English throne but no evidence existed to implicate her in any of the Catholic plots to overthrow the English queen. Elizabeth's solution was to confine Mary in a succession of castles and manor houses in the north of England while maintaining a system of state security to counter any Catholic plots against her. From 1573, state security came under the direction of Sir Francis Walsingham after he was appointed to the position of secretary of state in Elizabeth's court.

Walsingham had previously served as the queen's ambassador to France and in 1572 had witnessed the St. Bartholomew's Day Massacre in Paris in which mobs of Catholics had killed thousands of Protestants. He was a devoted Protestant who had lived in exile in Europe during the reign of Bloody Mary, so the brutality of what he had seen in Paris must have reinforced his awareness not only of the danger posed by Catholic plots to England and Elizabeth but also to his own position. Before going to France, he had been involved with state security under the direction of the queen's chief advisor, Lord Burghley. After his return to England, Walsingham made use of his experience and contacts to develop an extensive network of spies and informants in England and abroad. He would prove to be both ruthless and effective in uncovering and dealing with Catholic plots, employing spies to infiltrate Catholic groups in Rheims and elsewhere. The information he received from these spies led to the arrest of Catholic infiltrators, some of whom were turned into double agents once they had been caught and either sent back to Rheims or used as informers against Catholics in England.

THE BACKGROUND

The overall aim of the Babington Plot was to reinstate Catholicism in England by assassinating Elizabeth, rescuing Mary from her confinement, and installing her on the throne. Once Elizabeth was dead, the conspirators expected an uprising among Catholic recusants in England that would be supported by an invasion of Spanish and French forces, enabling them to take over the country. It was, to say the least, ambitious and it would later emerge that those members of the plot who had been in contact with representatives of Spain and France had overstated the willingness of those two countries to mount an invasion of England. Had the conspirators in England known this, they may well have been forced to abandon their plans. Instead, thinking that they had the necessary support, they decided to risk everything and go ahead with their conspiracy.

The plot was named for Anthony Babington because he was one of its main organizers in England, but it was most likely conceived in the English College in Rheims by John Ballard, a Jesuit priest who had studied in Rheims before moving surreptitiously to England in order to spread the faith. Babington was 24 years old at the time and had previously acted as a messenger, conveying letters from Catholics in France to Mary, Queen of Scots. He had met Mary personally on a number of occasions and appears to have become infatuated with her and with the idea of installing her on the English throne. His commitment to the cause may have blinded him to the dangers involved, but once he had been informed of the plot by Ballard, he agreed to become the leader of the English conspirators and to carry out the rescue of Mary, who was then being held at Chartley Hall, a moated manor house in Staffordshire.

CIPHER SHEET
One of the ciphers used by Mary, Queen of Scots, to send secret messages while she was being held at Chartley Hall.

What Babington and the Catholic friends he recruited to the plot did not know was that Walsingham's spies had infiltrated it right from the start. Ballard had come to England from Rheims with a man named Barnard Maude, who kept Walsingham informed about Ballard's intentions and who he was meeting. Once it had become clear that Babington was involved, one of Walsingham's agents, Robert Poley, managed to gain his confidence and become his close companion. As well as having these two spies shadowing the principal players in the plot, Walsingham also had an informer acting as a courier of letters between the plotters and Mary. Gilbert Gifford had studied at Rheims and in the previous year had been caught attempting to enter England in secret. Walsingham turned him into a double agent, presenting him with the choice of working for England or being executed. Gifford set up a system of smuggling letters to Mary in Chartley Hall by concealing them in the barrels of beer that were delivered to the hall every week and receiving replies in the empty barrels that were brought out. But before delivering letters in this way, he gave them to Thomas Phelippes, an expert codebreaker, who deciphered the codes used to write the letters and sent the details to Walsingham before resealing the originals and sending them on to the recipients.

With so much intelligence coming to him concerning every aspect of the plot, Walsingham could have put a stop to it at any moment. Instead he chose to wait, expecting that he would be able to gather evidence implicating Mary in the treasonous plot as well as the conspirators. It was a dangerous game; the aim, after all, was the assassination of Elizabeth. Had Walsingham lost track of the plot at any stage, it could have had disastrous consequences. The breakthrough came on June 28, when Babington wrote to Mary to tell her that a plot was being planned in which Elizabeth was going to be assassinated and he was going to rescue her from Chartley Hall and install her on the throne. Mary replied a few weeks later, agreeing to participate in the plot and, in doing so, sealing her fate. Phelippes deciphered Mary's letter and appears to have forged a few extra sentences in which Mary asked Babington to tell her more details of the plot and to supply her with the names of the men involved in it. He then underlined the incriminating nature of this letter by drawing a gallows on the copy of it he sent to Walsingham.

Walsingham did not wait for Babington's reply to reach Mary, considering it too risky to wait any longer when the plot was so far advanced. He may well have known the names of the plotters from his other sources and Mary's letter had provided him with the evidence he needed to implicate her in treason. Ballard was arrested immediately, on August 4, and a confession extracted by torture in which he named Babington and the other conspirators, all of whom had gone into hiding in the knowledge that their plan had been discovered. Over the course of the next few weeks, all were caught and Mary was arrested along with two of her secretaries. Babington, Ballard, and 13 other conspirators were sentenced to death and executed on September 20, 1586. Mary was put on trial at Fotheringhay Castle in Northamptonshire and, largely as a consequence of her letter to Babington, was found guilty of treason. On February 8, 1587, she was beheaded in the great hall of the castle after Elizabeth had personally signed her death warrant. Sixteen years later, Mary's son, King James VI of Scotland, succeeded Elizabeth to the English throne, ruling as King James I of England.

MOTIVATION

Murder
Assassination
Treason
Espionage
Robbery
Hijacking
Fraud
Kidnapping

THE MURDER OF JOHN NEWCOMEN

1630

Location: Plymouth Colony

Perpetrator: John Billington

Outcome: The first murder in the American colonies

This year John Billington the elder (one that came over with the first) was arrained, and both by grand and petie jurie found guilty of willfull murder, by plaine and notorious evidence. And was for the same accordingly executed. This, as it was the first execution amongst them, so was it a mater of great sadnes unto them... His fatte was, that he way-laid a yong-man, one John New-comin, (about a former quarell,) and shote him with a gune, wherof he dyed.

William Bradford (ca. 1590–ca. 1657), *Of Plymouth Plantation*

Little is known of the life of John Newcomen beyond the fact that in early September 1630 he was shot and killed by John Billington. We don't even know for certain if Newcomen was his surname or if it simply referred to the fact that he was a newcomer to the Plymouth Colony, the settlement established ten years previously by the group now known as the Pilgrim Fathers. The Fathers had arrived on board the *Mayflower* in December 1620, landing on the coast of what is now the state of Massachusetts. The colony they founded is now widely regarded as being the first stage in the creation of America. John Billington was one of these original settlers and a signatory to the Mayflower Compact, the document written during the Atlantic passage setting out regulations to govern the new colony. He also committed the first murder among the English settlers and subsequently became the first of them to be executed for his crime.

THE MAYFLOWER COMPACT
One of a series of 78 historical paintings by Jean Leon Gerome Ferris (1863–1930) entitled *The Pageant of a Nation.*

PLYMOUTH COLONY

Billington may have sailed on the *Mayflower*, but he was not one of the group of religious separatists who would later become known as the Pilgrim Fathers. He had joined the expedition with his wife, Elenor, and their two children, John and Francis, together with two other families, after the separatists had arrived in England from Leiden, the city in the Dutch Republic where they had settled after leaving England a decade earlier. They were followers of the Protestant cleric Robert Brown, who, along with other Puritans, did not think the Reformation had gone far enough in England so had moved to Holland in an attempt to find a place to live where they could practice their religion as they saw fit.

The religious persecutions, described in the previous chapter, that had begun during the reign of Queen Elizabeth I were continued by her successor, King James I, and were directed against all dissenters from the Church of England, Puritans as well as Catholics. The Brownists had chosen to go to the Dutch Republic because of its reputation for religious tolerance and had formed their own community in Leiden. Most had come from rural Nottinghamshire and appear to have struggled to settle in the city and to living in a foreign country. Rather than go back to England, they decided to go to the New World, where they could establish farms and would be free from persecution. The first group of these emigrants left the Dutch Republic in July 1620 on board the *Speedwell*, a ship they had bought themselves, with the intention of meeting the *Mayflower* in England and crossing the Atlantic Ocean together.

The *Speedwell* proved to be unseaworthy and so, after a series of delays, the *Mayflower* made the voyage alone, beginning in September. As a consequence of this late start, the ship experienced bad weather in the Atlantic Ocean during the crossing. The original intention had been to settle in Virginia, where they had purchased a lease from the London Virginia Company and where an English colony had previously been established at Jamestown, but for unknown reasons the decision was taken to settle in the region where the ship had arrived in America rather than to continue southward to join the Jamestown colony. After a few weeks of searching, they landed at what would become Plymouth Colony. It has been said that they came ashore at Plymouth Rock, although no contemporary accounts of this first landing actually mention the site.

PLYMOUTH ROCK
A hand-tinted lithograph by Sarony & Major, ca. 1846, showing the landing of the Pilgrim Fathers in December 1620.

The first winter proved to be extremely hard in the new colony. Half of the settlers died from disease and a lack of food and it is almost certain that the colony would have failed completely without the help of the Native American tribes in the region. After that terrible experience, the settlers held what is now called the "First Thanksgiving" after the success of the harvest in the following year and, while the modern celebration of Thanksgiving has rather more complicated roots than this, it can to some extent at least be regarded as a continuation of the practice of those first pilgrims in America.

Even before they had founded their first settlement, tensions existed between Billington and William Bradford, the leader of the separatists on board the *Mayflower* and the future governor of Plymouth Colony. Much of what we know about the early years of the colony is derived from the account kept by Bradford, later published as *Of Plymouth Colony*, in which he describes Billington as being critical of the way in which the colony was administered and recounts speeches made against Miles Standish, the man handed responsibility for the defense of the colony.

It is impossible to know the extent to which Billington deserved his reputation as a troublemaker; the only details we have come from Bradford's writing and may have been a result of some unknown personal animosity between the two. He appears to have been involved in a conspiracy against the colony's administration, which was uncovered by Bradford in 1624. Its orchestrators, John Lyford and John Oldham, were banished from the colony, but there was insufficient evidence to take action against Billington. The murder of John Newcomen by Billington in the summer of 1630 provided Bradford with the opportunity he may have been looking for to take action against a man who had threatened his position as governor of the colony six years before. According to Bradford's account, Billington had previously been involved in an argument with Newcomen over an unspecified subject and this disagreement, whatever its nature, led to Billington shooting Newcomen dead at their next meeting. Billington was then arrested and put on trial in front of a jury of his peers. Without giving any further details of the trial, Bradford writes that Billington was found guilty of murder and sentenced to death.

A history of the colony written 50 years later by William Hubbard, who was nine years old at the time of the incident, states that Billington had shot Newcomen in cold blood while he had been hunting deer and that, despite being found guilty at his trial, thought that he would escape execution either because the court did not possess the required authority to carry out the sentence or because the colony, being short of men, could not afford to execute him. Bradford apparently sought the advice of a number of others, including John Winthrop, a lawyer who had arrived from England that year. Winthrop was the governor of the nearby Massachusetts Bay Colony, the second settlement in New England, established in 1628 as an increasing number of Puritan colonists began to arrive in the region. Bradford's consultations with Winthrop apparently convinced him that, as governor of the colony, he possessed the required authority to carry out the sentence imposed by the court and, on September 30, 1630, John Billington was hanged. He was the first, but by no means the last, American to be executed for murder.

MOTIVATION

Murder

Assassination

Treason

Espionage

Robbery

Hijacking

Fraud

Kidnapping

CAPTAIN KIDD: PIRATE OR PRIVATEER?

1690s

Location: The Indian Ocean

Perpetrators: Captain William Kidd and his crew

Outcome: Kidd was hanged and gibbeted

We being desirous to prevent the aforesaid mischiefs and as far as in Us lies to bring the said Pirates, Freebooters, and Sea Rovers to justice, have thought fit and to hereby give and grant to you the said Captain William Kidd (to whom Our commissioners for exercising the Office of Our Lord High Admirals have Granted a Commission as a private Man of War bearing date the Eleventh day of december 1695, & unto ye Officers, Mariners and others shall we be under your command) full Power and Authority to apprehend, seize, and take into Your Custody all such pirates, Freebooters, and Sea Rovers being either Our Own Subjects or of other Nations associated with them.

From the commission given to Captain Kidd in 1695 in the name of King William III

The notoriety of Captain William Kidd, who was hanged in London on May 23, 1701, for piracy and murder, arose as much from the publicity surrounding the possibility of a royal and political scandal as it did from the nature of the crimes for which he was convicted. High-ranking members of the aristocracy and senior politicians in the Whig party were rumored to have financed Kidd's pirate activities and even the king, William III, was said to have been involved. As if that were not enough, it was reported that Kidd had buried the treasure he had stolen in various secret locations around the world, adding a layer of mystery and intrigue to what became one of the most sensational criminal cases of the period. As the captain of his own ship, Kidd had operated on the borderline between officially sanctioned privateer and outlawed pirate. The distinction was by no means always clear and this ambiguity would be at the heart of the charges laid against him.

Little is known of Kidd's early life, beyond the fact that he was born in the Scottish city of Dundee. The first reliable records concerning him date to 1689, at which time he was about 35 years old and the captain of a ship arriving at the Caribbean island of Nevis, a British colony. He had been sent there on commission by the island's governor to provide protection against possible French attack. At that time it was common practice for countries in times of war to take on ships owned by individuals or consortiums to supplement the regular navy, issuing these privateers with what were known as letters of marque, which effectively licensed them to attack and seize ships belonging to an enemy country and claim the ships and whatever cargo they were carrying as prizes by way of payment.

PRIVATEER OR PIRATE?

The War of the Grand Alliance, sometimes known as the Nine Years' War, had begun in 1688. Fought between France and an alliance of European powers, including England, it was the result of tensions caused by the attempts of King Louis XIV of France to expand French territory on the European continent. Much of the fighting occurred around the borders of France but also included some actions at sea and in the colonial possessions of the European belligerents. Kidd led raids on islands held by the French in the Caribbean and captured French ships as prizes before moving further north to operate against the French along the coast of New England, sailing out of ports in the English colonies of New York and Massachusetts. By this time he was targeting the pirates who were attacking commercial shipping of any nationality in the region and his success against both led to him gaining a reputation as a man who was capable of combating the threat of piracy.

By the 1690s, some pirates from the Caribbean and western Atlantic had begun to look further afield, sailing round the Cape of Good Hope at the tip of the African continent and into the Indian Ocean in order to attack merchant shipping that was carrying precious cargos from the Far East.

CAPTAIN KIDD
An illustration from *Howard Pyle's Book of Pirates* (1921) showing Kidd on the deck of the *Adventure Galley*.

Ships belonging to the influential East India Company were among those attacked, leading to the company lobbying the English parliament to take action against the pirates. In 1695 a group of wealthy English noblemen entered into an agreement with Kidd to provide him with the financial backing to mount an anti-piracy expedition into the Indian Ocean, also securing for him a letter of marque signed by King William III. The king does not appear to have invested any of his own money, but he was nevertheless given a 10 per cent share of the booty in what was clearly expected to be a profitable enterprise.

The investments allowed Kidd to purchase a brand new ship, the *Adventure Galley*. In September 1696, alongside a French ship captured previously, he embarked on the voyage to the Indian Ocean. Over the course of the following year he lost almost half of his crew, either forcibly pressed into service by the Royal Navy or dead as a result of a cholera epidemic. He had failed to find any pirates and therefore had not taken any prizes, leading to discontent among the remaining crew and raising the threat of mutiny. In one incident, Kidd physically attacked a crewman called William Moore, striking him over the head with a metal bucket and fracturing his skull. Moore died from his injuries, leading to charges of murder being brought against Kidd in London four years later.

It was about this time that rumors began to reach London and New York that Kidd had abandoned privateering for piracy. No evidence exists to support such claims, although in January 1698 he captured the *Quedagh Merchant*, an Indian-owned ship that had been chartered by Armenian merchants and was captained by an Englishman. It did not at first appear to be a legal prize for Kidd to take until he discovered that the ship had been issued with passes by the French, that guaranteed it safe passage, and thereby conceivably making it a legitimate target. It was carrying a valuable cargo, including silk and opium, as well as considerable amounts of gold and silver that the Armenian merchants had accrued from trade. Whatever doubts Kidd may have had, the prospect of turning a considerable profit for himself and his crew as well as for his backers in London appears to have persuaded him to keep the prize. He also retained the French passes as proof that taking the *Quedagh Merchant* was legal under the terms of his letter of marque.

After taking the *Quedagh Merchant* Kidd decided to return to New York to claim the prize and pay his investors. During the voyage he encountered the pirate captain Robert Culliford and, despite having now actually encountered a genuine pirate, made little apparent effort to capture him, even though he had the advantage of three ships to Culliford's one. A number of conflicting accounts of this encounter exist, but most agree that many of Kidd's crew, still dissatisfied with his captaincy, deserted him for Culliford. When he continued on his way to New York with a reduced crew, he left the *Adventure Galley* behind, which had become unseaworthy, and sailed in the *Quedagh Merchant* instead, renaming it the *Adventure Prize*. On the long voyage, he discovered that he had been declared a pirate and was being hunted by the Royal Navy and so left much of the booty he had accumulated in various locations in the Caribbean and in other places along the route he was following to New York, including burying some on Gardiner Island not far from his destination.

Kidd was hoping to negotiate a deal with Lord Bellemont, one of his backers who was also the governor of the English colonies on New York and Massachusetts. When Kidd traveled to see Bellemont, who was in Boston, he was arrested and thrown into jail, where he would remain for over a year before being extradited back to England. If he had thought that his backers would use their influence to help him, he was mistaken. They appear to have regarded him more as an embarrassment and a scapegoat for the failure of their venture. Some of the merchandise he had seized

ARREST AND TRIAL

BURYING TREASURE
Kidd and his men burying treasure on Gardiner Island, from *Howard Pyle's Book of Pirates.*

when taking the *Quedagh Merchant* had belonged to high-ranking officials of the Mogul Empire in northern India, who had close links to the East India Company. These officials now wanted to demonstrate to the Moguls that they were taking action against piracy in the Indian Ocean. As if that were not bad enough for Kidd, the Tories had recently taken control of the English parliament and were now intent on using his case to discredit the previous Whig administration, which had been in power when Kidd's expedition was first authorized.

In March 1701, Kidd appeared before the members of parliament in the House of Commons. It remains the only occasion in which a man accused of piracy has been summoned in this manner. Still apparently believing that his Whig backers would come to his aid, Kidd refused to answer questions put to him. He was subsequently charged with piracy and the murder of William Moore and sent for trial at the High Court of the Admiralty, which had jurisdiction over crimes committed at sea.

HANGING IN CHAINS
Kidd's gibbeted body was left hanging at Tilbury Point on the River Thames for three years after his execution in May, 1701.

During the trial proceedings a number of witnesses testified against him, including one of the Armenian merchants from the *Quedagh Merchant* and members of his crew, while one of the few pieces of evidence that would have gone some way to exonerating him on the piracy charges, the French passes he had taken from the ship, had gone missing in the period between his arrest and the beginning of the trial. In the circumstances, the guilty verdict handed down to Kidd was inevitable. On May 23, 1701, Kidd was hanged at Execution Dock on the bank of the River Thames. According to contemporary accounts, the rope broke during the first attempt to execute him and so he was hanged a second time. His dead body was left in a metal cage overhanging the river as a warning to others of the fate of pirates. More than 200 years later, in the early twentieth century, the French passes were found, apparently misfiled in a government archive, but the discovery of the evidence that may have saved Kidd from the gallows was not much use to him by then.

DICK TURPIN: THE HIGHWAYMAN

1730s

MOTIVATION

Murder
Assassination
Treason
Espionage
Robbery
Hijacking
Fraud
Kidnapping

Location: England

Perpetrators: Turpin and his criminal associates

Outcome: The death of a highwayman and the birth of a legend

Rash daring was the main feature of Turpin's character. Like our great Nelson, he knew fear only by name; and when he thus trusted himself in the hands of strangers, confident in himself and in his own resources, he felt perfectly easy as to the result.

William Harrison Ainsworth,
***Rookwood* (1834)**

The criminal career of Dick Turpin spanned about seven or eight years, beginning in the early 1730s and ending on April 7, 1739, when he was hanged in the English city of York after being convicted of horse theft. By that time he had gained a notorious reputation in England for the long string of offenses he had committed, both individually and as part of a criminal gang. But he would become much more famous after his death as a consequence of the publication of numerous accounts of his life, beginning within days of his execution when Richard Bayes, who had encountered Turpin a few years previously, published a widely distributed account of his life. It fed the public appetite for stories about the criminal underworld, elaborating some details and inventing others to present Turpin as a heroic figure, in the process establishing the character of the dashing highwayman. Almost a century later, in 1834, William Harrison Ainsworth wrote the novel *Rookwood*, in which Turpin appears as a character, providing us with what became one of the best-known episodes of his life, the entirely fictional overnight ride from London to York on his trusty mare Black Bess.

STAND AND DELIVER

The reality, as far as it can be established from the existing records, is rather more mundane. Turpin began as a petty criminal in the English county of Essex before graduating to more serious crimes, including burglary, armed robbery, and murder, with little to suggest that he bore any resemblance to later depictions of him as being a "knight of the road." He was born in September 1705 (the exact date is unknown) in the village of Hempstead, where his father was an innkeeper and butcher. He followed his father as a butcher and it would appear that this line of business first brought him into contact with the criminal gang he would later join, who were stealing cattle and sheep in Essex and the outskirts of London and poaching deer in Epping Forest. We don't know for certain, but it is not hard to envisage the gang disposing of stolen meat through the butcher's store run by Turpin.

By 1733, Turpin had given up his butcher's store and may have begun to run an inn. If he had not already done so, at this point he also became more heavily involved with the gang, joining the others in stealing livestock and poaching deer. Over the course of 1734, the gang became more ambitious, staging raids against isolated farms in Essex and in other locations around London. During some of these raids, Turpin participated in the torture of the gang's victims to force them to reveal the location of whatever valuables they possessed. After a particularly brutal attack in which a 70-year-old man was savagely beaten, most likely by Turpin, the authorities began to take notice. A reward of £50 was issued for information, leading to the arrest of three members of the gang. A full confession was obtained from one of them, including the names and descriptions of the others involved, with Turpin described as being about 5 feet 9 inches tall (1.75m) with numerous smallpox scars on his face.

The publicity surrounding the gang's crimes, together with the descriptions, led to a string of arrests. By the summer of 1735, all of them, with the exception of Turpin and one other, Thomas Rowden, had been caught, put on trial, and either executed or transported to the American colonies. After the gang had been broken up, Turpin turned to the crimes that would later make him famous, committing highway robberies from horseback, sometimes along with Rowden and sometimes alone. They held up coaches on the roads leading out of London to rob the passengers and also targeted individual travelers on horseback or on foot. The robberies continued over the course of the following months until Rowden was arrested toward the end of 1735 on separate counterfeiting charges and, after being found guilty at his trial, transported to America.

PENNY DREADFUL
This cover illustration from one of the pulp fiction serials from the 1860s known collectively as penny dreadfuls recounts Turpin's adventures.

After losing his partner, Turpin disappeared from view for more than a year, perhaps laying low to avoid arrest himself or living under an assumed name without committing any crimes that could be traced back to him. In February 1738 he reemerged in the company of another man sometimes identified as the well-known highwayman Tom King and sometimes as his younger brother Matthew King. The highway robberies began again, with Turpin and King apparently hiding out in Epping Forest between each attack. At the beginning of May, the two were tracked down by a group of men, including Richard Bayes, after a horse they had stolen was spotted in the Whitechapel area of East London. A shootout ensued in which King was fatally wounded. Bayes later wrote that the shot that killed King had been fired by Turpin, who then managed to escape. A few days later he was confronted in Epping Forest by Thomas Morris, a servant of one of the keepers of the forest, no doubt attempting to capture the wanted man and claim the reward. Turpin shot and killed Morris before disappearing again.

JOHN PALMER

On October 2, 1738, a man calling himself John Palmer shot a cockerel belonging to another man in the town of Brough in East Riding, Yorkshire, about 200 miles (320km) north of London. When he was challenged by a passerby, Palmer threatened to shoot the man as well, prompting him to contact the local magistrates. It was a relatively minor incident, but when Palmer refused to put up money for a bond he was taken to prison and an investigation began. The magistrates became interested in how he managed to live in some style when he had no obvious means of support, suspecting that he was involved in some illegal activity. He claimed to be a horse dealer from the neighboring county of Lincolnshire, but enquiries there uncovered evidence that he had actually stolen a number of horses in the county and then taken them to Yorkshire for sale. Horse theft was a much more serious charge and carried the death penalty at that time, even if most convictions were commuted to a prison term, particularly if it was a first offense.

As a consequence of the serious charges he was now facing, Palmer was transferred from the custody of local magistrates to the city of York, where he was held in the jail of the castle. While there, Palmer wrote a number of letters, including one to Turpin's brother-in-law in Hempstead, Essex. While this letter was being held in the post office of the nearby town of Saffron Walden, it was seen by James Smith, who would later say that he had recognized the handwriting as belonging to Turpin, who he had taught as a child. It was either an extremely unlucky coincidence for Turpin or Smith was not being entirely truthful; it is possible he had been watching for letters to the Turpin family in Hempstead in the hope of claiming the reward, which, after the murder of Morris, had increased to £200. Whatever the truth of the matter, the letter was passed on to magistrates in Essex, who opened it to find that it had been signed in the name of John Palmer and sent from the jail in York Castle. Smith traveled to York, where he visited the jail and identified Turpin, apparently picking him out from among a group of prisoners.

THE
TRIAL
Of the Notorious Highwayman
Richard Turpin,
At *York* Aſſizes, on the 22d Day of *March*, 1739, before the Hon. Sir WILLIAM CHAPPLE, Kt. Judge of Aſſize, and one of His Majeſty's Juſtices of the Court of King's Bench.
Taken down in Court by Mr. THOMAS KYLL, Profeſſor of Short Hand.
To which is prefix'd,
An exact Account of the ſaid *Turpin*, from his firſt coming into *Yorkſhire*, to the Time of his being committed Priſoner to *York* Caſtle; communicated by Mr. APPLETON of *Beverley*, Clerk of the Peace for the *Eaſt-Riding* of the ſaid County.
With a Copy of a Letter which *Turpin* received from his Father, while under Sentence of Death,
To which is added,
His Behaviour at the Place of Execution, on *Saturday* the 7th of *April*, 1739. Together with the whole Confeſſion he made to the Hangman at the Gallows; wherein he acknowledg'd himſelf guilty of the Facts for which he ſuffer'd, own'd the Murder of Mr. *Thompſon's* Servant on *Epping-Foreſt*, and gave a particular Account of ſeveral Robberies which he had committed.

YORK:
Printed by WARD and CHANDLER; and Sold at their Shop without *Temple-Bar*, *London*; and in *Coney-Street*, *York*, 1739.   (Price Six-pence.)

TURPIN'S TRIAL
Front page of a pamphlet published in 1739 describing the trial of Dick Turpin at the York Assizes.

Rather than being taken to either Essex or London to face charges of murder and highway robbery, Turpin remained in York to stand trial for horse theft. The trial occurred on March 22, 1739, at the York Assizes. He was charged with stealing three horses in Lincolnshire and evidence was given by both the man who owned the horses and an army officer who had bought two of them from Turpin. Smith was also called to give evidence concerning the defendant's true identity, saying that he had known Turpin since childhood, a statement that Turpin denied, claiming that he had never seen Smith before in his life. But there was no doubt that the man in the dock was Turpin and the evidence presented against him on the charges of horse theft was convincing. He was found guilty and sentenced to death after the judge rejected Turpin's final argument that he had not been given enough time to prepare his defense or to call character witnesses from Essex.

The sentence was carried out on April 7 in front of a large crowd at York racecourse. According to a contemporary account, Turpin had bought a new suit of clothes for the day and behaved with some assurance in the moments before he was executed. While climbing the ladder up to the gallows, he talked to the executioner and then, with the noose around his neck, threw himself off it. The account goes on to say that it took five minutes for him to die and then his body was left hanging for several hours to ensure that he was dead. It was the typical fate of most highwaymen of the period and, in truth, there was little to separate Turpin from the others, except perhaps the notoriety he had gained by evading capture for several years. The subsequent romantic stories written about him, in which he was made out to be a Robin Hood-like character, may bear little relationship to the facts as we know them, but it is these fictional versions, of the dashing highwayman rather than the violent criminal, that have endured in the public imagination.

THE DANDY HIGHWAYMAN
A romanticized view of a highway robbery carried out by a knight of the road, painted in 1860 by William Frith Powell.

MOTIVATION

Murder

Assassination

Treason

Espionage

Robbery

Hijacking

Fraud

Kidnapping

THE POYAIS FRAUD

1820s

Location: Britain and Honduras

Perpetrator: Gregor MacGregor

Outcome: The certain knowledge that no such place as Poyais existed

The climate is remarkably healthy, and agrees admirably with the constitution of Europeans; many of whom, having become much debilitated by a long residence in the West Indies, have been completely restored to health by a removal, for a short period, to the Bay of Honduras. The soil is extremely rich and fertile, bearing three crops of Indian corn a year.

**From an advertisement placed by the Poyais
Land Office in 1822 in the *Glasgow Herald***

In the summer of 1821 Brigadier-General Sir Gregor MacGregor arrived in London, having spent almost ten years in South America. He announced himself as the Cazique of Poyais, a title equivalent to that of "prince" that he said had been bestowed on him by King George Frederic Augustus I, the indigenous chief of the Miskito people of Central America, who had also granted him a huge tract of land on the Bay of Honduras that he called Poyais. MacGregor had fought in the South American wars of independence against the Spanish and had been promoted to the rank of general by none other than the great revolutionary hero General Francisco de Miranda and had married Josefa, now the Princess of Poyais, who was a cousin of the Liberator, Simón Bolívar. The cazique and the princess were the toast of London high society and he was invited to high society balls and parties, where he explained that he had come to Britain to raise finance to develop the abundant natural resources of Poyais by means of a bond issue and also to sell land rights to prospective settlers, who he encouraged to emigrate with descriptions of the favorable climate and fertile soils of the region. It appeared to be a great opportunity for investors, but there was a major drawback that would only become apparent a few years later: the country of Poyais did not actually exist.

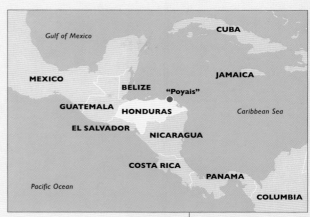

CARIBBEAN DREAM
The fictional country of "Poyais" was located in densely forested terrain on the coast of Honduras.

By the 1820s, London had become the financial center of the world on the back of the expansion of the British Empire and the exploits of the East India Company on the Indian subcontinent, together with the developing Industrial Revolution in which goods were manufactured and sold around the world. Victory in the Napoleonic Wars, culminating at the battle of Waterloo in 1815, together with the decline of the Spanish Empire had left Britain as the major world superpower and self-styled "ruler of the waves," keen to exploit whatever colonial and commercial opportunities arose around the world. As the independence movements pushed the Spanish out of both Central and South America, territories that had previously been the sole preserve of Spain were opening up to other financial interests and British investors were queuing up to cash in what

THE CONFIDENCE TRICKSTER

YOUNG MACGREGOR
A portrait from 1804 by George Watson showing the 18-year-old Gregor MacGregor as an officer in the British army.

was expected to be enormous returns for relatively modest initial outlays. Whether by accident or design, MacGregor's arrival in London coincided with a period of optimism in the financial markets, particularly with regard to business in the Americas. As a consequence, the investment opportunities he offered received a great deal of interest.

Gregor MacGregor was born in 1786 in Glengyle, Scotland, and was a descendant of the Scottish folk hero and outlaw Rob Roy MacGregor, even if he was not as closely related as he would later claim to be. He joined the British army as a junior officer in 1804 before getting married for the first time to Maria Bowater the following year, at which time he was sent to Spain and Portugal to fight in the Peninsular War against Napoleon Bonaparte's French Empire. It is difficult to know at what point he first began to elaborate on the truth. After buying himself out of the army in 1810 and returning to Britain, he would describe himself as a colonel and would later claim to have been involved in the Battle of Albuera, where his regiment, the 57th Foot, distinguished itself, earning the nickname of the Die-Hards. The battle had, in fact, been fought in May 1811, the year after he had returned to Britain, and he had not achieved the rank of colonel or, as he would also claim, been awarded a knighthood by the Portuguese.

In December 1811 Maria died and her wealthy family refused to have anything else to do with MacGregor, who by this time had gained a reputation for extravagance and boastfulness. With little means of support, he left Britain for South America, where he talked his way into a meeting with General de Miranda and a genuine commission as a colonel in the republican army of Venezuela. It is difficult now to separate fact from the tall tales MacGregor told about the years he spent as a soldier of fortune, but there appears to be little doubt that on occasion he demonstrated real leadership qualities, first under Miranda, who really did promote him to brigadier-general, and then, after Miranda died in 1816, as a staff officer with Bolívar. He had achieved one of his aims in coming to South America, to make his name, but the other, to make a fortune, had eluded him and it was perhaps this failing that his progression from being a boastful soldier who embroidered the truth to a fully fledged confidence trickster.

By the time he returned to London in 1821, MacGregor had certainly made that transition, setting up what, in scope and ambition as well as in financial terms, would become one of the largest confidence tricks of all time. One of the reasons why he was able to fool so many people was that his story contained enough truth for it to be convincing. Like all successful confidence tricksters, however, what really enabled him to get away with it was that people wanted to believe him. The prospect of becoming involved at the beginning of what, had it been true, could develop into a highly lucrative enterprise, offering significant returns on money invested, proved to be very attractive, as did the MacGregors themselves. The Scottish-born soldier of fortune and his beautiful Venezuelan wife became the toast of London at the receptions, balls, and dinner parties they attended and MacGregor set up an office in London called the Legation of the Territory of Poyais in order to facilitate his aim of promoting the country he claimed to represent, appointing Major William Richardson, an army officer who had also served in Venezuela, as *charge d'affairs*, with the primary purpose of dealing with the sale of bonds.

MacGregor's description of Poyais as an almost perfect country for development was supported in 1822 by the publication of a book by Captain Thomas Strangeways, *Sketch of the Mosquito Shore, Including the Territory of Poyais*. It was similar to many books written by army officers at the time. It gave details of the regions of the world where Britain had already developed or was in the process of developing colonial and commercial interests. Furthermore, it described Poyais in glowing terms, outlining opportunities there to establish gold and silver mines and describing the capital city, St. Joseph's, as already developed and possessing wide streets and an opera house, among other facilities. More than simply confirming what MacGregor had been saying, it arguably depicted Poyais even more positively than he had done. Nobody appears to have asked why such a valuable territory had been given away in the first place or why the Spanish, who had been the colonial power in the region for almost 300 years, had never made any effort to develop it.

The bond issue, scheduled for October 1822, raised £200,000, an enormous sum equivalent to around $750 million (£500 million) in today's money. However, MacGregor did not stop there. Even before the bonds were sold, he had begun to sell land rights in Poyais, opening offices in Edinburgh

THE POYARS

and Glasgow in order to target sales to his fellow Scots. The land was priced so as to attract people who could not afford to buy property in Britain, while professional people, including doctors and lawyers, were offered positions in the government of the newly established country. In November, 1822, the ship *Honduras Packet* left Scotland carrying the first 70 of the Poyars, as MacGregor named the citizens of Poyais, and was followed in January 1823 by the *Kennersley Castle*, carrying around 200 more prospective settlers on board.

The shock awaiting the settlers when they arrived in Poyais can only be imagined. Not only was there no opera house, there was no port, no town, and no roads. In fact, there was nothing at all other than a few ruins from a previous failed attempt to colonize the region 100 years before. The settlers had to start from scratch, building shelter from whatever natural materials they could find and enduring the hot and humid conditions they encountered as best they could. People began to fall ill after contracting tropical diseases and many died, while others fell into despondency at the situation they found themselves in. In April 1823, the survivors were rescued by a ship sent from the British colony of Belize. In October 1823, some 50 of them arrived back in Britain, while others decided to settle elsewhere in Central America and the Caribbean. Having given up their jobs and invested everything they had in emigrating, there was nothing for them to return to in Britain. However, of those

IDYLLIC POYAIS
An illustration from *Sketch of the Mosquito Shore* purporting to show a port in Poyais. Neither the country nor the port actually existed.

who had originally left Britain, almost two-thirds had died either on the Mosquito Coast of Honduras or during the long and arduous journeys they had undertaken.

News of what had happened to the settlers reached Britain before any of them got back, prompting an investigation into MacGregor's dealings. By that time, he had skipped the country, going to France and leaving Richardson to deal with the fallout. It would soon become apparent that almost everything had been a fabrication and that everybody, including Richardson, had been conned. Even the book purportedly written by Captain Strangeways, which had done so much to boost confidence in Poyais, was in reality written by MacGregor himself. The only part of the scheme that was actually true was that he had secured the land rights to a stretch of the coastline on the Bay of Honduras in the form of a handwritten piece of paper signed by King George Frederic Augustus, but it was a region of dense rainforests and mangrove swamps that remains largely undeveloped today.

MacGregor attempted to set up another Poyais scheme in France, issuing bonds and selling land rights, but before any more unfortunate people set out for the non-existent country, the French government stepped in. MacGregor and several other people who had worked with him in Britain before joining him in France were arrested and charged with fraud. At the subsequent trial, one of his colleagues was found guilty and sentenced to a year in jail, while MacGregor was acquitted. It was the only occasion he faced any charges for the frauds he had instigated, even after returning to Britain in 1826 and attempting to sell land rights in Poyais again. By this time most people were well aware of the nature of his business practices, so there was little chance of him succeeding in defrauding anybody else. Incredibly, he managed to squander all the money he had made, estimated to be in the region of £1.3 million—about $5.25 billion (£3.5 billion) today. After his wife died in 1838, he emigrated to Venezuela, where he was awarded a pension as a former brigadier-general in the republican army. He died at the age of 58 on December 4, 1845, in Caracas and his funeral was attended by the president of Venezuela and numerous other dignitaries, no doubt paying their last respects to a hero of the independence movement in their country rather than remembering the Cazique of Poyais, the man who had perpetrated one of the biggest confidence tricks in history.

MOTIVATION

Murder
Assassination
Treason
Espionage
Robbery
Hijacking
Fraud
Kidnapping

THE ANATOMY MURDERS OF BURKE AND HARE

1828

Location: Edinburgh

Perpetrators: William Burke and William Hare

Outcome: Burke was hanged and Hare set free

A neat little man of about five feet five, well-proportioned, especially in his legs and thighs... Nothing repulsive about him, to ordinary observers at least, and certainly not deficient in intelligence. Hare was the most brutal man I have ever seen. His dull blackish eyes, one rather higher than the other; his large thick or rather coarse lipped mouth; his high, broad cheekbones and sunken cheeks... all steeped in a sullenness not born of the jail but alive to the almost deformed face.

Descriptions of Burke and Hare respectively by Professor John Wilson, writing under the name of Christopher North in *Blackwood's Magazine* in 1829

Over the course of a ten-month period, from February to November 1828, William Burke and William Hare murdered 16 people in Edinburgh, Scotland, in a case that would become known as the Anatomy Murders. They sold the bodies to Dr. Richard Knox, a distinguished anatomist, who gave lectures at the medical school in the Scottish capital during which he dissected the bodies in front of his students. The extent to which Knox was aware of the source of these bodies is not known for certain, even if it is difficult to believe that a doctor who specialized in anatomy would not have known how the individuals had died. But bodies of people who had recently died that were suitable for dissection were not easily acquired and it would appear that few questions were asked of Burke and Hare, allowing their gruesome business to continue for much longer than might otherwise have been the case.

Up until 1832, when the law was changed, partly in response to the Burke and Hare murders, there were few ways for doctors to obtain human bodies for the purpose of medical research. If unknown vagrants or destitute inmates of workhouses died and their remains were not claimed by relatives, the bodies could be sent to medical schools to be used for research and dissection purposes. The only other source was the bodies of executed criminals, but the number of executions being held in Britain had declined in the early nineteenth century as less serious crimes such as horse theft were no longer held to be capital offenses. At the same time, a rapid rise in the population of Britain was occurring, which meant that more doctors were needed and medical schools were expanding. The result was a shortage of bodies that could be obtained by legitimate means and the corresponding development of a black market that was supplied by body snatchers, or resurrectionists, as they were sometimes called, who disinterred recently buried bodies in cemeteries in order to sell them to medical schools.

THE ANATOMY MURDERS

Resurrectionists were certainly at work in Edinburgh during the 1820s and it was not unusual for the relatives of a recently deceased person to mount a vigil over their grave to prevent the body being stolen. The authorities in Edinburgh were doing very little to prevent it; they may even have been turning a blind eye to the crime because they were aware of the need for bodies at the city's medical school, one of the most prestigious in Britain at the time. Body snatching became so prevalent that the price of a body had become standard: £8 (about $1500, or £1000 today) in the summer and £10 (about $1800, or £1200 today) in the winter, when the colder conditions preserved bodies for longer so that they would be in better condition for dissection. On November 29, 1827, an elderly tenant with no known relatives died of natural causes in the lodging house run by Hare and his wife Margaret in Tanner's Close in the West Port district of Edinburgh. The man, named only as Donald, died owing rent and one way for Hare to recoup the money was to sell the body to the medical school.

Hare enlisted the help of Burke, who had recently moved into the lodging house, and together they removed the body from its coffin before it was taken away for burial, weighting the empty coffin with tanner's bark from the tannery that at the time stood immediately behind the lodging house. Once they had obtained the body, the two of them went to the medical school to try to sell it, initially asking for Dr. Alexander Munro, a senior anatomist at the school. They were directed instead to the nearby offices of Dr. Knox at No. 10 Surgeon's Square. A deal was agreed with Knox's assistants and the body was delivered, where it was inspected by Knox himself before Burke and Hare were paid £7 and 10 shillings, a considerable sum of money. Knox and his assistants were clearly accustomed to acquiring corpses in this way from the resurrectionists and presumably they assumed that their new suppliers were another pair of body snatchers.

Burke and Hare had both come to Scotland from Ireland in 1818 to work as laborers, or navvies as they were called, on the construction of the Union Canal to link Edinburgh to Falkirk. After the canal was completed in 1822, both worked at a variety of laboring jobs in and around Edinburgh but do not appear to have been acquainted with each other before Burke moved into Hare's lodging house. Hare had been a lodger in the house himself before marrying his landlady after her first husband died, while Burke arrived at the lodging house in the company of a woman called Helen MacDougal, having abandoned his wife and two children in Ireland.

The next opportunity to make some easy money presented itself to Burke and Hare the following February when another of Hare's lodgers fell ill. When the man, known only as Joseph, began to recover, Burke and Hare took matters into their own hands, plying him with whiskey until he became unconscious, at which point one of them smothered him with a pillow while the other lay across his chest, preventing him from moving or taking a breath. They then took the body to Surgeon's Square in a tea chest and were paid £10 for it by Knox's assistants. Once they had crossed the line into murder, they began to kill regularly, mostly targeting people who had come to stay in the lodging house or those they met elsewhere and invited back there with the offer of accommodation. Once they had identified a victim, they then employed the same method to murder them, getting them drunk and then suffocating them.

Shortly after the first killing, Burke and Hare murdered an old woman named Abigail Simpson and then an unnamed Englishman who sold matches on the streets of Edinburgh. In each case they arranged to meet a porter from Surgeon's Square at a designated spot below Castle Rock, the hill in the middle of Edinburgh, who would then take the tea chest with him. The murderers went with the porter so that they could collect the money they were owed from Knox's assistants. Over the course of the

spring and summer, they sold a succession of bodies to Knox in this way, with no questions being asked. Their victims were mostly from Edinburgh's transient underclass and, if they were missed at all, nobody appears to have made any great effort to enquire where they had gone.

The murder of Mary Paterson, an attractive young woman who may have been working as a prostitute in Leith Street, Edinburgh's red light district, was

SURGEON'S SQUARE
An engraving from 1829 by Thomas Hosmer Shepherd of Surgeon's Square as it was at the time of the murders.

an exception to this routine. One day in mid-April, she and her friend Janet Brown chanced to meet Burke in a public house. After buying them several drinks, he invited them both to accompany him to his brother's house nearby. They went with him, but when Helen MacDougal arrived at the house and flew into a rage at finding Burke with two young women, Janet Brown left. By this time Mary Paterson had fallen into a drunken sleep and when Hare turned up at the house shortly afterward, he and Burke suffocated her. In some accounts of this murder it has been suggested that, after the body had been delivered to Surgeon's Square, one of Knox's assistants recognized it as being Mary Paterson, but no questions were asked as to how a young and apparently healthy young woman had died.

The murders continued into the fall with no indication that Burke and Hare were close to being discovered. The money they made funded a drunken and dissolute lifestyle and, perhaps having convinced themselves that they would never be caught, they began to take more risks. In October they murdered 18-year-old James Wilson, who suffered from some form of mental disability and was a well-known character on the streets of Edinburgh, where he was universally known as Daft Jamie. His sudden disappearance did not go unnoticed and, when his body was being dissected by Dr. Knox, some of the students attending his anatomy lecture are said to have recognized him, who had been seen alive and apparently healthy only a few days before. According to some later accounts, once Knox became aware that the body had been identified, he hurriedly finished the dissection to make it unrecognizable, which, if true, would indicate that he knew more than he ever admitted about how Burke and Hare were obtaining the bodies they sold to him.

ARREST AND TRIAL

The murder of James Wilson should have raised suspicions about Burke and Hare, but it was actually their next murder, the sixteenth, that finally led to their arrest. On October 31, Mary Docherty, a middle-aged Irish woman, was invited to the house Burke was now living in for a Halloween party, where she was seen by a number of other people. The following day a couple who lodged in the house found her dead body on a bed, where it had been covered in blankets. They went to the police, but by the time the police arrived at the house Burke and Hare had delivered the body to one of the porters from Surgeon's Square. When the police enquired about the whereabouts of Mary Docherty they were told she had left the house. Crucially, the stories told by Burke and MacDougal differed as to the time she had departed. With their suspicions aroused, the police searched the house and found bloodstains in the bed where Docherty had been killed. On November 2, police investigators visited Surgeon's Square, most likely as the result of a tip-off, and in the cellar found the body of a woman in a tea chest that was then identified as being Mary Docherty by the couple who had seen her in Burke's house.

Burke and Hare, together with their respective partners, were arrested, but the doctors who carried out a post-mortem on Docherty's body could not confirm that she had been murdered. The public prosecutors decided to offer Hare immunity from prosecution if he gave a full confession and testified against Burke. They apparently considered the evidence to be too weak to guarantee convictions and did not want to risk a trial in which all four defendants might have been acquitted. Hare's subsequent confession led to Burke and MacDougal being charged with the murders of Mary Paterson, James Wilson, and Mary Docherty. The trial began on Christmas Eve and considered the Docherty case first, with both William and Margaret Hare taking the stand to testify against Burke and MacDougal. Proceedings lasted for almost 24 hours and, on Christmas Day, the jury found Burke guilty and returned a verdict of "not proven" against MacDougal. Burke was sentenced to death and on January 28, 1829, he was hanged at a public execution in Edinburgh, after which his body was sent to the medical school for dissection.

The other three defendants were released from custody and forced to leave the city because of the threat of mob violence against them. The Hares returned to Ireland and MacDougal, after moving to England, is thought to have emigrated to Australia. Dr. Knox did not face any charges and did not give evidence at the trial. He was later exonerated by a committee of enquiry set up to investigate his dealings with Burke and Hare and continued to work in Edinburgh despite public anger over his role in the affair. In 1856, almost 30 years after the murders, he moved to London to take up a research position and died there in 1862 at the age of 71. He never spoke publicly about the case.

DR. KNOX
An illustration showing Dr. Robert Knox giving a lecture, taken from a biography published in 1870, eight years after his death.

After details of Burke and Hare's crimes became known, similar murders were committed in other British cities. The perpetrators of these crimes were known as "burkers" and their method of murder by suffocation as "burking." A law passed in 1832, which allowed medical schools to acquire bodies for anatomical research by legal means, brought the black market trade to an end, putting the burkers and body snatchers out of business. In 1836, in a strange and, to this day, unexplained occurrence, 17 miniature coffins containing carved wooden figures were found in a cave on Arthur's Seat, one of the hills that overlooks Edinburgh. No connection with the Anatomy Murders was made at the time, but, if the confessions given by Burke and Hare were correct, then they sold a total of 17 bodies to Dr. Knox. It is impossible to know what, if anything, these coffins had to do with Burke and Hare, but it has nevertheless added a note of mystery to the most notorious criminal case in Scottish legal history.

MOTIVATION

Murder

Assassination

Treason

Espionage

Robbery

Hijacking

Fraud

Kidnapping

THE ASSASSINATION OF ABRAHAM LINCOLN

1865

Location: Washington, D.C.

Perpetrators: John Wilkes Booth and his fellow conspirators

Outcome: The conspirators succeeded in killing Lincoln but not in their long-term aim of prolonging the Civil War

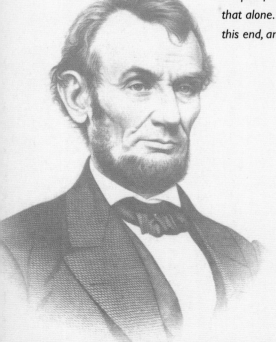

I hoped for no gain. I knew no private wrong. I struck for my country and that alone. A country that groaned beneath this tyranny, and prayed for this end, and yet now behold the cold hands they extend to me.

From a diary entry written by John Wilkes Booth after he had assassinated President Abraham Lincoln

On Palm Sunday, April 9, 1865, the Confederate General Robert E. Lee surrendered his forces to General Ulysses S. Grant of the Union army at Appomattox Court House in Virginia. It may not have marked the official end of the American Civil War but after four years of fighting it was nevertheless a clear signal that the Union had won. Five days later, on Good Friday, April 14, President Abraham Lincoln was assassinated by the well-known actor John Wilkes Booth shortly after 10 o'clock in the evening as he was attending a performance of the play *Our American Cousin* by Tom Taylor at Ford's Theater in Washington. Booth had entered the box to the side of the stage where Lincoln, his wife, and several other people were sitting and had then shot the president in the back of the head at point blank range with a single-shot Philadelphia Derringer pistol before jumping from the box onto the stage brandishing a knife and escaping through the back of the theater, riding away on a horse that was being held for him in the street.

THE ASSASSINATION
An illustration from 1865 by Alfred Pharazyn showing John Wilkes Booth leaping to the stage in Ford's Theater after shooting Lincoln.

Lincoln was attended by two doctors in the audience that night. He had not been killed instantly by the gunshot, but the doctors quickly determined from the nature of his head wound that he would not survive. He was taken to a nearby house in a coma and died there nine hours later without regaining consciousness. By that time it had become apparent that the assassination had been part of a wider conspiracy. Booth may have been the lone gunman in Ford's Theater, but not long after he shot Lincoln an attempt was made on the life of Secretary of State William H. Seward at his home in Washington. At the time, Seward was recovering from the injuries he had received in a serious carriage accident nine days previously. A man later identified as Booth's associate, Lewis Powell, forced his way into Seward's house, stabbed the secretary of state a number of times in the head and neck, and also injured a number of other people who were in the house without killing any of them. It would later emerge that the full plot

THE CONSPIRACY

THE CONSPIRATORS
A contemporary poster
offering a $100,000 reward
for information leading
to the arrest of Booth,
Surratt, and Herold.

had also involved an attack on Vice-President Andrew Johnson that was not carried through after the intended assassin, George Atzerodt, lost his nerve and spent the night drinking and walking the streets of Washington instead.

The investigation into the assassination of Lincoln and the attack on Seward focused on known associates of Booth and resulted in numerous arrests, although most of the people held were later released without charge. But the police also discovered a connection to the Washington boarding house run by Mary Surratt, who was arrested there along with Lewis Powell. He arrived at the house shortly after police detectives, telling them that he had come to dig a ditch, and was arrested after Mrs. Surratt claimed not to know him. He was then identified by members of the Seward family as being the man who carried out the attack on the secretary of state. It emerged that the boarding house had been used by the conspirators as a meeting place to discuss what had originally been a plan to abduct Lincoln with the intention of exchanging him for Confederate prisoners-of-war. Mary Surratt's son John was undoubtedly involved in the conspiracy and was an agent of the Confederate Secret Service, but the extent of his mother's involvement, beyond providing lodgings and a place to meet, is less certain and remains controversial today.

By the time of these arrests Booth was hiding out in an area of dense forest and wetland in southern Maryland known as Zekiah Swamp. After the assassination he had ridden south from Washington into Maryland, meeting up with his fellow conspirator David Herold and heading first for Surratt's Tavern, 9 miles (15km) from Washington, which had been established by Mary Surratt's late husband and was still owned by her. Booth and Herold picked up a stash of weapons and supplies they had previously stored at the tavern and then traveled on into Maryland to the house of Dr. Samuel Mudd near Bryantown, arriving in the early hours of the morning. At some point during the escape, Booth's horse had tripped and thrown him, resulting in a break to the fibula bone in his left leg just above the ankle. By the time he reached Mudd's house his leg was swollen and he must have been in considerable pain. Mudd set the bone, later saying that he had not recognized Booth despite the fact that he had met him on at least two occasions in November and December of the previous year.

The following day Booth and Herold continued their journey, relying on the help of Confederate sympathizers to hide them in Zekiah Swamp while Union soldiers conducted an extensive manhunt through Maryland after receiving information that the fugitives were in the state. Five days later the two crossed the Potomac River into Virginia and were escorted to a farm owned by Richard Garrett, who was apparently unaware of the assassination and was told that Booth was a wounded Confederate soldier. Union soldiers tracked Booth and Herold to Garrett's farm, arriving there on April 26 and surrounding them in a tobacco barn on the property. After the soldiers threatened to set light to the barn, Herold surrendered. Booth refused to come out and, after the fire had started, he was shot in the back of the neck and died two hours later from the wound. The soldier who fired the shot, Sergeant Boston Corbett, would later say that Booth had raised the guns he was carrying, while accounts from other witnesses suggest that, while Booth had been armed, the guns were by his side at the moment he was shot.

In total, eight people were charged with being involved in the conspiracy to assassinate President Lincoln. As well as David Herold, Lewis Powell, George Atzerodt, and Mary Surratt, two other men, Samuel Arnold and Michael O'Laughlen, who were implicated with Booth in the original plan to kidnap Lincoln, had been arrested, as had Dr. Samuel Mudd and Edmund Spangler, a stagehand from Ford's Theater whom Booth had asked to hold his horse for him at the back of the theater. In the event, Spangler had been busy and given the horse to a boy named Joseph Burroughs, who also worked at the theater and was commonly known as Peanuts. John Surratt, wanted as an accomplice, had been in New York at the time of the assassination and, as soon as he heard of the event, fled first to Canada, then to Europe and then on to Egypt. He was located there by American agents in November 1866 and brought back to America, where he was tried for the murder of Lincoln and found not guilty.

President Andrew Johnson, who had been sworn into office within hours of Lincoln's death, ordered that the trial of the conspirators be heard by a military tribunal. The exact reason for this is not clear; given that most of the defendants were not military personnel, it has been argued that the trial should have been heard by a civilian court. The number of people prosecuted was also a point of contention. With the exception of Dr. Mudd,

THE TRIAL

those who had helped Booth and Herold travel through Maryland and into Virginia were not charged. Similarly, a close friend of John Surratt, Louis Weichman, who had been a lodger in the boarding house throughout the period of the conspiracy, was called only as a witness.

The trial began on May 1, 1865, and the evidence presented against Herold, Powell, and Atzerodt made for a compelling case against them. The same cannot be said of the case made against the other five defendants; had the trial been held in a civilian court, it is possible that they would all have been acquitted due to a lack of evidence. The case against Mary Surratt relied on the testimony given by Weichman, who said that he had accompanied her to the tavern she owned in Maryland with a consignment of weapons and supplies, which were to be retrieved later by Booth and Herold. This testimony was supported by the landlord who leased the tavern from Surratt. Weichman also testified that he had seen Booth and Mudd talking together in Washington in December 1864, which clearly suggested that Mudd was lying when he stated he had not known who Booth was when he arrived at his house with a broken leg.

There was little doubt that Arnold and O'Laughlen had been involved in the initial conspiracy to kidnap Lincoln, but both denied having anything to do with the plot and there was little evidence that tied them to the other conspirators on the day of the assassination. Spangler was accused of helping Booth to escape from Ford's Theater. He denied the charge, claiming not to have had any knowledge of nor involvement in Booth's plan. The lawyers for the defense demonstrated that Booth was well known by everybody who worked at the theater and had previously arranged for Spangler to look after horses for him in nearby stables when he was away from Washington. Spangler, they contended, had been an entirely unwitting accomplice who had helped Booth with his horses in the past and was simply doing the same on the night of the assassination.

The trial lasted for seven weeks and, in total, more than 350 witnesses were called. The tribunal, made up of a panel of nine senior military officers, found all eight defendants guilty. Herold, Powell, Atzerodt, and Surratt were sentenced to death and all hanged on July 7, 1865, at Fort McNair in Washington, while Mudd, Arnold, and O'Laughlen were sentenced to life imprisonment. Spangler was given a prison term of six years. O'Laughlen died in prison in 1867 and the remaining three received a presidential pardon two years later. Questions were asked at the time of the trial as to the exact roles played by these men in Lincoln's assassination, together with wider questions concerning the extent of the conspiracy. Furthermore, doubt surrounded the genesis of the plot—had it been primarily the idea of John Wilkes Booth, who then recruited the others, or had there been a much larger conspiracy, involving figures in the Confederate government such as President Jefferson Davies and Secretary of State Judah Benjamin? After all, at least two of the known conspirators, Lewis Powell and John Surratt, were agents of the Confederate Secret Service. However, only circumstantial evidence linked Booth to that organization, including his contacts with Powell and Surratt, and the fact that he made regular trips to Confederate states to act in theatrical productions, which could conceivably have been used as a cover for espionage.

DEATH SENTENCE
An illustration from 1865 of the executions of David Herold, Lewis Powell, George Atzerodt, and Mary Surratt at Fort McNair.

Even if it is not possible to say for certain whether Booth was acting on orders from the Confederate government, he was the driving force behind the conspiracy as it developed from a plot to kidnap Lincoln into one of assassination. His motivation appears to have been what he saw as an attempt by the North to destroy the culture of the South and, in particular, the institution of slavery. He came to regard Lincoln as the man responsible for this, the embodiment of all that he hated. The surrender at Appomattox Court House may have been the catalyst for the assassination attempt. By killing its three most senior figures, Booth perhaps intended to disable the Union government and rally the remaining Confederate forces to continue the fight. In truth, the war was already lost and, by killing Lincoln, Booth had removed one of the principal advocates of a moderate approach to the period of reconstruction that would follow the war. Rather than becoming a hero of the Confederacy, as he seems to have imagined he would become, Booth is now remembered as the murderer of one of the most revered figures in American history.

MOTIVATION

Murder

Assassination

Treason

Espionage

Robbery

Hijacking

Fraud

Kidnapping

THE KELLY GANG

1870s

Location: Australia

Perpetrators: Ned Kelly, Dan Kelly, Joe Byrne, and Steve Hart

Outcome: The creation of an Australian legend

All doubts as to the presence of the Kelly gang in the colony – a fact which has been to some extent a matter of dispute – were set at rest yesterday by the intelligence that they had re-appeared at Beechworth, and had added yet another murder to the crimes already resting upon their heads. Since the gang so successfully plundered the bank at Jerilderie and escaped across country, no trustworthy information as to their whereabouts has been obtained. At various intervals it has been intimated that they were in the country, but the information as to their being in a particular locality at any set time was always many days late, and generally even then of an un-certain character.

From a report in the *Melbourne Argus* on June 28, 1880, concerning the murder of Aaron Sherritt

Since first gaining notoriety in Australia in the late 1870s, Ned Kelly has provoked a wide range of reactions. He has been variously described as a violent and dangerous outlaw whose crimes included cold-blooded murder or as a man driven to extremes after he and his family had been the victims of persecution and injustice at the hands of a police force acting on behalf of wealthy and well-connected landowners. As far as it is possible to know the real story now, there appear to be elements of truth in both of these versions of events and it is perhaps this uncertainty about him that has led to an enduring fascination with his life story among many people in Australia and around the world.

Edward "Ned" Kelly was born in late 1854 or early 1855 (the precise date is not known) on a small farm near the town of Beveridge in the state of Victoria, Australia, about 35 miles (55km) north of Melbourne. His father, John Kelly, who was known as "Red," was Irish and had been transported to Australia after being convicted of stealing two pigs. Following his release from penal servitude after four years, he settled in Victoria, married Ellen Quinn, and rented a small farm where the couple raised a family of eight children. Red Kelly became involved in stealing cattle, or "duffing," as it was known, and in 1866, shortly after serving a prison sentence for that offense, he died and the family moved to a farm at Eleven Mile Creek near Greta, an area that has since become known as Kelly Country.

KELLY COUNTRY

Northern Victoria was undergoing a period of rapid social change at this time, partly as a consequence of the discovery of gold in the region in 1851, which led to an influx of people hoping to make their fortune, but also because of a series of land laws passed in the Australian colonies to allow for what was known as the "selection" of land claims by settlers. By that time, much of northern Victoria had already been claimed by "squatters," people who had settled in the region and laid claim to large tracts of land without any legal basis beyond the right of possession. The squatters had become relatively wealthy and did not appreciate the arrival of "selectors" making legal claims on what they considered to be their land. Many of the selectors were poor and, like the Kelly family, of Irish-Catholic descent, while the squatters were predominately British and Protestant. Ned Kelly grew up against this background of antagonism between these two groups and, after he had been declared an outlaw by the Victorian authorities, stated that he had been forced into a life of crime by the police, who had acted against him because of his Catholic background and because of the influence of the squatters.

Kelly's accusations against the Victorian police may have had some substance, but it is also possible that he and his extended family contributed to what he described as their persecution by continually breaking the law. Numerous members of the Kelly and Quinn families had been arrested and charged with various crimes, mostly involving cattle duffing or other similar offenses, and Ned would later say that he had himself stolen hundreds of horses in his youth. While still a teenager, he is also thought to have been an accomplice of Harry Power, a well-known bush-ranger who committed a string of robberies in Victoria during 1870, before being caught and sent to prison. The 15-year-old Kelly was also arrested at the time but was released without charge because witnesses to Power's robberies were unable to identify him.

THE KELLY GANG

Over the next few years, Kelly was constantly in trouble, serving a six-month sentence of hard labor for assault and then, three years later, being found in possession of a stolen horse. Kelly claimed that he had no idea the horse was stolen and would later say that, as the man who had actually taken it received a jail sentence of only 18 months, it was clear that he was being victimized by the police. After he was released from prison in 1874, he continued to get into trouble until, on April 15, 1878, an incident occurred that would lead to him becoming an outlaw. On this occasion at least, his claims of police provocation against his family appear to have had some justification.

In the afternoon of that day, Constable Alexander Fitzpatrick went to the Kelly farm with the intention of arresting Ned's younger brother, Dan Kelly, who was wanted on a charge of horse stealing. On arriving there, the officer found that Dan was not at home and so decided to wait for him there. When Dan arrived, an altercation occurred in which the constable was injured in the wrist. He reported that he had been shot by Ned Kelly and, when police officers later arrived at the farm to find neither Ned nor Dan there, they arrested Ellen Kelly and two other men who had been there at the time. All three were charged with being accomplices to the attempted murder of a police officer and, despite evidence that Fitzpatrick had been drinking before arriving at the farm and the inability of a doctor to confirm that his wrist injury, which appears to have been minor, was caused by a gunshot, they were found guilty. The two men were sentenced to six years for their part in the incident and Ellen Kelly was given three years, with the judge saying that if Ned Kelly had been caught he would have gotten 15 years.

The severity of the sentences and the remarks of the judge convinced Kelly that, if he turned himself in, he would

not receive a fair trial. So he went into hiding with his brother Dan in a hut in the Wombat Ranges, now known as the Tolmie Tablelands, which lie between Greta and the town of Mansfield, where they were joined by two friends, Steve Hart and Joe Byrne. On October 25, four police officers—Sergeant Michael Kennedy and constables Thomas Lonigan, Michael Scanlan, and Thomas MacIntyre—set out from Mansfield into the Wombat Ranges in search of the two Kelly brothers, unaware that Hart and Byrne had joined them. That night they camped at Stingybark Creek, apparently unaware of the location's proximity to the hut where the Kelly Gang were hiding. In the morning, Kennedy and Scanlan began a search of the area, leaving Lonigan and MacIntyre at the camp, where they were discovered by the gang that afternoon. They attempted to capture the two police constables, entering the camp with their guns raised. The unarmed MacIntyre surrendered immediately, but Lonigan reached for his gun and was shot and killed by Ned Kelly. Some time later, Kennedy and Scanlan returned to the camp and a short gun battle ensued in which they were both killed. Kennedy, wounded while attempting to get away, was finished off by Ned Kelly at close range. In the chaos, MacIntyre managed to mount a horse and escape into the bush.

After the killing of the police officers, the Kelly Gang were declared to be outlaws in Victoria who could be shot on sight and a reward of £2000 was posted for their capture, dead or alive. The support they had enjoyed among the Irish selector community must surely have been damaged, not least because all of the policemen they murdered were of Irish descent. However, either out of loyalty or fear, very little useful information about the whereabouts of the gang was passed on to the police. On December

10, 1878, they staged their first bank robbery in the town of Euroa, having the day before invaded a sheep station outside the town, taking the family who lived there and their workers hostage and then cutting the telegraph wires before entering the town. After robbing the bank, they returned to the sheep station, sat down to eat with their hostages, and then rode away.

On February 10, 1879, the gang raided the town of Jerilderie, this time capturing the police station and setting themselves up in a hotel near the bank before robbing it. Afterward they went back to the hotel and bought drinks for their hostages. Before leaving the town, Ned Kelly left a long letter he had previously dictated to Byrne, the best educated of the four, in which he described the events he had taken part in and attempted to justify his actions, saying that he and his family had been unfairly targeted by the police and that he had fought back on behalf of poor Irish Catholics. The Jerilderie Letter, as it is now known, was not published in full until 1930, and since then it has come to be regarded as an important document in the history of Australia.

GLENROWAN | After the bank robbery at Jerilderie, the gang went to ground. Little is known about their movements for the following 15 months beyond some unsubstantiated reports that they may have attempted to buy passage on a ship bound for California. During this period the police had little success in tracking them down, attracting the derision of the public. The gang reappeared in dramatic fashion on Saturday June 26, 1880, when Joe Byrne murdered Aaron Sherritt at his farm at Woolshed Creek, near the town of Beechworth. Sherritt had been closely associated with the gang but was killed after being suspected of having betrayed them.

The next day the gang raided Glenrowan, taking about 50 hostages in a hotel and sabotaging the railway line in the expectation that a force of police officers would be sent to the town by train. All four members of the gang were wearing suits of armor that had been fashioned out of iron plow shares and covered their heads and bodies, leaving their arms and legs free. The suits, intended apparently to protect the gang from gunshots, together with the sabotaging of the train tracks, indicate that their intention in raiding the town was to take on the police rather than to rob the bank. It has since been suggested that Kelly wanted to start an insurrection against the Victorian government that would lead to the northeastern region of the state breaking away from the colonial administration in Melbourne.

However, there is little evidence to support this claim. It may simply be an exaggeration of his intention promoted by people who would prefer to think of him as a revolutionary of some sort rather than simply as an outlaw.

As the gang had expected, the police arrived in the town the following day by train, but had been alerted to the sabotaged tracks and stopped before the train was derailed. They surrounded the hotel and a gun battle broke out that continued throughout the day and into the night. In the dark, Ned Kelly escaped from the hotel and in the morning, wearing his iron armor, attacked the police from the rear. He was shot in his exposed legs and arms and was then captured. Later that morning Byrne was shot and killed in the hotel and, after they had released the hostages, Dan Kelly and Hart appear to have committed suicide rather than surrender. Their charred bodies were later found in the ruins of the hotel, which had been set on fire by the police in an attempt to drive them out, although they were most likely dead before the fire started.

Ned Kelly was tried in October 1880 in front of the same judge, Sir Redmond Barry, who had previously presided over the trial of his mother. He was charged with the murder of three police officers, the bank robberies, the raid on Glenrowan, and a string of other offenses and, after being found guilty of the murder of Constable Lonigan, he was sentenced to death. On November 11, 1880, Kelly was hanged in Melbourne Jail and his body buried in an unmarked grave within the grounds. In 2011 his remains were identified by DNA analysis after bones were recovered during an excavation of the graveyard and were returned to his descendants for reburial in Greta cemetery. More than 130 years after his death at

KELLY CAPTURED
Contemporary engraving from the *Illustrated Australian News* showing Victorian police officers capturing the wounded Ned Kelly.

the age of 25, Kelly still divides opinion between those who regard him as an Australian folk hero and those who think of him as nothing more than a common criminal and murderer. But, whatever opinion is held of him now, there can be little doubt that he has become an iconic figure in the history of Australia.

MOTIVATION

Murder

Assassination

Treason

Espionage

Robbery

Hijacking

Fraud

Kidnapping

THE OUTLAW JESSE JAMES

1860s–1882

Location: Western Missouri

Perpetrators: Jesse and Frank James, the Younger brothers, and numerous other bushwhackers and outlaws

Outcome: The civil war finally ended for James when he was shot dead by Bob Ford

Poor Jesse had a wife who mourned for his life
Three children, they were brave
But that dirty little coward who shot Mister Howard
Has laid poor Jesse in his grave

**From the traditional
song "Jesse James"**

In May 1864 the 16-year-old Jesse James joined his older brother Frank in a band of Confederate guerilla fighters, or bushwhackers as they were commonly called, in Clay County, western Missouri, where the two brothers had grown up. By that time Frank James, only 20 years old himself, had been involved in the Civil War for almost three years, first in the regular Confederate army and then with various groups of bushwhackers. The guerilla war in Missouri was a brutal and dirty affair in which neither side observed the usual rules of war and the murder of civilians and unarmed soldiers was a common occurrence. For Jesse James it was an introduction to a life of violence and to living outside the law, a path he would follow long after the war was over and for much of the remaining 16 years of his life.

THE BUSHWHACKER
Jesse James in 1864, aged 16, after he had joined the Confederate guerilla group led by Bloody Bill Anderson.

Frank and Jesse's parents, Robert and Zerelda James, had moved to western Missouri from Kentucky after they were married in 1841 and had bought a farm where they grew hemp and tobacco. As well as farming, Robert James was a minister in the Baptist Church, traveling widely in Missouri to deliver sermons. In 1850, when Jesse was three years old, his father went to California to find his fortune in the Gold Rush but contracted cholera shortly after arriving there and died, leaving his family in serious financial trouble. Zerelda James gained a reputation as a strong-minded and outspoken woman who married a wealthy older man not long after her first husband had died and then married for a third time after his death.

During this period many migrants were settling in Missouri, some of whom, like the James family, came from the southern states of America and brought their slaves with them. Others came from the north and from Europe, principally Ireland and Germany, and many of these new arrivals were opposed to the institution of slavery. It created a tense political situation that regularly turned violent, and the issue of whether western states such as Missouri and the neighboring Kansas should be free states or slave states would become one of the main causes of the Civil War. After the war started in 1861, Missouri remained in the Union, but many people

FROM BUSH-WHACKER TO OUTLAW

in the state supported the secessionist Confederacy in the South, including the James family, who, at the start of the war, owned six slaves. A number of battles were fought in Missouri between the armies of the North and South, which resulted in the Confederate forces being pushed out of the state and prompted the beginning of a guerilla war by those Confederates who remained. It was in this conflict that Frank and Jesse James would later fight.

By the summer of 1864 Frank and Jesse had joined the bushwhacker band led by William T. Anderson, who had a murderous reputation and was known as Bloody Bill. They participated in the Centralia Massacre, in which 22 unarmed Union soldiers were killed and a further 100 armed cavalrymen died in a subsequent ambush. Bloody Bill was himself ambushed and killed a month after the massacre and his second-in-command Archie Clements, a man with an even worse reputation, took over. After the Confederate general Robert E. Lee surrendered on April 9, 1865, effectively bringing the civil war to an end, Clement continued to hold out. Jesse James was shot in the chest during an encounter with Union soldiers in May 1865 and spent time convalescing under the care of his cousin Zee Mimms, who he would later marry. At the same time, Clements led his band in attacks against Union targets, which, for the most part, involved robbing banks owned by northern Republicans, in the process converting guerilla fighters into civilian criminals.

Missouri remained in turmoil during this period of postwar Reconstruction, split along the same lines as during the war. At the two extremes, radical Republicans advocated the imposition of harsh measures against former supporters of the Confederacy, while the ex-Confederates themselves envisaged a resurgence in their political power in the future that would enable them to take control of the Missouri state government. The former bushwhackers turned bank robbers became a force in the political struggle, intimidating some because of the threat they posed but supported by others because they targeted the assets of the wealthy Republican elite.

Jesse James appears to have rejoined his former comrades at some point during the summer of 1866 but did not begin to emerge as a prominent figure until December 7, 1869, when he and his brother robbed the bank in Gallatin, Missouri. Jesse apparently mistook the cashier of the bank, a man named John Sheet, as the man who had killed Bloody Bill Anderson and shot him dead in cold blood. The brothers then escaped from a pursuing posse and for the first time their exploits brought their names to the attention of both newspapermen and the governor of Missouri, who declared them to be outlaws with a price on their heads.

One newspaperman who would become closely associated with the James brothers was John Newman Edwards, the founder and editor of the *Kansas City Times*. He had been a senior officer in the Confederate army and was using his newspaper to mount a campaign in favor of the Democrats and against what he described as the oppressive policies of Reconstruction pursued by the ruling Republicans. After the Gallatin raid, Edwards met the James brothers and began what we might now call a publicity campaign in their favor, presenting their crimes as being committed by Confederates who had not surrendered and were "striking back" against injustice. He was particularly keen to promote Jesse, the more extrovert of the two brothers, and would go on to publish a series of letters written by him in which he either denied being involved in the crimes he was accused of committing or defended himself by stressing the political aspects of his exploits. It was this collaboration, between the newspaper editor and the charismatic outlaw, that would result in Jesse James becoming well-known throughout America and further afield and would be the source of numerous stories about him, many of which have endured despite having only a very distant connection to the truth.

By the summer of 1870, the James brothers had joined with Cole Younger, another former bushwhacker, and his three brothers, John, Jim, and Bob. Together with a number of other Confederate veterans, they formed what became known as the James-Younger Gang. Over the course of the following six years the gang carried out numerous raids in Missouri and the surrounding states, initially robbing banks and holding up stagecoaches before in 1873 carrying out what would be the first of a number of train robberies. Throughout this period Jesse James continued to write letters to newspapers and John Newman Edwards published articles and editorials glorifying the exploits of the gang, despite the fact that a number of people had been killed in their raids. It is difficult to assess whether the support the

HOLLYWOOD LEGEND

Poster from a 1921 movie of James' life, which starred his son, Jesse James Jr., in the title role.

THE JAMES-YOUNGER GANG

THE YOUNGERS
From the left, Bob, Cole, and Jim Younger, together with their sister Henrietta, in a group portrait taken about 1889.

gang enjoyed with many people in the state played a part in the election of the Democratic candidate as governor of Missouri in 1873, the first Democratic victory after the war, but the new administration brought a bill before the state legislature to grant an amnesty to both the James and Younger brothers once they were in power. The bill was narrowly defeated and afterward political support for the gang began to ebb away, the Democrats and the ex-Confederates affiliated to them now holding power and the responsibility for maintaining law and order in the state.

As the gang became increasingly successful, the Pinkerton Detective Agency was engaged to track them down, paid for by the banks and railway companies they had targeted. A violent feud developed between the gang and the Pinkerton agency, which resulted in the deaths of several agents without any significant impact on the number of crimes being committed. In one incident in January 1875, Pinkerton agents raided the James Farm in Clay County, believing that Frank and Jesse were visiting their mother. An explosive device was thrown into the house in an attempt to drive them out, but it would transpire that they were not actually there and the bomb, when it exploded, killed their 9-year-old half-brother Archie and seriously injured their mother. Three months later a neighboring farmer who had allowed the Pinkerton agents to use his house as a base for the raid was found murdered by an unknown assailant. The overall effect was to increase popular support for the gang. With little to show for their work and the loss of agents, Alan Pinkerton decided to call a halt to the agency's pursuit of the gang.

On September 7, 1876, eight members of the gang raided the bank in the town of Northfield, Minnesota, the furthest they had traveled from Missouri. Three members of the gang, including Jesse James, entered the bank while two kept guard outside and three others waited on horseback outside the town. It was similar to the way they operated in previous bank raids, but the element of surprise was lost when the two gang members outside the bank were spotted. Rather than be intimidated by the presence of armed bank robbers in their town, the citizens of Northfield fought back. While the robbers inside the bank unsuccessfully attempted to force the cashier to open the safe, a furious gun battle erupted outside. The robbers found themselves in an exposed position in front of the bank, while the town's defenders were able to take cover in nearby houses. The three robbers waiting outside the town rode in only to find themselves caught in the crossfire. Two of the robbers were shot dead and the others wounded. As the three inside the bank ran out, the last one turned back and shot the cashier through the head, killing him, and in the chaos an unarmed bystander was also shot dead, most likely by Cole Younger.

Of the six who escaped from the town, only Frank and Jesse James evaded capture. The Younger brothers all survived but after being caught were sentenced to life imprisonment and only avoided the death penalty by pleading guilty. For almost three years after the disastrous bank raid, Frank and Jesse lived under assumed names near Nashville, Tennessee, becoming farmers. Frank appears to have settled down with his family into this new peaceful life, but farming was not enough for Jesse. In 1879 he recruited a new gang, including the brothers Charley and Bob Ford, and set out on a crime spree, beginning with the hold-up of a train in Glendale, Missouri. In 1881 one of the new gang was caught and, fearing that this man would talk, the James brothers left Tennessee, Frank traveling to Virginia and Jesse going back to western Missouri.

In December 1881 Jesse and Zee James rented a house in the town of St. Joseph, not far from where Jesse had been born, and moved in with their two children. It was here that, on April 3, 1882, he was killed at the age of 34, shot in the back of the head by Bob Ford, who had apparently agreed with his brother Charley to kill Jesse so that they could collect the reward. Shortly before he was shot, Jesse is said to have taken off his coat because of the hot weather that day and as a consequence had also put down the pistols he had been wearing under the coat in case anybody should chance to see him. Then, noticing dust on a picture hanging on the wall, he stood on a chair to clean it, giving Bob Ford, who is popularly said to have been too much of a coward to take Jesse on "face to face," the opportunity to shoot him from behind.

MOTIVATION

Murder

Assassination

Treason

Espionage

Robbery

Hijacking

Fraud

Kidnapping

THE UNION PACIFIC BIG SPRINGS ROBBERY

September 18, 1877

Location: Big Springs, Nebraska

Perpetrators: Sam Bass and the Black Hills Bandits

Outcome: The Texas Rangers got their man

A Daring Robbery. Capture of a station by thirteen highwaymen. The passenger Train stopped by a danger-signal and the express car and passengers rifled. Pursuit by sheriff's posse from several counties.

Headline from the New York Times on September 20, 1877

At around 10:30pm on September 18, 1877, six men raided the office of the station agent in Big Springs, Nebraska, at that time no more than a few houses clustered around a water stop on the Union Pacific railroad. They cut the telegraph wire and forced William Bradford, the station agent, to put out a red signal to stop the express train from San Francisco to New York, due through Big Springs a few minutes later. Once the train had been stopped, the men boarded it and robbed the passengers of their valuables and took about $450 from a small safe in the mail car. They were, however, unable to open the main safe in the express car because it was secured by a timer lock that would not be released until the train reached its final destination in New York. But they also found three wooden crates stacked next to the safe that contained 3000 newly minted Double Eagles, gold coins each with a face value of $20, making for a total worth of $60,000. It was the first time a Union Pacific train had been robbed and remains the largest robbery in the history of the company.

The railroad running through Big Springs had been built between 1863 and 1869 to link San Francisco to Council Bluffs, Iowa, from where it connected to the already existing lines of the railway network in the east. It created the first transcontinental railway in America, facilitating the settlement of the western United States as well as the carriage of passengers and freight. The gold coins on the train in September 1877 were from the San Francisco Mint, established in 1854 after the Californian gold rush, beginning in 1848, which had seen a huge movement of people westward. At the time of the robbery, a gold rush was underway in the Dakota Territories, where gold had been discovered in the Black Hills, immediately to the north of the railroad. It had brought numerous miners and prospectors into the region, causing trouble with the Great Sioux Nation and leading to confrontation between the Sioux and the US army, which included the Battle of the Little Bighorn, fought in 1876, in which General George Armstrong Custer and 268 of the men under his command were killed.

As well as drawing prospectors to the Black Hills, the gold rush attracted the usual entourage of saloon keepers, gamblers, and prostitutes to

UNION PACIFIC

DOUBLE EAGLES
Sam Bass and the Black Hills Bandits stole 3,000 of these $20 gold coins from the Union Pacific train they robbed at Big Springs.

the Dakotas. The town of Deadwood had been established only a few years previously and had come to national attention in 1876 when the notorious gambler and gunslinger Wild Bill Hickok was murdered there, shot in the back of the head while playing poker in a saloon. As the town had been illegally settled in territories belonging to the Lakota people of the Great Sioux Nation, it was beyond the reach of US law enforcement, so it also attracted outlaws. In the *New York Times* report on the robbery quoted at the beginning of this chapter, it was suggested that Frank and Jesse James had been responsible for holding up the train, but, as has already been described in the previous chapter, at the time the James brothers were lying low near Nashville, Tennessee, after the failed bank raid in Northfield, Minnesota, in September 1876, which had caused the break-up of the James-Younger gang. In fact, the robbery had been carried out by a gang led by Sam Bass and Joel Collins known as the Black Hills Bandits. They had held up the Deadwood stage on at least four occasions and appear to have decided that the time had come to rob a train.

THE BLACK HILLS BANDITS

Bass and Collins had initially come to the Dakota Territory in 1876 for what appeared to be legitimate reasons. They had been hired by ranchers in Texas to drive cattle to Dodge City, Kansas, intending to sell the cattle there. However, after they had arrived they decided to continue further north to take advantage of the higher prices available in the towns and settlements in the Dakota territory that had been established as a consequence of the Black Hills gold rush. It is impossible to know now if they had ever intended to return to Texas to give the profits from the sale of the cattle to the ranchers who had employed them, but, whatever the truth of the matter, after making what is reputed to have been $8000, they stayed in the Dakota Territory and tried their hand at prospecting.

After failing to find any gold and squandering what remained of their money gambling in Deadwood, Bass and Collins recruited four other desperate characters, named as Jack Davis, Tom Nixon, Bill Heffridge, and Jim Berry, with the intention of robbing stagecoaches. However, the money taken from the passengers, once divided six ways, did not amount to very much, which may have been why they decided to target the train at Big Springs. There is no indication, however, that they were expecting it to be carrying a shipment of gold coins.

After the robbery, the gang divided the gold and money they had stolen equally between them, split up into pairs, and headed off in three different directions. Collins and Heffridge were recognized in Buffalo Station, Kansas, a week after the robbery. They had claimed to be cattlemen returning to Texas, but after they were spotted, both were killed in a shootout with the sheriff and a detachment of ten US army soldiers who happened to be in the town that day. Nixon and Berry traveled to Berry's home town of Mexico, Missouri, where they were tracked down and Berry apprehended. He was wounded during his capture and died two days later, while Nixon escaped and is thought to have gone to Canada.

Bass and Davis went to Texas, traveling there in a horse-drawn buggy and disguised as farmers. Davis may well have continued going south to Mexico and was never heard from again, but Bass remained in Texas and, presumably having blown all his money again gambling, formed another gang to rob trains and stagecoaches in the state. At least four train robberies ensued and a special unit of the Texas Rangers was formed in order to track the gang down. Acting on information from a member of the gang who had been arrested, Bass and two others were located in Round Rock, Texas, on July 19, 1878, where they are thought to have been intending to rob the bank before crossing the border into Mexico. The sheriff of the town confronted all three in a store and was shot and killed, prompting a furious gun battle when the three encountered other members of the sheriff's office and several Texas Rangers. One of the gang and a deputy sheriff were killed in the exchange of fire and Bass was severely wounded, shot in the back as he attempted to ride away. He was later found propped up against a tree in a field outside the town and died two days later from his injuries.

UNION PACIFIC
Title page from a book published in 1870 to mark the opening of the first transcontinental railroad, which passed through Big Springs.

MOTIVATION

Murder
Assassination
Treason
Espionage
Robbery
Hijacking
Fraud
Kidnapping

THE WHITECHAPEL MURDERS OF JACK THE RIPPER

1888

Location: London

Perpetrators: An unidentified man known only as Jack the Ripper

Outcome: One of the world's most famous unsolved series of crimes

I was not codding dear old Boss when I gave you the tip, you'll hear about Saucy Jacky's work tomorrow double event this time number one squealed a bit couldn't finish straight off. Had not got time to get ears off for police thanks for keeping last letter back till I got to work again.

Jack the Ripper. Text of the "Saucy Jack" postcard received by the Central News Agency on October 1, 1888

The murders of five women in the area of Whitechapel in London's East End between August and November 1888 were notorious at the time and have since become among the most famous unsolved crimes ever committed. Part of the reason for this, besides the brutality of the killings, was the proliferation of mass-circulation newspapers in the late nineteenth century that brought all the gruesome details to a mass readership. Competition between the various newspapers resulted in sensationalist reporting of the case and generated huge public interest at the time, which continues today. In order to flesh out stories about the unknown assailant, the name of Jack the Ripper was invented for him and, over the years since, numerous theories have been put forward in an effort to identify him. Every last detail of the murders has been studied in great detail by so-called ripperologists and books and movies continue to appear, making the Whitehall murders some of the most discussed and analyzed crimes in history, perhaps second only to the assassination of President John F. Kennedy.

The police files on the Whitechapel murders contained details of the murders of 11 women, most of whom were known to have worked as prostitutes in the area. Of these, the "canonical five" murders, as they are known, show all the hallmarks of being committed by the same person, employing what we would now describe as the modus operandi of a serial killer. A variety of methods were used in the murders of the other six and, while it is not possible to say that they were definitely not victims of Jack the Ripper, this variance suggests that they were killed by a number of different assailants. It also provides us with an indication of the regularity of attacks on women in the East End of London at that time. The area, and in particular Whitechapel, was composed of overcrowded slums where poverty and dereliction were commonplace, accompanied by widespread drunkenness and crime. Over the previous few decades mass immigration of poor people from other parts of Britain and Ireland had created a largely

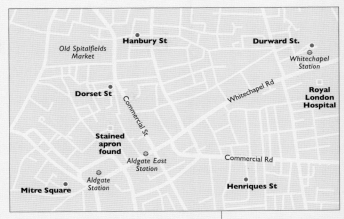

THE FIVE MURDERS
This map of the Whitechapel area of East London as it is today shows the locations (marked with red circles) of the five murders.

THE CANONICAL FIVE

ignored underclass that, over the course of the 1880s, was supplemented by the arrival of many Jewish refugees from the anti-Jewish pogroms then occurring in the Russian Empire. This sudden influx led to a rise in anti-Semitic feeling in the East End that, once the publicity surrounding the murders had begun, added a further dangerous dimension to what was already an incendiary situation.

The first of the five murders now attributed to Jack the Ripper occurred at about 3am on Friday August 31, 1888, in front of the gates of a stable in Buck's Row, a narrow side street in the heart of Whitechapel. Mary Ann Nichols was a 43-year-old prostitute who lived in a nearby lodging house. Her throat had been cut with a knife that had then been used to inflict several slash wounds on her abdomen, setting a pattern that would be repeated in subsequent murders. The police investigation established her movements up until about 2:30am and found that she had been seen in the company of an unknown man, but little further progress had been made. A week later, in the early hours of Saturday, September 8, the body of a second prostitute, Annie Chapman, was found in the back yard of a house in Hanbury Street, less than half a mile from the first murder. Her throat had been cut and abdomen slashed, but this time the wound in her stomach was more extreme and her intestines had been pulled out and thrown over her right shoulder.

The third and fourth murders both occurred in the early hours of Sunday, September 30, in what has come to be known as the double event. The body of Elizabeth Stride was found in a yard off Berner Street, to the south of the first two murders, and it is thought that the man who found the body disturbed the killer because Stride's throat had been cut in the usual manner but her body had not been mutilated. Not much more than half an hour later, a policeman found Catherine Eddowes in Mitre Square, a short walk from where Elizabeth Stride had been killed. The killer appears not to have been disturbed this time, disfiguring Eddowes's face and disemboweling her then throwing her intestines over her right shoulder. He also cut out part of her uterus and removed her left kidney.

About an hour later a piece of bloodstained cloth from the apron she had been wearing was found in the doorway of a house not far away, apparently discarded by the killer after he had wiped clean his hands and the knife he had used. A cryptic message had been written in chalk on the wall above the cloth that is thought to have read, "The Juwes are the men that will not be blamed for nothin." The police washed the chalk off the wall shortly afterward because of fears it would incite further incidents of anti-Semitism in the East End, even though it is far from clear whether the message was actually blaming or defending Jews over the murders and, in doing so, they were destroying one of the few pieces of direct evidence relating to the case.

The last of the canonical five murders occurred on Friday, November 9, and, unlike the other four, was committed in the room in a lodging house where the victim, Mary Jane Kelly, lived. Perhaps the killer, knowing how close he had come to being caught during the double event, had decided to find a less risky way of murdering his victims or perhaps the opportunity simply presented itself to him.

BLIND-MAN'S BUFF.

BLINDMAN'S BLUFF
Cartoon from the September 22, 1888, edition of *Punch* magazine satirizing the inability of the police to identify Jack the Ripper.

Whatever the truth of the matter, with little fear of being discovered, the killer appears to have taken his time, severely mutilating the body and removing the victim's intestines and organs, which were found thrown around the room. It was the most savage of the attacks and it would also prove to be the last. The murders of a number of prostitutes after Mary Jane Kelly had been killed were initially attributed to Jack the Ripper, but are now generally considered either not to be connected or to be the work of a copycat killer.

At the time, the police received a great deal of criticism for failing to catch the killer or solve the mystery of his identity. Almost from the start the investigation was led by Inspector Frederick Abberline of Scotland Yard, who appears to have done everything that could have been done in the absence of the investigative techniques of forensic science now available, but tracking down a random killer relied on either catching him in the act, which nearly happened, or on information provided by witnesses. Descriptions obtained from those people who had seen the victims in the company of a man were often contradictory or so general in nature as to be of little use, so scant progress was made. The lack of success by the police led to the formation of the Whitehall Vigilance Committee by

INVESTIGATING THE CRIME

FROM HELL
The letter received by George Lusk on October 16, 1888. It was delivered together with part of a human kidney.

FINDING A NAME

local residents, a group led by a local builder, George Lusk, who patrolled the area at night in an effort to catch the killer themselves.

At first the investigation focused on a man who came to be known as Leather Apron, leading to the arrest of a local Jewish shoemaker called John Pizer who was sometimes known by that name and had gained a reputation for hating prostitutes. He was interviewed and eliminated from the investigation by Inspector Abberline, who continued to believe that the man he was looking for was from the Whitechapel area because the killer appeared to use knowledge of its backstreets to avoid being caught. Other theories suggested that, as the attack had shown some skill in the use of a knife, he could be a doctor or a butcher, but this did not lead to the identification of a suspect.

Over the course of the investigation, numerous letters were received by the police and by newspapers, the vast majority of which were obvious hoaxes and some most likely written by unscrupulous journalists attempting to sensationalize the story. Three of these letters were treated more seriously and still divide opinion today as to their authenticity. The first two are known as the "Dear Boss" letter and "Saucy Jack" postcard and were both sent to the Central News Agency in London. The third, the so-called "From Hell" letter, was received by George Lusk and contained part of a human kidney, the writer saying that it had belonged to Elizabeth Eddowes and that he had eaten the rest of it. But none of the letters cast any light on the identity of the killer, which continues to be a compelling mystery.

Over the years more than 100 people have been identified as Jack the Ripper, made possible because libel laws cannot be used to protect the reputations of people who have died. One of the best known of these suspects was Prince Albert Victor, the Duke of Clarence, who was the grandson of Queen Victoria and, at least according to one theory, had fathered a child with one of the women murdered and, after killing her, went on to kill the others because they knew what had happened. The problem with this theory is that there is not one single shred of evidence to back it up and the prince is known to have been at Balmoral, the royal residence in the north of Scotland, at the time of some of the murders. Rather than bring the speculation to an end, the knowledge of his whereabouts has led to a widening of conspiracy theories about him and to the identification of other well-known Victorians as being the killer, including Sir William Gull, the doctor to the royal family, and the artist Walter Sickert.

In 1959 researchers for a TV documentary on Jack the Ripper came across a previously unpublished report written in 1894 by the assistant commissioner of the Metropolitan Police, Sir Melville Macnaghten, which reviewed the Whitehall murders and named three principal suspects. Aaron Kosminski was a Polish-born Jew who worked as a barber in Whitechapel at the time of the murders and was later committed to a mental asylum. It is not clear why he was suspected by police at the time of being the murderer, but recent forensic analysis of a scarf thought to have been worn by Catherine Eddowes at the time of her murder found traces of what could well be Kosminski's DNA on it. If correct, this would link him to the scene of the crime. While the evidence does not appear to be conclusive, it nevertheless indicates that Kosminski is a more likely candidate to be the Ripper than had previously been thought.

The second man named was the Russian-born Michael Ostrog, a petty criminal and conman who, it would later emerge, was serving a prison sentence in France at the time of the murders. The third suspect, Montague John Druitt, was considered the most likely candidate by Sir Melville Macnaghten. Druitt was a barrister and also worked as a teacher in Blackheath, an affluent area of London on the other side of the River Thames from Whitechapel, who drowned in the river in early December 1888, apparently committing suicide after being dismissed from his teaching post. In the report Macnaghten stated that he had seen information confirming that Druitt had been the killer without specifying what that information was or where it had come from. As nothing has since come to light, his assertion that Druitt was Jack the Ripper relies on little more than the coincidence of his suicide occurring not long after the last of the murders had been committed. In the absence of any more substantial evidence it is impossible to know if Macnaghten was correct about Druitt, just as the DNA evidence does not confirm the guilt of Kosminski. More than 130 years after the events, the true identity of Jack the Ripper still remains in the shadows.

MOTIVATION

Murder

Assassination

Treason

Espionage

Robbery

Hijacking

Fraud

Kidnapping

THE DREYFUS AFFAIR

1894–1906

Location: France

Perpetrators: Major Ferdinand Walsin Esterhazy and numerous senior politicians and military leaders

Outcome: Deep divisions in French society were exposed; Dreyfus was exonerated

*The government of the Republic has given me back my freedom.
It is nothing for me without my honor.*

**Statement made by Alfred Dreyfus
after he was pardoned in 1899**

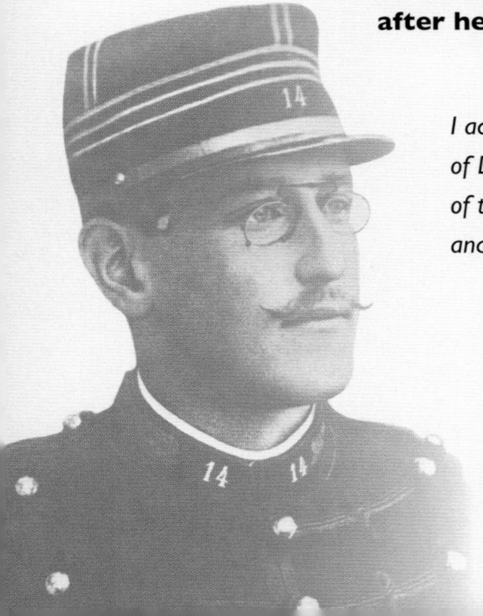

*I accuse General Billot of having held in his hands absolute proof
of Dreyfus's innocence and covering it up, and making himself guilty
of this crime against mankind and justice, as a political expedient
and a way for the compromised General Staff to save face.*

**One of the accusations made by
Émile Zola in the article "J'Accuse,"
published in January 1898**

On December 22, 1894, a French military court convicted Alfred Dreyfus, an artillery captain, on charges of treason and sentenced him to life imprisonment, also stripping him of his rank and cashiering him, which involved a ceremony of degradation in front of his regiment. An unsigned note, now known as the *bordereau*, addressed to Max von Schwartzkoppen, the German military attaché in Paris, had been recovered from a trash can in the German embassy by a cleaner working for French military intelligence in which a French officer offered to pass on secret information, including details of the design of a new French artillery piece. It was clearly an act of treason, but had that been all there was to it, then it would probably have remained a relatively minor incident in Franco-German relations in the period between the Franco-Prussian War of 1870 and the outbreak of the First World War in 1914. In the event, the Dreyfus Affair, as it became known, rumbled on for 12 years, exposing deep divisions in French society and a disturbing undercurrent of anti-Semitism in both military and civilian life.

THE MILITARY COURT
Cover illustration from the Parisian daily newspaper *Le Petit Journal* from December 23, 1894, the day after Dreyfus was convicted of treason.

THE AFFAIR

The primary evidence against Dreyfus was a comparison between the handwriting of the author of the *bordereau* and his own. Significant differences between the two existed, explained by an expert witness as being the result of Dreyfus attempting to disguise his handwriting when communicating with Schwartzkoppen. It was hardly convincing, but a secret dossier was passed to the seven military judges of the court shortly before they reached their verdict that appears to have swayed their decision. The contents of this dossier were not made fully public until 2013, showing that it contained crude attempts to undermine the character and reputation of the accused, some clearly forged, and nothing that had any great bearing on the case. The trial had been conducted behind closed doors so the nature of the evidence against Dreyfus was not widely known and his conviction was at first welcomed in newspapers and among the general public. Dreyfus continued to protest his innocence, supported by his family and a small number of others who claimed that he had been the victim of a miscarriage of justice and that he had been scapegoated because senior military leaders and politicians needed a quick resolution to the case. They also alleged that he had been targeted because he was Jewish and came from Alsace.

DEVIL'S ISLAND
Print from about 1890 showing the French penal colony where Dreyfus was held for almost five years.

After suffering a humiliating defeat to the Prussians in 1870, the French had been forced to cede much of the province of Alsace and some of neighboring Lorraine to Germany in the peace settlement signed following the Franco-Prussian War. It caused a great deal of bitterness in France, manifested as anti-German feeling and what became known as "revanchism," the desire to recover the lost territory and restore the honor of France. The Dreyfus trial, in which a Frenchman was accused of spying for Germany, had aroused a great deal of anger in France and, because he was from the Alsace region near the border with Germany and could speak fluent German, it was widely assumed that Dreyfus held pro-German views and must be guilty.

Dreyfus was sent to the notorious penal colony of Devil's Island off the coast of French Guiana in South America, where he was kept in solitary confinement and subjected to a harsh disciplinary regime. In France, his supporters began a campaign to clear his name that attracted the support of the more radical sections of French society, forming a loose association of secular republicans, intellectuals, and members of socialist movements who were labeled as "Dreyfusards." The anti-Dreyfusards, as Dreyfus's opponents were known, were made up of those people who supported the military and political establishment and included a faction who were against Dreyfus simply because he was Jewish. It transformed the affair from a dispute between France and Germany over spying to one between radical and reactionary forces within France of the sort that had existed since before the French Revolution of 1889 and that had contributed to both the revolution itself and to the turbulent political history of the country in its aftermath.

J'ACCUSE ...!

In the summer of 1896, by which time Dreyfus had been on Devil's Island for more than a year, Georges Picquart, the recently appointed new chief of the Deuxième Bureau, the French counter-intelligence agency, uncovered evidence that exposed the French officer who had actually written the *bordereau*. He discovered an unsent telegram written by Schwartzkoppen addressed to Major Ferdinand Walsin Esterhazy, a French army officer, and on comparing Esterhazy's handwriting with the *bordereau* found it to be identical. Picquart became convinced that Dreyfus was innocent and that a great miscarriage of justice had occurred. He investigated Esterhazy in secret after being warned by senior officers to leave the matter alone, finding a relationship between Esterhazy and Schwartzkoppen dating back a number of years and involving numerous leaks of military intelligence.

After receiving no support from senior officers, Picquart gave the details of the evidence against Esterhazy to lawyers working for the Dreyfusards. He was removed from his position in the Deuxième Bureau, demoted, and posted to the French colony of Tunisia, but his actions also forced the trial of Esterhazy, which began in January 1898 and was again conducted by a closed military court. New documents were presented to the court during this trial that appeared to show that Dreyfus really had been involved in espionage, which were later shown to be forgeries made by an intelligence officer in an effort to discredit him. Esterhazy was acquitted by the court, sparking celebrations by anti-Dreyfusards across France, which in some cases turned into anti-Semitic riots. Two days after the trial, the author Émile Zola published what has become one of the most famous newspaper articles in history in the liberal newspaper *L'Aurore* under the headline of "J'Accuse...!." In the article Zola did exactly what the headline said, accusing the French government and military of anti-Semitism and, specifically, naming the minister of war and senior commanders of the general staff of the French army as being complicit in framing Dreyfus and then covering up the conspiracy that had resulted in his conviction while knowing that he was innocent.

Zola's article was the first occasion when the Dreyfus Affair was set out as a whole in front of the French people. His intention in publishing it had been to force those he accused to sue him for libel so that the case could be heard in a public court. It had the desired effect, with the minister of war, General Jean-Baptiste Billot, issuing a writ for libel against Zola that was heard in February 1898 against a background of increasing civil unrest between the two factions in cities across France. The trial judge refused to allow the defense to ask questions about anything to do with Dreyfus even though it was clearly relevant to the libel case, resulting in Zola's conviction and the imposition of a one-year jail sentence. While an appeal was being heard, he left France, going to London to avoid being sent to jail, but the publicity generated by the trial had made the Dreyfus Affair the burning political issue in France that, at least in some quarters, led to fears of a civil war or a military coup d'état.

The Dreyfus Affair had a key influence on the presidential election in February 1899, which was won by the Republican candidate Émile Loubet. The change in government to one more favorable toward the Dreyfusards led to an overall change in attitude by the French establishment. By that time the forged documents presented at the Esterhazy trial had been exposed and their author, Major Hubert-Joseph Henry, had committed suicide, leading to a full review of the case against Dreyfus. In July 1899 he was brought back to France after almost five years on Devil's Island to stand trial again on lesser charges. Inexplicably, given that all the evidence against him had been discredited, he was found guilty again, this time of "treason with mitigating circumstances," and sentenced to ten years in prison. Shortly afterward he was offered a pardon in exchange for an admission of guilt, which he accepted despite clearly not being guilty because the years of confinement on Devil's Island had taken a toll on his health and a pardon would mean an immediate release from prison.

In the end, the affair did not reach a final conclusion until 1906, when all the convictions against Dreyfus were quashed and he was rehabilitated into the army with the rank of major. By that time the furore over the affair had largely died down. The republican principles of liberty, equality, and fraternity had been reestablished in the country, including freedom from the sort of arbitrary justice that had been inflicted on Dreyfus. He resigned from the army in 1907 but remained on the reserve list and was recalled in 1914, when he was 55, at the start of the First World War.

Later French governments appear to have had little desire to reopen the affair by prosecuting any of the senior officers of the General Staff who had been involved in the affair. It was an understandable decision given the divisions the affair had opened up in French society, but it meant that, even though Dreyfus was fully exonerated, he did not receive full justice by seeing those who had committed crimes against him brought to account for what they had done. He faded from French public attention later in life, dying in 1935 at the age of 75, and did return to the fore until after the Second World War, by which time the extreme consequences of anti-Semitism in France and in other parts of Europe had become all too clear.

THE ASSASSINATION OF ARCHDUKE FRANZ FERDINAND

June 28, 1914

MOTIVATION

Murder

Assassination

Treason

Espionage

Robbery

Hijacking

Fraud

Kidnapping

Location: Sarajevo

Perpetrators: Gavrilo Princip and other members of Young Bosnia and the Black Hand

Outcome: The outbreak of the First World War

So this is how you welcome your guests? With bombs?

Archduke Franz Ferdinand after the first unsuccessful assassination attempt on June 28, 1914

The lamps are going out all over Europe.
We shall not see them lit again in our lifetime.

Sir Edward Grey, the British foreign secretary, speaking on the eve of the First World War while watching street lamps being extinguished in London

At about 10:45am on June 28, 1914, Archduke Franz Ferdinand and his wife Sofie, Duchess of Hohenberg, were shot and killed by the 19-year-old Bosnian-Serb Gavrilo Princip in Sarajevo, then the capital city of the Austro-Hungarian province of Bosnia-Herzegovina. The double assassination led to five weeks of political and diplomatic tension between the great European powers of the day, known as the July Crisis, which culminated in declarations of war at the beginning of August and the onset of the First World War. The exact sequence of events and the responsibility for the escalation of the crisis remain hotly debated by historians today, as are the reasons why the killing of Franz Ferdinand and his wife, two people that many in the rest of Europe had never heard of before, in a city they would struggle to locate on a map, led to one of the most devastating wars in human history in which almost 10 million soldiers and service personnel were killed.

THE POWDER KEG

It was by no means apparent at the time that the assassination would lead to a major European war, but it was nevertheless a significant event. The archduke was the heir to the throne of the Austro-Hungarian Empire, in line to succeed his uncle Emperor Franz Joseph, head of the Habsburg dynasty, which had ruled a huge territory across Central Europe for centuries. Relationships between the Habsburgs and both the Tsarist Russian Empire to the east and the Turkish Ottoman Empire to the south had long been strained and, in the years leading up to 1914, tensions were particularly high in the Balkan region, where the three empires intersected.

Over the course of the nineteenth century, the power of the Ottoman Empire declined to such an extent that it was often referred to as the "Sick Man of Europe." It had previously controlled much of the territory of the Balkans and its decline opened up a power vacuum in the region that Austria-Hungary and Russia both hoped to exploit. The situation was complicated further by rising nationalism in the Balkans and by the ethnic and religious differences that existed in that region. Bosnia-Herzegovina was split between Muslims and Christians, who were themselves divided between Orthodox Serbs and Catholic Croats. It had come under Austro-Hungarian control in 1878, at the same time as Serbia gained its independence from the Ottoman Empire, and the tensions between people from different backgrounds within the country were exacerbated by anti-Austrian feeling and by agitation from Serbia.

In 1903 nationalist officers in the Serbian army staged a coup, overthrowing the relatively pro-Austrian King Alexander I and replacing him with King Peter I, who shared the ambition of the army officers involved in the coup to create a larger state of Greater Serbia, which would include all the territories where ethnic Serbs lived, including neighboring Bosnia. One of the leaders of this group of officers

AUSTRIA-HUNGARY
The borders of the Austro-Hungarian empire as they existed on the eve of war in 1914.

was Dragutin Dimitrijević, known as Apis because of his bull-like stature, who would go on to become the head of Serbian military intelligence. He used his position to further his aims of expanding Serbia, creating secret organizations to carry out covert actions in neighboring regions in support of those ethnic Serbs who wanted to become a part of a Greater Serbian state. One of these secret organizations was known as the Black Hand, an underground society made up of extreme nationalists in the army dedicated to using whatever methods were necessary to expand Serbian territory.

Tensions between Austria-Hungary and Serbia were exacerbated in 1908 when Austria-Hungary formally annexed Bosnia-Herzegovina into its empire, exploiting what was perceived as the military weakness of Russia, the long-term supporter of Serbia, after its disastrous defeat in a war against Japan a few years previously. With little chance of support from Russia against Austria-Hungary, Apis and his fellow nationalists concentrated on agitating in the territory still controlled by the Ottoman Empire. In two wars fought in the Balkans in 1912 and 1913, Serbia almost doubled its territory, giving it the confidence to turn its attention toward Bosnia.

In June 1914 dissension in Sarajevo against the rule of Austria-Hungary by Bosnian Serbs was high. It may well have been the reason behind Austria-Hungary's decision to stage military maneuvers in Bosnia toward the end of the month, most likely as a show of strength to the people of Bosnia as well as to Serbia and Russia. Archduke Franz Ferdinand was scheduled to

THE SPARK

observe these maneuvers before traveling on to Sarajevo with his wife for an official visit. The date chosen for this visit, June 28, could hardly have been more symbolic. It was a public holiday in Bosnia ostensibly to mark the feast day of St. Vitus, but was also recognized by Bosnian Serbs as the anniversary of the Battle of Kosovo, fought in 1389 between a Serbian army and the invading Ottomans. The battle was ultimately lost and Serbia occupied by the Ottoman forces, but it involved a suicidal attack on the Ottoman sultan by a Serbian knight that succeeded in killing him and became the source of an enduring national legend concerning the sacrifice of the individual for the greater good of Serbia.

Despite the obvious potential for trouble, the security measures taken to protect the archduke and duchess were relatively lax, and much less stringent than when Emperor Franz Ferdinand had visited Sarajevo in 1908 after the annexation. The royal party arrived in the city by train and were driven in a motorcade through the streets to an official reception in the city hall, the archduke and duchess sitting in the back seat of an open-topped car. Before they had reached the reception, a small bomb was thrown at their car by somebody in the crowd that was lining the street. It bounced off the car and exploded under the following vehicle, injuring the people in it together with a number of bystanders but not hurting the archduke and duchess.

THE FATAL SHOTS
An illustration from *La Petit Journal* on July 12, 1914, showing Gavrilo Princip shooting at Archduke Franz Ferdinand and his wife.

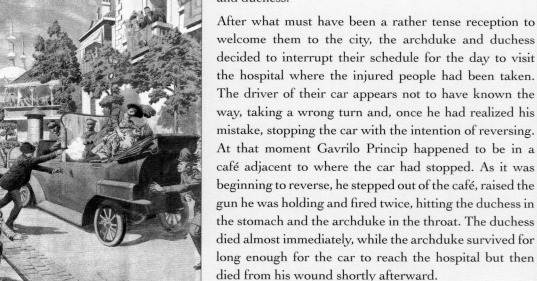

After what must have been a rather tense reception to welcome them to the city, the archduke and duchess decided to interrupt their schedule for the day to visit the hospital where the injured people had been taken. The driver of their car appears not to have known the way, taking a wrong turn and, once he had realized his mistake, stopping the car with the intention of reversing. At that moment Gavrilo Princip happened to be in a café adjacent to where the car had stopped. As it was beginning to reverse, he stepped out of the café, raised the gun he was holding and fired twice, hitting the duchess in the stomach and the archduke in the throat. The duchess died almost immediately, while the archduke survived for long enough for the car to reach the hospital but then died from his wound shortly afterward.

Princip was grabbed and disarmed by people in the crowd and arrested. It would later emerge that he was a member of a secret organization called Young Bosnia, which he had joined while he was at school in Belgrade, the capital of Serbia, and which was made up of young Bosnian Serb nationalists. At some point earlier in the year they had made contact with the Black Hand, who were then in the process of recruiting young men to carry out missions in Bosnia and had identified Franz Ferdinand as a possible target. The members of Young Bosnia met with Major Vojislav Tankosić, an officer in Serbian military intelligence, and at no time appear to have met Apis or even have known that he was the leader of the Black Hand. Tankosić supplied them with handguns and bombs, together with the training they needed to use them, and then arranged for them to travel to Sarajevo with the assistance of Serbian border guards sympathetic to the cause.

Altogether about ten members of Young Bosnia were involved in the attack, positioned at various places along the route of the motorcade. The cars drove past the first few without incident, the potential assassins apparently losing their nerve at the last moment, until one of them threw the bomb that bounced off the archduke's car. In the ensuing chaos, the car containing the archduke and duchess drove past the remaining assassins, including Princip, before any of them could take any action. After this failure, Princip decided to go home, stopping in a café on the way when the archduke's driver took that fateful wrong turn and pulled up next to him. What Princip did then would make him infamous as the man who fired the shot that started the First World War.

Almost all of the members of Young Bosnia who had taken part in the assassination plot were caught, either at the time or shortly afterward. Five of them were executed, but not Princip, who under Austrian law was too young to face the death sentence, instead being sentenced to 20 years in jail, where he died in April 1918 after contracting tuberculosis. All of the men who had been caught were Bosnians, technically making them subjects of the Austro-Hungarian Empire, but it was apparent that they had come to Sarajevo from Belgrade and were using Serbian military weapons. Austrian investigators suspected the involvement of the Serbian government and military, but beyond the role played by Major Tankosić and Serbian border guards, could not find conclusive evidence of government involvement in the plot.

THE JULY CRISIS

Some senior figures in the Austro-Hungarian government and in its army had been advocating a military attack on Serbia, even before the assassination, to punish it for its perceived support of agitators in Bosnia. They were intent on exploiting the situation in its aftermath to achieve their aims. The government decided to seek German support before taking any action and received it in what has become known as the "blank check," an undertaking by Germany to back Austria-Hungary no matter what it did. Much to the annoyance of the Germans, the Austro-Hungarians vacillated, finding reasons why they should delay military actions while the Russians became increasingly vocal in their support for Serbia.

Over the course of the preceding decades the Great Powers of Europe had split into two power blocs, the Triple Alliance of Germany, Austria-Hungary, and Italy, and the Triple Entente of Britain, France, and Russia. What made the diplomatic exchanges following the assassination so dangerous was that the disagreements were between states on either side of the division, principally between Austria-Hungary and Russia. The role played by Germany in escalating the diplomatic dispute into war is still hotly debated by historians today, but, at least according to one school of thought, the Germans made use of the situation in which Russia began to take military preparations in support of Serbia as a pretext for initiating a war on two fronts against Russia and France.

The Schlieffen Plan, as it was known, envisaged a swift attack by the German army on France first and, once France had fallen, the transfer of German forces to the east to take on the Russians. The first stage was the transfer of German forces through Belgium in order to invade France from across its northern border rather than the heavily defended Franco-German border, but the plan was compromised almost immediately by much stiffer resistance from the Belgian army than had been anticipated and by the reaction of the British. They had been one of the signatories of a treaty dating back to 1839 that guaranteed Belgium neutrality, and it was partly this that led to Britain issuing an ultimatum to Germany to withdraw its forces or face war. Germany ignored the British ultimatum and, on August 4, 1914, Britain declared war on Germany. The shots fired in Sarajevo, then, did not actually start the First World War, but caused the crisis between the Great Powers of Europe that escalated into war, making the crime committed by Gavrilo Princip the one with the most serious consequences of any in this book.

THE BLACK SOX SCANDAL

1919

MOTIVATION

Murder

Assassination

Treason

Espionage

Robbery

Hijacking

Fraud

Kidnapping

Location: America

Perpetrators: Eight Chicago White Sox players and various gamblers and gangsters

Outcome: No convictions, but the eight players were banned from playing Major League baseball for life

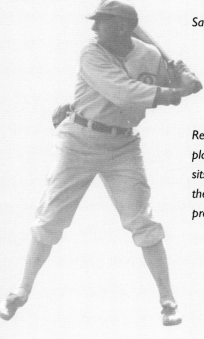

Say it ain't so, Joe.

Reportedly said by a young boy to Shoeless Joe Jackson after he admitted his part in the fix to a grand jury

Regardless of the verdict of juries, no player who throws a ballgame, no player that undertakes or promises to throw a ballgame, no player that sits in conference with a bunch of crooked players and gamblers where the ways and means of throwing a game are discussed and does not promptly tell his club about it, will ever play professional baseball.

Statement released by the Commissioner of Baseball after all eight Black Sox players had been acquitted on charges of conspiracy to defraud

The 1919 World Series of baseball was played by the Chicago White Sox and the Cincinnati Reds in October of that year over a best-of-nine-game format rather than the more usual best-of-seven. The White Sox were the hot favorites. They had won the World Series in 1917 and, after a season in 1918 in which several of their players had been on war service, could again field an all-star team that included the legendary left fielder Shoeless Joe Jackson, whose batting average of .356 remains third on the all-time list to this day. The first game began on October 1 at Redland Field in Cincinnati, where the Reds defied the odds to gain an easy 9–1 victory after a disastrous fourth inning for the White Sox in which their pitcher, Eddie Cicotte, served up such terrible pitches that the Reds scored five unanswered runs. This, combined with a number of uncharacteristic mistakes in the field by some of the Chicago players, fueled rumors that had begun before the game had even started that the series had been fixed by gamblers, who were said to have paid the favorites to throw the game. The White Sox went on to lose the series 4–2, which served to intensify the rumors, although it would be almost a year before the real story began to emerge. As it did so, it became the greatest sporting scandal in history.

THE FIX IS ON

Numerous stories and legends have grown up over what became known as the Black Sox Scandal, so that it is now almost impossible to separate fact from fiction. Even the origin of the name is disputed, some baseball historians contending that "Black Sox" had come into use as a nickname for the team before the scandal because the owner, Charles Comiskey, refused to allow the kit worn by the players to be sent to the laundry any more often than was strictly necessary.

Comiskey had a reputation for being extremely tight-fisted, even when compared to other owners, who, as a group, were not known for their generous natures. His penny-pinching is often cited as one of the reasons why some of his players were prepared to take bribes to throw the World Series. He is thought, for example, to have insisted that Eddie Cicotte be left out of the side toward the end of the season in 1917 and 1919 after he had pitched 29 wins because he was due a large bonus if he pitched 30. The truth of this is not known, but low wages and poor conditions certainly set the players against Comiskey, a situation exacerbated by the nature of player contracts at the time, which prevented them moving to another team without the permission of the owner even after their contracts had expired.

The atmosphere in the dressing room was poisoned even further by the division of the players into two factions based on social status. Regardless of ability, those players who came out of the college system were paid more than those from a lower social background.

The involvement of gamblers and gangsters in fixing sporting events was by no means a new phenomenon at that time in America. Gangs involved in racketeering and extortion had flourished as America's economy boomed and were becoming more structured and organized. Gambling was an obvious area of interest for these gangs and, while boxing matches and horse races may have been the most common targets for the fix, large quantities of money were regularly placed on baseball games.

High-rolling gamblers were always on the lookout for ways of shortening the odds, paying sportsmen for inside information as well as bribing them to influence the outcome. One of these gamblers was Joseph "Sport" Sullivan, a well-known figure in the betting world who had developed relationships with numerous sportsmen, including Chick Gandil, the first baseman for the White Sox. On September 18, 1919, the two met in Gandil's hotel room in Boston while the White Sox were in the city to play the Red Sox. Accounts differ concerning which one of them first brought up the subject of fixing the World Series, for which the White Sox were almost certain to qualify at that time. Between them they arrived at a figure of $80,000 for the players to throw the games. With an agreement in place, Sullivan then began to put a syndicate of his fellow gamblers together to raise the initial stake while Gandil came up with a plan of how he would throw the games.

GANDIL, CHICAGO AMER.

CHICK GANDIL
Baseball card showing the ringleader of the group of Chicago White Sox players who threw the 1909 World Series.

One player on his own could not guarantee the result of a baseball game, so in order for the fix to work, Gandil needed to recruit others and, in particular, the pitchers, the individuals with the most influence on the game. Three days later, Gandil held a meeting with five other players to discuss the plan, including two of the three pitchers who would play in the upcoming World Series games. One was Eddie Cicotte, who had recently bought a farm and needed money to pay the mortgage, and the other was Lefty Williams, while the three other players at the meeting were Swede Risberg, Fred McMullin, and Oscar Felsch. Shoeless

Joe and Buck Weaver, who were later implicated in the scandal, were most likely not present and do not appear to have accepted any of the money that was given to Gandil, so it is debatable how far their involvement went beyond being aware that the fix was on.

By the time of the first game in Cincinnati, word of the fix had spread to other gamblers and, according to some accounts, two of them, Billy Maharg and Sleepy Bill Burns, set up a rival syndicate to the one organized by Burns, using the former world campion boxer Abe Attell as a go-between with the players. All three were known associates of the New York mob boss Arnold Rothstein, who afterward denied any involvement in the fix but nevertheless made a large amount of money betting on the games.

In that first game, Cicotte's second pitch of the day hit the Reds batsman on the back. It is said to have been a signal to the gamblers that the fix was on, so that those listening to play-by-play news of the game as it was telegraphed around the country and then read out knew what was happening. After losing the first game by a wide margin, the second game was closer, but the White Sox lost. They then staged a comeback to leave the series poised at 4–3 to the Reds going into the eighth game. It is said that Cicotte, the pitcher for that game, was threatened by a mob enforcer the night before to make sure he threw it. Whether that is true or not, he certainly had a nightmare on the day, gifting the Reds four runs in the first innings and enabling them to win the game 10–5, sealing the series victory.

ARRAIGNED AND BANNED

Rumors of the fix intensified after the White Sox lost the series and by the summer of the following year several of the gamblers involved had talked to the press, including Billy Maharg, who gave the name of at least four of the players involved. With so many details of the Black Sox Scandal, as it was now being called, already in the public domain, the authorities in Chicago were compelled to act, forming a grand jury to investigate the matter. Eddie Cicotte, Shoeless Joe Jackson, and Lefty Williams all confessed, implicating themselves, five other players, and some of the gamblers. Sport Sullivan and Abe Attell left the country, going to Mexico and Canada respectively, so that they did not have to appear, their trips allegedly paid for by Arnold Rothstein, who appeared in front of the grand jury himself to deny having anything to do with the scandal.

The Grand Jury indicted all eight players and five gamblers on charges of conspiracy to defraud the public and certain named individuals, including Charles Comiskey and one of the players not involved in the fix who claimed to have lost income because of it. At some point between the indictment and the opening of the trial in June 1921, the confessions signed by the three players went missing, allegedly stolen from the courthouse, either by one of the defense lawyers or by somebody working on his behalf. The documents were key evidence for the prosecution and in their absence the defendants were acquitted on all charges. The euphoria that must have been felt by the players would prove to be short-lived. The day after the verdicts were given, the recently appointed Commissioner of Baseball, the federal judge Kenesaw Mountain Landis, released a statement indicating that none of the players would play professional baseball again and subsequently banned all of them for life.

BLACK SOX TRIAL
Swede Risberg, far left, Buck Weaver, middle, and Oscar Felsch, far right, with two of their defense attorneys during the trial in June 1921.

Shoeless Joe Jackson is sometimes referred to as being the great lost talent of baseball, even if he was 33 years old at the time of the scandal and had been playing in the major leagues for more than a decade. Despite the confession he had made to the Grand Jury in 1920, he would protest his innocence for the rest of his life, saying that he had been offered a bribe of $5000 on several occasions but had refused to take it, pointing out that he had achieved the highest batting average of either team during the World Series games. In the aftermath of the scandal the White Sox went into a long period of decline that only came to an end in 2005 when they won the World Series for the first time since 1917. The wider impact of the scandal on society is not easy to quantify, but it certainly led to the erosion of people's faith in the ideals of baseball and of sport in general and perhaps also a wider realization that gangsters were becoming ever more powerful in America. If the crooks could fix the World Series, then was there anything left in the country they could not reach?

MOTIVATION

Murder

Assassination

Treason

Espionage

Robbery

Hijacking

Fraud

Kidnapping

THE MAN WHO SOLD THE EIFFEL TOWER

1925

Location: Paris

Perpetrator: Robert Miller, aka Count Victor Lustig

Outcome: The Eiffel Tower is still standing

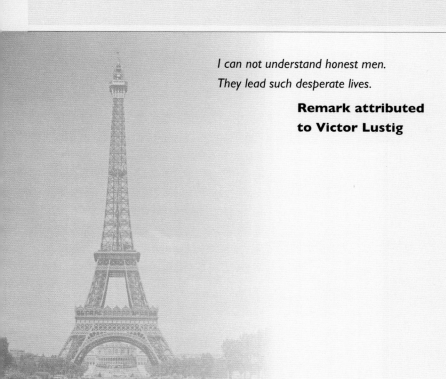

I can not understand honest men.
They lead such desperate lives.

**Remark attributed
to Victor Lustig**

In May 1925, an article appeared in a French newspaper on the declining state of the Eiffel Tower. The iconic landmark had been in public ownership since 1909 and had been neglected for years by the Ministry of Post and Telegraph, the government body responsible for its upkeep, so that it had become an embarrassment to the city of Paris. The article caught the eye of a man who called himself Victor Lustig, or "the Count." He was charming and sophisticated, capable of mixing easily with all levels of society and fluent in English, French, German, and several other European languages. But Lustig was not interested in the article out of concern for the appearance of the city in which he sometimes lived. In reality, he was a confidence trickster and it had given him the idea for a scam on an epic scale, one that would lead to him becoming known as "the man who sold the Eiffel Tower."

THE CONMAN

Lustig was actually Robert Miller, born in 1890 in the Bohemian town of Hostinne, then within the territory of the Austro-Hungarian Empire and now in the Czech Republic. He had initially gone to Paris at the age of 19 to attend university but had dropped out to pursue a career as a conman, traveling between numerous European cities and finding his victims from among the wealthy elites of the day, who could be found in the casinos and at the race tracks. As a well-spoken and well-dressed young man, Count Victor Lustig moved effortlessly into these social circles, and out again, typically with somebody else's money. He also regularly sailed across the Atlantic on the huge ocean liners of the day, fleecing first class passengers at the card table and coming up with schemes that would see some of them handing over large sums of cash shortly before the ship arrived in port, allowing him to make a rapid exit before the people he had scammed realized what had happened.

In what he called the "money box scam," Lustig showed a large box containing a mechanical device he had brought with him on the passage across the Atlantic to somebody he had picked out as a mark, explaining that it copied dollar bills. He would then demonstrate how the box worked by feeding a high denomination note into a slot in the box, saying that it would take six hours for the copy to be ready. Six hours later, he retrieved a second note from the machine, which had, of course, actually been in the box all along. He would then allow the mark to talk him into selling the box, negotiating until the last moment and finally agreeing to part with it for sums that could reach tens of thousands of dollars when the ship was within sight of land. By the time the unlucky buyer had fed a note of their own into the box and waited the required six hours to discover that nothing had happened, Lustig was long gone. It may sound ridiculous, the sort of scam that nobody in their right mind would fall for, but plenty of people did, giving an idea of how credible Lustig could make himself and how persuasive he could be, giving his marks the impression that they were talking him into deals rather than the other way around.

SCRAP METAL SALESMAN

Lustig was in New York when he read the article about the Eiffel Tower. He traveled to Paris and took a suite in the luxurious Hôtel de Crillon on the Place de la Concorde in the center of the city, near many of the ministries of the French government. He then had headed stationery and business cards printed that stated he was a senior official in the Ministry of Post and Telegraph. The next step was to send letters out on the headed paper to invite six of the largest scrap metal merchants in Paris to a meeting in his suite, explaining that the nature of the business he wanted to discuss was confidential, which was why he was holding the meeting away from the ministry. Once the merchants were assembled, he told them that the government had decided that it was too expensive to refurbish the Eiffel Tower and intended to sell it off to the highest bidder for scrap. But, he continued, the deal must be done quickly and in secret to avoid any public protests.

All six of the scrap metal merchants submitted closed bids to Lustig, no doubt recognizing the potential to make a huge profit on the 7000 tons of iron used in the construction of the landmark. By that time, Lustig had picked his mark, a man called Andre Poisson, who had recently arrived in Paris and had given the impression that he was particularly keen to pick up some government business. Lustig invited Poisson to a private meeting, at which he dropped hints that he was open to being bribed, suggesting that his salary was much less than might be expected for a man of his position. Poisson took the bait, perhaps thinking that the payment of backhanders was a necessary expense in order to secure government contracts. The exact sum of money involved is not known for certain, and has been estimated as being in the region of $50,000, but Poisson gave some of it to Lustig as cash and the remainder in a check. He cashed the check immediately and left Paris for Vienna with a suitcase full of money, having had no intention from the start to try to collect any money that would have been forthcoming for the actual sale of the Eiffel Tower. That would have involved drawing up a contract and the payment of the money to the French government. Even the most gullible of businessmen would have become suspicious if he had suggested that they give him cash or make out a check in his name for a government contract.

Lustig waited in Vienna, expecting to hear that Poisson had reported him to the police. After a month had gone by with no news, he returned to Paris intent on running the scam again with a different group of scrap metal merchants. Poisson had either been too embarrassed to admit that he had been conned or had reasoned that, if he went to the police, he would have had to explain that he had lost his money attempting to bribe what he thought was a government official. The second attempt was not quite so successful, his intended mark reporting Lustig to the police rather than offering him a bribe. It required him to make a rapid exit from Paris, an inconvenient but not unusual situation for him to be in because he was well used to leaving places in a hurry.

Lustig went back to America, where he continued his criminal career for another ten years, branching out into counterfeiting before being arrested by the FBI in 1935 in possession of a large quantity of forged dollars. It resulted in a long custodial sentence, and he died in prison in 1947 at the age of 57 having gained a reputation as one of the greatest conmen ever to practice the art. In truth, he didn't actually sell the Eiffel Tower, just gave the impression that he was in a position to do so, which enabled him to extract a bribe from a man who was not behaving in an entirely honest way himself.

THE COUNT
Lustig, on the left, being escorted into court in New York in November 1935 to face counterfeiting charges.

MOTIVATION

Murder

Assassination

Treason

Espionage

Robbery

Hijacking

Fraud

Kidnapping

THE ST. VALENTINE'S DAY MASSACRE

February 14, 1929

Location: Chicago

Perpetrators: Al Capone and the Chicago Outfit

Outcome: The massacre remains officially unsolved

7 Moran Gangsters Slain: Victims are Lined Against Wall;
One Volley Kills All.

Headline from the late edition of the *Chicago Daily News* on February 14, 1929

Only Capone kills like that.

Remark made by Bugs Moran to reporters two days after the massacre

Everybody in Chicago knew who was behind the St. Valentine's Day Massacre in which seven men were lined up against the back wall of a garage at 2122 North Clark Street at about 10:30am on February 14, 1929, and then cut down by a burst of fire from two Thompson machine guns and two shotguns. Five of the men were members of Bugs Moran's North Side and the other two associated with them, so it was not hard to work out that the Chicago Outfit, formerly known as the South Side Gang, was responsible and that the orders for the massacre must have come from Al Capone, the mob boss of the Outfit. But identifying the four men who had been seen marching the victims into the garage and then establishing that they were connected to Capone was no easy matter for the Chicago Police Department. Even Frank Gusenberg, one of the victims, who had survived for several hours despite being shot 14 times, refused to talk before he died. And even if evidence had been found against him, Capone had enough police officers, politicians, and judges in his pocket to ensure that any charges brought against him were unlikely to stick. With Chicago in the grip of the mob and a prevailing atmosphere of intimidation and violence, it is unsurprising that nobody was brought to account for the massacre, which remains unsolved to this day.

The introduction of Prohibition in America had the unintended consequence of handing control of the liquor trade to the underground gangs that organized much of the illegal activity going on in the larger cities of the country. Up until then, most of these gangs had been relatively small-time and were now intent on cashing in on this multimillion-dollar business by securing for themselves what Al Capone described as "a slice of the pie." As well as setting up illegal breweries and distilleries, gangs began bootlegging alcohol, principally whiskey and beer, across the border from Canada, where alcohol remained legal, and also set up distribution networks across America that mirrored those previously used for the legal trade. The proximity of Chicago to the Canadian border made it the ideal base for the illegal operations, enabling those gangs controlling the city to supply much of the eastern side of America.

Capone had initially gone to Chicago from New York to act as an enforcer for Johnny Torrio, the mob boss who took control of the Outfit just as the profits from bootlegging began to roll in. Capone proved to be both intelligent and ruthless, establishing himself as Torrio's right-hand man,

THE ROAD TO WAR

and was undoubtedly involved in a number of mob hits that occurred in the city. An uneasy truce existed between the largely Irish North Side Gang run by Dean O'Banion and the Italian-dominated Outfit, whereby both sides operated exclusively in their own territories. However, the peace was shattered in November 1924 when Sicilian associates of the Outfit murdered O'Banion over a gambling debt, sparking a gangland war that would continue sporadically for more than four years until it effectively came to an end with the St. Valentine's Day Massacre. After Torrio was seriously wounded in an attempted hit by members of the North Side Gang in January 1925, he decided to retire and passed control of the Outfit over to Capone, handing him a business that has been estimated to have been worth $100 million a year.

THE MASSACRE

The two sides in the war rarely targeted anybody who was not involved with the gangs, but, as limited as it may have been, it was nevertheless brutal. Both regularly brought in hitmen from out of town to murder a member of the opposition and any attempts to investigate the crimes by police officers who were not on the take were routinely met with a wall of silence. Capone held a number of peace conferences with Bugs Moran, who had emerged as the leader of the North Side Gang, aimed at establishing a truce that would have been mutually beneficial, but, every time terms were agreed, one side or the other would break them, committing an act of arson against the business premises of the other side or hijacking a liquor delivery.

By the summer of 1928, Capone appears to have decided to settle the war once and for all by hitting Moran and his chief lieutenants at the same time. It would be six months before a plan came together to achieve his ambition. According to one of a number of different versions of the story, Moran was to be lured to the garage on St. Valentine's day by members of the Purple Gang of Detroit, who claimed to have hijacked a liquor delivery belonging to the Outfit and were offering to sell it to him. On the day, however, it is said that Moran was running late and, while on his way to the garage, saw a police car parked nearby so decided not to attend the meeting with the Purple Gang. In the meantime, five other members of the North Side Gang had arrived at the garage and an Outfit lookout had mistakenly identified one of them as being Moran. The lookout called his associates to say that the hit was on and, shortly afterward, a car pulled up outside the garage and four men got out, two of whom were said by witnesses to have been dressed as policemen and were carrying shotguns as if about to stage a police raid. They entered the garage and there was an intense burst of gunfire, then the four came out again, the two fake policemen apparently escorting the others to the car and then driving away.

The real police arrived shortly afterward to find the garage turned into a slaughterhouse. Frank Gusenberg may have survived, if not for long, but the other four gang members and the two mechanics who had been in the garage working on two trucks that were to be used to pick up the liquor had been cut to pieces by the machine gun fire, before two of them had been finished off with shotgun blasts to the head at close range. The police knew as well as anybody else who was behind the massacre. They investigated a number of Capone's associates in relation to the crime and arrested several of them, but no charges were ever brought because of a lack of direct evidence.

Capone himself was in Florida when the massacre took place and was all but immune from prosecution in Chicago at the time anyway, but he had failed in his attempt to kill Moran and the nationwide publicity that the massacre attracted resulted in a federal investigation led by Eliot Ness of the Bureau of Prohibition which would eventually lead to Capone's conviction on charges of tax evasion. The repeal of Prohibition in 1933 brought the involvement of the gangs in the liquor trade to an end, but by that time they had grown wealthy and had become involved in numerous other illegal activities, including drugs trafficking, in the process evolving into the crime syndicates that still dominate organized crime in American cities today.

BUGS MORAN
The boss of the North Side Gang and the probable intended target of Al Capone's gunmen on St. Valentines day.

MOTIVATION

Murder

Assassination

Treason

Espionage

Robbery

Hijacking

Fraud

Kidnapping

THE LINDBERGH KIDNAPPING

March 1, 1932

Location: New Jersey

Perpetrators: Richard Hauptmann and possibly several others

Outcome: Charles Lindbergh Jr. died on the night of the kidnapping; Hauptmann was sent to the electric chair

Have 50.000 $ redy 25,000 $ in 20 $ bills 15000 $ in 10 $ bills and 10000 $ in 5 $ bills. After 2–4 days we will inform you were to deliver the mony.

We warn you for making anyding public or for notify the Police the child is in gut care.

Indication for all letters are signature and three holes

Text of the ransom note found at the scene of the Lindbergh kidnapping

Over the course of May 21 and 22, 1927, Charles Lindbergh completed the first nonstop flight by airplane from New York to Paris, taking 33 hours 30 minutes and, in the process, becoming famous around the world and a national hero in America. It was not the first nonstop transatlantic flight—that had been achieved by John Alcock and Arthur Whitten Brown, who flew from Newfoundland to the west coast of Ireland in 1919—but it was nevertheless considered to be one of the great pioneering feats in the early history of aviation, demonstrating to the world the enormous potential of powered flight. The success of the flight resulted in Lindbergh's name appearing in headlines on the front pages of newspapers around the world. When he got back to New York, he was greeted with a ticker-tape parade through the city. A little under five years later, Lindbergh's name would return to the front pages of those same newspapers under very different circumstances. On the evening of March 1, 1932, his 20-month-old son Charles Lindbergh Jr. was kidnapped from the family home of Hopewell in East Amwell, New Jersey.

One newspaper editor described the story as being "bigger than the Resurrection" and others dubbed it the "crime of the century." In among the hyperbole and the media circus that developed around the case, the fact that a young child had been kidnapped appeared to become almost incidental compared to the fame of his father. What actually happened was that Charles Lindbergh Jr., known as Charlie to the family, had been put to bed in his crib by his nurse at about 8pm and, when she returned to check on him at 10pm, was found to be missing. At first she assumed that either his father or mother, Anne Morrow Lindbergh, had picked him up, but it soon became apparent that this was not the case. A search of the house ensued and, in the baby's bedroom, one of the windows was found to be ajar and an envelope was discovered on the windowsill. The police were called and recovered a homemade ladder composed of three separate parts that had been thrown into a bush in the grounds of the house. The police opened the envelope to find a ransom note demanding $50,000. It contained numerous spelling mistakes, such as "anyding" for "anything"

THE AVIATOR
Lindbergh, second from the left, photographed in front of his plane, *Spirit of St. Louis*, shortly before his transatlantic flight.

THE CRIME OF THE CENTURY

FAMILY PORTRAIT
Anne Morrow Lindbergh, on
the right, with her mother
and grandmother, who is
holding Charles Jr.

and "gut" instead of "good," which were interpreted as indicating that it had been written by somebody whose native language was German. The note concluded with the writer saying that future notes would carry the same signature, composed of circles and lines with three holes punctured through the paper.

Lindbergh effectively took over the police investigation into the kidnapping, converting Hopewell into a center of operations, and, while it was understandable for him to do everything he could possibly do, his involvement probably only hindered the police. Several more ransom notes containing the correct signature arrived by mail, all posted in Brooklyn. At this point a retired schoolteacher from the Bronx called John F. Conlon, who became known as "Jafsie" after his initials, involved himself in the case by offering $1000 of his own money for the return of the baby. He received a letter from the kidnappers, accepted as genuine by Lindbergh, saying that he could act as an intermediary for the handover of the ransom and then arranged a meeting in Woodlawn Cemetery in the Bronx.

The first of what would be two meetings in the cemetery between Jafsie and a man who said his name was John, becoming known as "Cemetery John" from then on, occurred on March 12 in which the two talked for an hour, apparently amicably, but beyond noticing that he spoke with a foreign accent, Jafsie could not provide a detailed description of him because he kept his face in the shadows. Cemetery John said that the baby was in good health and that he was a member of a group of six who had kidnapped him, claiming to be a Scandinavian sailor rather than a German national. He also said he would provide evidence that he really did have Charlie, sending Jafsie a package in the mail a few days later containing a baby's sleeping suit that was identified by Lindbergh. Another meeting was arranged in the cemetery for April 2 during which Jafsie gave John a package containing $50,000 in gold certificates, a form of paper currency then in circulation in America that was due to be withdrawn in the following year so that the kidnappers would have to exchange the notes at a bank at some point. The numbers on the notes were also recorded in the hope that they would be recognized should the kidnappers attempt to spend them before changing them.

John gave Jafsie an envelope in exchange for the money containing the location of a boat called the Nelly off the Massachusetts coast. An extensive search ensued, but the boat, if it had existed at all, was not found, leading Lindbergh to the conclusion that he had been duped. On May 12 a sack containing the body of a baby was found in woodland a few miles from Hopewell. The body was identified by Lindbergh as being that of his son, who was determined to have died from a blow on the head that had fractured his skull. From the state of decomposition of the body it also appeared that the baby had been dead for some time, most likely dying on the night of the kidnapping, although it was not possible to say for certain if the injury had been caused by an intentional blow or had been sustained accidentally. One theory suggested that the ladder used to climb up to the window of Charlie's room had broken during the kidnapping and that the baby had died at the scene from the subsequent fall, but there was no specific evidence to back this up and it was certainly possible that the kidnappers had murdered the baby on the night they took him and hidden the body rather than have to look after him until the ransom was paid.

The police investigation made little progress after the baby's body had been found. Attention initially turned to Violet Sharpe, who worked for the Lindberghs, and when questioned by the police had appeared to become agitated, giving evasive answers to questions concerning her whereabouts on the night of the killing. On June 10 she committed suicide, swallowing a type of polish containing cyanide, in an apparent attempt to escape the ordeal of further questioning. It would later be established that she had been attempting to conceal a relationship with the family's butler because she thought its discovery would lead to her losing her job. Suggestions were made later that she may have inadvertently revealed to the kidnappers the movements of the Lindbergh family, who stayed at Hopewell most weekends and lived in New York during the week, perhaps by answering a query about them made by telephone, but this is no more than speculation.

HOPEWELL HOME
A state trooper outside the Lindbergh's house in New Jersey from where Charles Jr. was kidnapped.

HAUPTMANN

Little further progress was made by the police. Some of the gold certificate notes turned up at various locations around America, but they proved to be dead ends. A breakthrough came in September 1934, two and a half years after the kidnapping, when a $10 bill was used by a man at a garage and the garage attendant, concerned that it might be a forgery, had written the license plate number of his car on it. After the bill was recognized in a bank, it led the police to Richard Hauptmann, who had come to New York from Germany ten years previously and lived in Brooklyn, where he worked as a carpenter. A search of his premises recovered almost $15,000 of the gold certificates concealed in a box in his garage, leading to his arrest and indictment on charges of kidnaping and murder.

The trial was held in Flemington, New Jersey, beginning on October 19, 1934, and was inevitably dubbed the "trial of the century" by the huge press pack that had assembled in the town. As well as the box of gold certificates, the prosecution introduced evidence to show that some of the wood used to make the ladder matched wood in Hauptmann's attic and that his handwriting was almost identical to that used to write the ransom notes. In addition, a telephone number found written inside a closet in Hauptmann's house was shown to be that of John Conlon, who identified Hauptmann as being Cemetery John, and a number of other witnesses testified that they had seen him in the vicinity of Hopewell on the night of the murder. Hauptmann maintained his innocence throughout, claiming that the box containing the money had been left with him by a fellow German immigrant called Isidor Fisch who had subsequently returned to Germany and then died.

RICHARD HAUPTMANN
At his trial in Flemington, New Jersey, Hauptmann was found guilty of the kidnapping and murder of Charles Lindbergh Jr.

Hauptmann was found guilty of murder and sentenced to death. Before being sent to the electric chair, he was offered a deal in which the sentence would be commuted to life imprisonment if he confessed and revealed the names of anybody else who had participated in the kidnapping. He refused, still maintaining his innocence, and was executed on April 3, 1936. Ever since, intense speculation has surrounded the question of whether he acted alone or had accomplices, or if he was in reality not guilty and the evidence against him had been fabricated and planted on him by the police. Numerous theories have been put forward over the years in an attempt to tie up the loose ends of the case, including one that proposed that Lindbergh himself had been involved in a conspiracy to murder his own son. This theory does not appear to have been based on any actual evidence, but was rather constructed because of Lindbergh's apparent interest in the now discredited science of eugenics, the purpose of which was to investigate human breeding with the objective of "improving" the heredity of the human species.

Needless to say, the advocates of eugenics considered that "desirable" human characteristics were in fact those they possessed themselves, which were usually concerned with race and position in society. In their view, if people who possessed these "superior" characteristics did nothing, humanity would become swamped by what were described as "inferior" traits. Charles Lindbergh Jr. had been born with some minor physical deformities and may have suffered from a mild form of rickets, a disease caused by a deficiency of vitamin D that can affect bone development in children. Lindbergh's interest in eugenics, together with the numerous anti-Semitic statements he made and his partial support for Nazi Germany in the years before the Second World War, were used by some to support a theory that he could not stand the thought of fathering a son who was not physically perfect.

Revelations about Lindbergh's private life, which came out after he died in 1974, have tended to increase the speculation about him. Between 1957 and 1967 he fathered seven children with three different German women during numerous visits to the country, as if he were conducting his own experiment in heredity. But his interest in eugenics or his racist opinions, however unsavory they may have been, do not offer any proof that he was in any way involved in the murder of his son. The evidence as it stands today still points most convincingly to the guilt of Richard Hauptmann, who most likely kidnapped Charles Lindbergh Jr. in collaboration with a number of other people who were never brought to justice and remain unknown today. In such a high-profile case in which numerous loose ends exist, speculation is inevitable, but for the most part it has served only to confuse the matter even further rather than shed any light on what actually happened.

MOTIVATION

Murder
Assassination
Treason
Espionage
Robbery
Hijacking
Fraud
Kidnapping

THE PAPIN SISTERS

February 2, 1933

Location: Le Mans, France

Perpetrators: Christine and Léa Papin

Outcome: Christine Papin could not live without her sister and died in prison. Léa Papin was released in 1941 and lived anonymously afterward

I have seen the photographs of those two pretty girls, these servants who killed and battered their mistresses. I've seen the photos before and after. Before, their faces hovered like two docile flowers above their lace collars...After, their faces glowed like a blaze.

Jean-Paul Sartre, *The Wall* (1939)

The two murders committed by the sisters Christine and Léa Papin at No. 6, rue Bruyère in the French city of Le Mans in the early evening of February 2, 1932, caused a level of shock and revulsion in French society beyond that of almost any other criminal act ever committed in the country. It was not only the brutal and gruesome nature of the killings that gripped the attention of the public but the fact that the perpetrators were young women, aged 27 and 21 respectively at the time, and that their victims were also women. There was also the suggestion of an incestuous lesbian relationship between the two sisters. Some of the leading intellectuals of the day, who then played a prominent role in French society, attempted to explain both the meaning and significance of the murders, including the philosophers Jean-Paul Sartre and Simone de Beauvoir and the psychoanalyst Jacques Lacan, while writers and artists also responded to the crime, perhaps most famously in the play *The Maids* by Jean Genet, which was loosely based on the case.

RUE BRUYÈRE

The house on rue Bruyère was the property of Monsieur and Madame Lancelin, who lived there with their 27-year-old daughter Geneviève. René Lancelin was a retired solicitor and, while the family could not be described as wealthy, they lived comfortable lives as members of the bourgeoisie who were by no means extravagant but could nevertheless afford to employ the Papin sisters as maids. Christine was primarily responsible for the cooking in the household and her younger sister Léa was the chambermaid. They worked for at least 12 hours a day, six and a half days a week, with only a half-day off on Sunday to attend church, and lived together in a single room at the top of the house. It may now sound like harsh working conditions, particularly in view of the minimal wages paid to the girls, but it was not an unusual arrangement at the time. The fact that the sisters hardly ever spoke to their employers about anything other than the running of the household—something that emerged at their trial—was also not as strange then as it appears now, the family and the maids being divided by a barrier of social class.

In the early evening of February 2, 1932, René Lancelin returned to the house after spending the afternoon playing cards with friends, expecting to meet his wife and daughter so that they could go out to dinner. He found the front door locked and the house in darkness and, growing worried after failing to get any response to repeated knocking, went to the police.

Three officers came to the house and broke in, finding the bodies of the two women in the hall. Both had been brutally murdered, beaten so severely that their faces were unrecognizable. The maids were in their room at the top of the house, the door locked; when the police broke it down, they found the sisters naked in bed together. When asked what had happened, they immediately confessed to the murders.

From the somewhat confused statements made by the sisters, it appears that Christine Papin had got into an argument with Madame Lancelin over a faulty electric iron that she had taken to an electrician to be repaired and which had subsequently blown a fuse in the house, plunging it into darkness. Madame Lancelin threatened to dock Christine's wages for the cost of the repair to the iron, provoking a furious response and the ensuing argument then escalated into a physical fight in which Christine grabbed a pewter vase and began hitting Madame Lancelin with it, knocking her to the ground. The noise brought Geneviève Lancelin to the hall, where she was also attacked by Christine. When Léa arrived, Christine shouted at her to join in before going to the kitchen to find other weapons to use on the two women, both of whom were now prostrate on the floor. Léa returned with a hammer and a knife and continued the assault along with her sister, taking turns to attack the victims with the hammer, the knife, and the pewter jug.

What the two sisters could not explain was why such a minor domestic incident had escalated into such a brutal and frenzied attack. Christine did almost all of the talking; she was characterized as being the more outspoken and argumentative of the two. Léa was described as quiet and withdrawn, her personality, according to a psychiatrists who examined her, having been completely subsumed into that of her dominant older sister. Investigations into the circumstances of their childhood appeared to suggest some unresolved family trauma that may have influenced their behavior. Their mother had left their alcoholic father when they were both young, accusing him of raping their elder sister Emelia, and had then neglected them while going on to engage in a promiscuous lifestyle. The sisters moved between relatives and an orphanage until each was old enough to decide for themselves what they wanted to do. Emelia became a nun, living for the rest of her life in a convent, while Christine and Léa took jobs as maids, preferring to work together in the same households and giving most of their wages to their mother. They appear to have lived secluded lives within the households where they worked, rarely leaving except to go to church or on errands for their work, and otherwise spending their time in each other's company, keeping their own company and spending their time making elaborate dresses, which they had few opportunities to wear.

The sisters were kept apart during the eight months it took for their case to be brought to trial. It appears to have had little affect on Léa but deeply upset Christine, who became severely depressed and, at one point, had to be restrained in a straitjacket after she attempted to tear her own eyes out. The psychiatrist who examined them declared both to be fit to stand trial, which was held in September 1933 in the midst of intense public and media interest. As both had confessed to the murders, the trial was over quickly, concluding in guilty verdicts for both of them. As Christine had instigated the attacks and was considered to be the dominant sister, she was considered more accountable and was sentenced to death, later commuted to life imprisonment, while Léa received a sentence of ten years with hard labor.

Christine's mental health declined rapidly after she was sent to prison, apparently incapable of living without her sister and regularly refusing to eat. She was transferred to a mental hospital after a few months and died there on May 18, 1937, suffering from a condition called cachexia, a syndrome in which the body wastes away whether the patient eats anything or not. Léa was released from prison after serving eight years of her sentence and lived with her mother under a false name. She is reported to have died in 1982, although a French TV documentary about the case claimed that she was still alive in 2000, living in a hospice after suffering from a stroke and dying the following year.

THE PAPIN SISTERS
Christine, on the left, and Léa Papin at their trial for murder, held in Le Mans in September 1933.

Almost as soon as the case was made public, numerous theories were put forward in efforts to explain the murders. Left-leaning intellectuals, for instance, described the case as being a symptom of the class struggle in which the downtrodden maids had risen up against their oppressors, while Jacques Lacan described it as being a *"folie à deux,"* a psychotic condition in which two people share paranoid and delusional beliefs, in the process enlarging and reinforcing those beliefs. He also suggested that the dominance shown by Christine and the sexual nature of the relationship between the two sisters could have been symptoms of this syndrome, even if this does suggest fitting the symptoms to the theory rather than making a diagnosis based on the facts of the case.

Yet another theory suggests that Christine had become jealous of Geneviève Lancelin, perceiving her as a threat to her own relationship with her sister and, being in a somewhat fragile mental state as a consequence of unspecified childhood traumas, suffered from some sort of psychotic episode when confronted by Madame Lancelin over the problem caused by the electric iron. Whatever the truth of the matter, the case gripped France at the time and continues to hold a great fascination for many people in the country today. It has inspired numerous books and movies over the years, perhaps in part because of the gory and salacious details of the case, but also because it defies a rational explanation and so invites speculation as to what could have prompted those two young women to commit such a terrible crime.

JOHN DILLINGER: PUBLIC ENEMY NO.1

1933–1934

MOTIVATION

Murder
Assassination
Treason
Espionage
Robbery
Hijacking
Fraud
Kidnapping

Location: The American Midwest

Perpetrators: Dillinger, together with numerous other bank robbers

Outcome: A crime wave and the development of the FBI to combat it

Dillinger Gang Captured Here

**Arizona Daily Star,
January 26, 1934**

*Dillinger Shoots Way Clear; Three of Gang Best
Officers in Gun Battle*

**Chicago Daily News,
April 24, 1934**

Dillinger Led To Death By Girl Dressed In Red

**Baltimore News,
July 23, 1934**

On May 10, 1933, John Dillinger was released on parole from the Indiana State Prison after serving more than nine years of a sentence handed down for the violent robbery of a man in Mooresville, Indiana. During his time in prison Dillinger had met many hardened criminals and he used this experience to learn as much as he could from them with the intention of beginning a career as a bank robber after his release. The fact that his release coincided with the height of the Great Depression ensured that, even if he had looked for work, there would have been little chance of him getting a regular job. Instead, he embarked on a crime spree that lasted for a year and involved numerous bank robberies, shootouts with the police and the FBI, and two jailbreaks. These exploits made him famous in Depression-era America, the sort of antihero whose contempt for authority and devil-may-care attitude toward risk apparently struck a chord with people struggling to get by. And this despite the fact that, before he was shot and killed by federal agents himself, his spree had cost the lives of at least 12 people.

PUBLIC ENEMY

Newspaper stories about Dillinger made him into a household name across America. He became the most famous of a group of outlaws responsible for an unprecedented crime wave in the Midwest during 1933 and 1934. As well as Dillinger, the group included Pretty Boy Floyd, Babyface Nelson, Machine Gun Kelly, Ma Barker and the Barker-Karpis Gang, and Clyde Barrow and Bonnie Parker. But there was something about Dillinger that lifted him above the others in the minds of the American public. He appears to have possessed a quality that attracted people to him in spite of the nature of the crimes he committed, affording him the sort of celebrity status usually reserved for movie stars. It also attracted the attention of J. Edgar Hoover, the director of the federal law enforcement agency that would later become the FBI. Hoover recognized that the crime wave engulfing the Midwest represented an opportunity for him to centralize the various federal agencies involved in domestic crime prevention into one bureau under his control. The publicity Dillinger generated represented the ideal pretext for Hoover's plan and would lead to the outlaw becoming America's first "Public Enemy No.1"—a newspaper-friendly title for the country's most serious offenders.

Six weeks after being released from prison, Dillinger pulled his first bank job, raiding the National Bank in New Carlisle, Ohio, and stealing about $10,000. Three more robberies occurred in quick succession before he was arrested by the police after a raid in Bluffton, Ohio. At some point before this arrest, he had arranged to have guns smuggled into the prison in Indiana where he had previously been held, as part of a prearranged plan to help others escape. How he managed to get the guns into the prison is not known; he may have bribed people working in the prison or simply had the guns thrown over the prison walls to an accomplice on the inside. On September 26, ten convicts used these guns to take a number of prison guards and the warden hostage so that they could simply walk out of the prison gates. Four of the escapees were Pete Pierpont, Charles Makley, Red Hamilton, and Russell Clark, the bank robbers who had tutored Dillinger and who would go on to form the core of Dillinger's gang, named for him by the press even though Pierpont, the most experienced bank robber among them, probably acted more like its leader.

At the time of the prison break by Pierpont and the others in Indiana, Dillinger was being held in Lima, Ohio, after his arrest for bank robbery. As soon as they were free, Pierpont, Makley, and Clark robbed a bank and then used the money they stole to fund an attempt to break Dillinger out as well. They entered the jail in Lima posing as officials from the Indiana prison service and saying that they had come to take Dillinger back to prison in Indiana for breaking parole. When the local sheriff asked to see some paperwork, Pierpont pulled out a gun and shot him in the stomach, a wound from which he would later die. They then forced the deputies in the jail to release Dillinger and made their getaway, heading to Chicago while an extensive manhunt began for them in Indiana. At some stage Pierpont and Dillinger rented an apartment in the city together with their girlfriends, Mary Kinder and Billie Frechette, where they lived quietly between bank raids.

PUBLIC ENEMY
A photograph from 1933 of John Dillinger posing for the camera with a Thompson machine gun and a pistol.

Shortly after freeing Dillinger, the gang raided a couple of police stations in Indiana, stealing an arsenal of arms, including Thompson submachine guns, ammunition, and bulletproof vests, which they would use in future bank raids. A bank-robbing spree ensued, beginning with the Central National Bank in Greendale, Indiana, on October 23, 1933, which is reputed to have netted the gang more than $70,000. The day after the robbery a policeman spotted a car seen at the scene at a garage and, after waiting for the driver to come back to it, challenged him. It was Red Hamilton, who shot the policeman dead, the second murder committed by a member of the gang.

Pierpont was the chief planner of the robberies, casing out the banks and the escape routes beforehand. The usual method involved one of the gang, often a woman, going into the chosen bank to ask a cashier to change a banknote. If the coast was clear, she was followed by two or three others while another waited outside in a car with the engine running. With everybody in the bank ordered at gunpoint to remain still, one of the gang leaned over the counter and filled a sack with cash. The police and federal agents soon established the identities of these robbers from fingerprints, thanks in no small part to the reforms Hoover had initiated at his bureau to gather together in one place as much data as possible on known criminals. National alerts were put out, even though the crimes were a state issue rather than a federal one, and mug shots were released to the newspapers. Despite the publicity, Pierpont and Dillinger continued to live in Chicago between robberies, going to the movies and restaurants with their girlfriends as if oblivious to the risk of them being recognized.

On January 25, 1934, after laying low in Florida for a month, Dillinger and Hamilton stuck up a bank in east Chicago, while another member of the gang waited in a car outside. On this occasion one of the bank employees managed to press an alarm button and the police arrived while the robbery was in progress. Dillinger grabbed two hostages and ran out of the bank toward the car, which the police outside the bank appear not to have noticed. Despite the presence of the hostages, one of the policemen, Officer Patrick O'Malley, began to shoot at Dillinger, who returned fire with his submachine gun, hitting O'Malley eight times and killing him. Witnesses and fingerprint evidence both confirmed that Dillinger was the shooter, the first time he is known to have used such extreme violence and the only occasion in which he is confirmed to have killed somebody.

After the east Chicago robbery, the gang traveled to Tucson, Arizona, apparently with the intention of crossing the border into Mexico. However, they were recognized in a hotel by firemen who had been called to tackle a small blaze. It led to the arrest of Pierpont, Dillinger, Makley, and Clark. Dillinger was extradited from Arizona to Crown Point, Indiana, where he was held in jail charged with the murder of Officer O'Malley, while the other three were sent to Ohio to be charged with the murder of the sheriff killed during the jailbreak that had freed Dillinger. Pierpont would subsequently be executed, while Makley was killed during an escape attempt and Clark was given a life sentence, of which he would serve more than 30 years. But Dillinger was not finished. On March 3, he used a wooden gun he had carved himself to take hostages in the jail in Crown Point and then escaped by stealing the sheriff's car. He drove to Chicago to stay with Billie Frechette, thereby taking a stolen vehicle across a state line and enabling federal agents to become officially involved in the hunt for him for the first time.

After this latest escape, Dillinger, together with Red Hamilton, joined Nelson's gang and began robbing banks again. Nelson was not as cool under pressure as Pierpont had been and his robberies almost always involved gunfire, causing casualties among the police, bystanders, and the gang. Dillinger was himself shot in the shoulder during one raid and, as the bodies began to stack up, a nationwide manhunt was instigated under the leadership of Special Agent Melvin Purvis. On April 20, most of the gang, including Nelson and Dillinger, were seen playing cards at the Little Bohemia Lodge near Manitowish Waters, Wisconsin. Purvis came the following day with other special agents, arriving there at the same moment as a car with three occupants was leaving. When the car failed to stop after being challenged, the agents opened fire, killing all three men inside who, it would transpire, had nothing to do with the gang. A brief gun battle erupted with the gang in which an agent was killed, before Dillinger, Nelson, and the others made their escape unscathed.

The last bank raid Dillinger is known to have participated in occurred on June 30, 1934, at South Bend, Indiana. After the robbery, he dropped out of

THE END OF THE ROAD

The scene of the shootout in Manitowish Waters, Wisconsin, in which Dillinger, Baby Face Nelson, and others exchanged fire with FBI agents.

sight for almost two months while the FBI dragnet continued. It would later emerge that he had lived quietly in Chicago during this period, changing his physical appearance on a number of occasions and undergoing plastic surgery on his face and fingers. On July 22, he went to the movies at the Biograph Theater with two women who worked as prostitutes, Polly Hamilton and Anna Sage, whose real was Ana Cumpănaş. She was originally from Romania and was under the threat of deportation at the time, leading to her making a deal with federal agents to inform them of Dillinger's whereabouts in return for permission to stay in America. That day, she had told the agents that she would be going to the movies with Dillinger that night, an act of betrayal that would result in her being labeled as the "Woman in Red" by the press, despite the fact that she was not wearing a red dress at the time.

Once they had been alerted by Sage, federal agents assembled outside the theater while Dillinger watched the movie. Purvis positioned himself by the main exit in order to signal to his colleagues when Dillinger came out. As Dillinger left the theater with the two women, Purvis lit a cigar, the agreed signal, and Dillinger is said to have looked straight at him. He made a run for it and was confronted by three agents in a nearby alley, who opened fire as he was attempting to pull a gun from his pocket. He was shot four times, one of the bullets hitting him in the back of the neck. It severed his spinal cord, killing him almost instantly and bringing the year-long spree involving around 20 bank raids to a sudden and dramatic end.

Dillinger's death did not mark the end of the crime wave, but most of the others involved who were not already in prison or dead were either caught or killed by December 1934, including Babyface Nelson and Pretty Boy Floyd. After that, bank robberies in the Midwest became much less frequent, partly as a consequence of the successes achieved by the FBI but also because the New Deal policies initiated by President Franklin D. Roosevelt after his election in March 1933 led to an economic recovery in America. In more prosperous times, there was less incentive for men to turn to robbery and less likelihood of those that did receiving the sort of public support Dillinger had enjoyed. Perhaps his story, exhaustively retold, also contributed to preventing others from following in his footsteps. He may have achieved some sort of fame, but he had died in a hail of bullets at the age of 31 and not much more than a year after being released from prison.

THE CAMBRIDGE SPIES

1930s–1960s

MOTIVATION

Murder

Assassination

Treason

Espionage

Robbery

Hijacking

Fraud

Kidnapping

Location: Britain

Perpetrators: Kim Philby, Donald Maclean, Guy Burgess, Anthony Blunt, and possibly John Cairncross

Outcome: The most extensive spy ring ever uncovered in Britain

The watchers failed to pick up Maclean since his departure for the country on Friday and we now learn from the Foreign Office that he was given a day's leave on Saturday. He has not apparently been seen since...

Extract from the diary entry made by MI5 agent Guy Liddell for May 29, 1951, four days after Burgess and Maclean defected

On the evening of Friday, May 25, 1951, Guy Burgess and Donald Maclean left Maclean's house in Kent and traveled to France using false passports. From there, they traveled on to Moscow, confirming the suspicions of the British Security Service, or MI5 as it is often called, of the presence of a Soviet spy ring in the British intelligence and foreign services. Maclean had worked at the Foreign Office since leaving Cambridge University in 1934 and had come under suspicion after secret Soviet diplomatic messages that had been decrypted in America pointed in his direction. The VENONA intercepts, as the transcripts were known, mentioned the movements of a Soviet agent codenamed Homer, which corresponded with those of Maclean, who had served in the British Embassy in Washington, but did not actually provide enough evidence to arrest him on charges of espionage. He was put under surveillance by MI5 during weekdays, but this did not continue at the weekend, allowing him to defect together with Burgess, who was not under suspicion at the time but had been ordered by his Soviet handlers to accompany Maclean. It could not have been a clearer confirmation of the existence of a spy ring and, once Burgess and Maclean had gone, attention turned to the so-called "Third Man," the person who had warned the two defectors.

THE CAMBRIDGE CONNECTION

The media in Britain and around the world reported the defections of Burgess and Maclean at the time, even if their presence in Moscow was not officially acknowledged by the Soviet Union until 1956, but the British government's obsession with secrecy has meant that, more than 60 years later, many of the files relating to the incident, and to the spy ring in general, still have not been disclosed. This means that the story of the Cambridge Spies, as the ring is now widely known, has yet to be told and, while the secretive nature of spying means that the full details may never be known for certain, it would appear likely that more revelations about them will come to light at some point in the future. What we can say now, from the information that is in the public domain, is that these spies were all recruited by the Soviets in the early 1930s while they were attending Cambridge University.

In 1961 the KGB defector Anatoliy Golitsyn spoke of a "ring of five," which has been taken by some to mean that the Cambridge Spies were made up of a total of five people. It is more likely, however, to refer to five specific spies rather than the total number recruited from the university.

The backgrounds of four of the five of them were very similar, each coming from relatively privileged upper-middle-class families and attending public schools (which in the UK are in fact private fee-paying schools), before going on to Cambridge and, at some point, becoming interested in Marxism, which by the 1930s had become fashionable in some intellectual circles in Britain.

Most of the members of the spy ring would later say that the origins of their left-leaning sympathies were in their opposition to the rise of fascism in Europe during the early 1930s rather than in a purely ideological attraction to communism. They claimed to have been particularly concerned with helping the Soviet Union in its fight against Nazi Germany during the Second World War. There may be an element of truth in this, even if it now sounds like an attempt to justify committing treason. Whatever their reasons, each of the Cambridge spies followed the well-worn career path from Cambridge University to a job in the British Civil Service in the mid-1930s and, in some cases, into the intelligence services during the war. The fact that Civil Service recruitment relied heavily on this pathway, as it still does to some extent today, ensured that secret agents from foreign countries who came to Britain would find it difficult to penetrate the Foreign Office or intelligence services. However, if foreign governments could recruit people from the appropriate background, not only would they have the opportunity to get inside the British establishment and gain access to secret information but the recruits would be less likely to come under suspicion should a leak occur.

THE THIRD MAN

Once Burgess and Maclean were confirmed as having defected to the Soviet Union, Kim Philby came under suspicion as being the third man because of his association with the two of them going back to their days together at Cambridge University. During the Second World War, Philby had joined the Secret Intelligence Service, also known as MI6, the agency concerned with foreign intelligence, and had been promoted over the years to become the head of the counter-intelligence division that dealt with the Soviet Union. In that position he was authorized to read the VENONA intercepts and so would have realized that the information contained in one message implicated Maclean. Rather than join the two defectors in Moscow, Philby withstood interrogation from MI6 about his association with them. No concrete evidence was uncovered to show that he was a

Soviet agent, but the suspicions raised about him forced him to resign his position in MI6 in July 1951, at which point he moved to the Lebanese city of Beirut and began to work as a journalist for several British newspapers as a correspondent on Middle Eastern affairs.

During his time in Beirut, Philby continued to work sporadically for MI6, despite the suspicions over his loyalties, until he was finally exposed by Anatoliy Golitsyn in 1961, forcing him to defect to Moscow. Two years later, the fourth man in the ring came to light when Michael Straight, an American who had been part of the same Cambridge circle in the early 1930s, confessed to his involvement with the KGB. Straight claimed to have been recruited by Anthony Blunt, a don at the university who was a few years older than the other members of the ring and, though he always denied it, may have been the one who originally introduced the recruits to his KGB handler. When confronted with Straight's confession, Blunt admitted his own role in the spy ring in exchange for immunity from prosecution. By that time he had become a respected art historian, holding the position in the royal household as Surveyor of the Queen's Pictures, and was not publicly exposed until 1979, at which point the knighthood he had been awarded in 1956 was stripped from him.

With four of the supposed "ring of five" identified, the British intelligence services turned their attention to the fifth man. Numerous individuals were investigated, but it would later emerge that the most likely candidate was John Cairncross, who had known Blunt at Cambridge but was not from the same social background as the others and does not appear to have associated with them after they left university. Cairncross had been implicated as being a KGB agent as early as 1951, his name mentioned in papers found in Guy Burgess's flat after he defected, at which point he was forced to give up his civil service job with the Treasury, but did not give a full confession until 1963. Both he and Blunt had worked for MI5 during the Second World War at Bletchley Park, the house in Buckinghamshire where the Enigma codes used by the German military to transmit secret messages were broken. The British restricted access to the information gained from this codebreaking, known as ULTRA intelligence, in what would prove to be a successful effort to prevent the German military from realizing that their secret messages were being deciphered. This extended to the information they gave to the Soviet Union, but, unknown to the British, Soviet agents in the country were receiving other ULTRA intelligence because Blunt and Cairncross were copying documents at Bletchley Park and passing them on to their KGB handlers. After the war neither Blunt nor Cairncross gained positions in the intelligence communities so no longer had access to secret documents.

The intelligence supplied by Burgess and Maclean was most likely more of a background nature rather than being top secret, used by the Soviets in conjunction with intelligence gathered from other sources in an effort to establish an overall picture of what the British were doing. Some of the most important information they passed on concerned British involvement in the development of the atomic bomb during and after the Second World War, passing on details of the progress of the British research being carried

THE SPY RING
Clockwise from the top left: Anthony Blunt, Donald Maclean, Kim Philby, and Guy Burgess.

out under the code name of "Tube Alloys" and then of the Manhattan Project, the joint effort by the Allies that successfully built the first bomb. But neither Burgess nor Maclean had access to the technical details of the research, which was later obtained by the Soviet Union from a number of other agents from within the project itself.

Burgess and Maclean both worked in the British Embassy in Washington in the late 1940s, as the Cold War between the Soviet Union and the West was getting underway, and passed on important information about the nature of British and American relations at the time, particularly concerning how they were intending to deal with the Soviet Union. But, as with Blunt and Cairncross, neither possessed the necessary clearance to have access to the most sensitive secret intelligence. Philby, on the other hand, held senior positions in MI6 both during the Second World War and afterward, until his resignation in 1951, and is thought to have supplied the KGB with information about the identity of British agents working behind the Iron Curtain, leading to the capture and execution of dozens of them.

The full extent of damage done to British interests by Philby and the other Cambridge spies remains one of the many questions surrounding them that has yet to be fully answered. It has been suggested that the Soviets did not entirely trust any of them, suspecting that they may have been part of an elaborate plot by British intelligence to feed disinformation to the KGB or to place double agents into their ranks. The three defectors were certainly never allowed to hold positions in Moscow that would have given them access to sensitive information and were kept under surveillance by the KGB. The fact that no prosecutions have ever been brought in Britain against any of the Cambridge spies or anybody else involved with them might also suggest that there is more to the story than is currently in the public domain. Equally, it could be explained in terms of a reluctance on the part of the British government and intelligence services to invite yet more scrutiny on their failure to catch the spies. Whatever the truth of the matter, the Cambridge Spies represent the most serious breach of British security by agents working for a foreign country.

Numerous non-fiction books, novels, movies, and TV shows examining the case have appeared over the years and the media reports any new piece of information on them as soon as it becomes public, no matter how insignificant it may be. The public fascination with the secret world of espionage in general and, in particular, with those spies who committed acts of treason against their own country still has the capacity to cause intrigue because their motivation is far from clear. More twists and turns in the story may yet be revealed and, while it is impossible to predict what these may be, it would appear certain that the Cambridge spies will continue to make headlines long after all the main protagonists have died.

THE ATOM SPIES: JULIUS AND ETHEL ROSENBERG

1940s

MOTIVATION

Murder

Assassination

Treason

Espionage

Robbery

Hijacking

Fraud

Kidnapping

Location: America

Perpetrators: Julius and Ethel Rosenberg, together with other atomic spies

Outcome: Both were executed. Ethel Rosenberg may have been the victim of a miscarriage of justice

LIBERAL [Julius Rosenberg] recommended the wife of his wife's brother, Ruth GREENGLASS, with a safe flat in view. She is 21 years old, a TOWNSWOMAN [American citizen], a GYMNAST [member of the Communist Party] since 1942. LIBERAL and his wife recommend her as an intelligent and clever girl. Ruth learned that her husband [David Greenglass] was called up to the front. He is a mechanical engineer and is now working at the ENORMOZ [Manhattan Project] plant in SANTA FE, New Mexico.

Extract from one of the VENONA intercepts dated September 21, 1944, which, when decrypted, implicated the Rosenbergs in espionage

THE ROSENBERGS
Julius and Ethel Rosenberg after being found guilty of treason at their trial.

On June 19, 1953, Julius and Ethel Rosenberg were executed in the electric chair at the Sing Correctional Facility in New York State after being found guilty of passing secret information on American research into nuclear weapons to the Soviet Union. They were the only two people executed for espionage in America during the Cold War and their deaths occurred at the height of McCarthyism, the period named for Senator Joseph McCarthy and sometimes known as the Red Scare, which developed in America in the aftermath of the Second World War and as the Cold War between the Western and Eastern Blocs was beginning. Thousands of Americans were accused of being communist sympathizers who were disloyal to their country. Furthermore, secret agents of the Soviet Union were considered by some to be attempting to exert a malign influence over many different aspects of American life.

The Rosenberg case epitomized the climate of fear that had developed in America at the time and showed how deep the divisions had become between the political right and those people with left-leaning tendencies. Those of the right considered the case to be a demonstration of the threat posed by the Soviet Union, while the Rosenbergs were seen as being scapegoats by the left, sacrificed by a government desperate to show that it was doing something to combat the perceived threat. The political differences between the two sides only served to obscure the central issues: were the Rosenbergs guilty or innocent of committing acts of treason against America? And would the death sentence be justified in the event of a guilty verdict?

THE RED MENACE

On August 29, 1949, the balance of power in the Cold War was changed fundamentally by the detonation of a nuclear device at the Semipalatinsk Test Site in what is now Kazakhstan, then part of the Soviet Union. Up until the test was carried out, the Americans and their Western allies had thought that the Soviet Union had been four or five years away from constructing a viable atomic bomb, but the test made it abundantly clear that their nuclear research was much further advanced than had been previously thought. Soviet attempts to develop an atomic bomb had begun during the Second World War and were then increased after the success of the Manhattan Project, the huge nuclear research program undertaken by America, Britain, and Canada, which in August 1945 produced the bombs that were dropped on the Japanese cities of Hiroshima and Nagasaki. The immense power of these bombs and the strategic advantage they conferred on those countries possessing them were apparent to everybody and, as the Cold War developed, the Soviet ambitions to obtain their own bomb intensified.

As well as conducting their own research, the Soviets made use of information they had obtained from the work done in Nazi Germany, compelling those German scientists who had been involved to continue their research in secret within the Soviet Union. Having been made aware of the progress of the Manhattan Project by secret agents, including some of the Cambridge spy ring described in the previous chapter, the Soviet intelligence services had also begun operations to penetrate the site in America where the Allied research was being carried out. The extent of this penetration did not begin to become apparent until after the Soviet nuclear test in 1949 and, while it is difficult to know exactly to what extent the information gained through this source speeded up the Soviet research program, it has been estimated that it may have knocked years off the length of time it took them to develop their own atomic bomb.

Julius Rosenberg joined the American Communist party in New York as a young man while at college studying electrical engineering. After graduating in 1939 he married Ethel Greenglass, who he had met at Communist party meetings. The following year, he joined the US Signal Corps, working in the radio research laboratories at Fort Monmouth, New Jersey. Through contacts in the Communist party, he was introduced to Soviet secret agents and established a spy ring at Fort Monmouth, passing on numerous documents concerning the work then in progress there. Ethel's brother David Greenglass and his wife Ruth were also members of the Communist party and Julius Rosenberg recommended his sister-in-law, Ruth Greenglass, to his Soviet handlers as a potential recruit, initially suggesting that her apartment could be used as a safe house for copying documents but also probably as a means of drawing her husband into the ring.

TRINITY SHOT
The first test of the atomic bomb developed by the Manhattan Project, detonated in the New Mexico desert on July 16, 1945.

ATOM SPIES

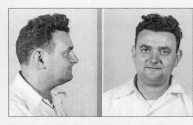

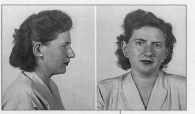

THE GREENGLASSES
Mugshots of David
and Ruth Greenglass,
whose confessions led
to the conviction of
the Rosenbergs.

In 1943, David Greenglass was called up to the US army and initially worked as a machinist at an ordnance facility before being transferred to the huge nuclear research laboratory that had been established in Los Alamos, New Mexico, as part of the Manhattan Project. In November 1944, Greenglass began making sketched copies of the plans he was using to make parts for the project, which he passed on to Harry Gold, another Communist party member and employee of the laboratory, who in turn gave them to Anatoli Yakovlev, a member of the Soviet intelligence services posing as a diplomat in the Soviet Consulate in New York.

The level of intelligence gained by the Soviet Union from Greenglass, who was not a nuclear physicist, is not thought to have been very great, but he was not the only person passing on secret information from the Los Alamos laboratory. Klaus Fuchs, a naturalized British citizen and nuclear physicist, worked on the Manhattan Project in America during the war and had also used Harry Gold as a courier to pass on the details of his work to Yakovlev. In 1950, he was implicated in spying by the VENONA intercepts, decrypted secret Soviet military and diplomatic telegrams. Fuchs provided British intelligence with a full confession of his spying activities and named Gold as the courier. Once this information had been supplied to the Americans, Gold in turn implicated Greenglass. The chain continued when Greenglass named Julius and Ethel Rosenberg, later claiming that he had done so in order to protect his wife and family, and the Rosenbergs were then arrested in New York. As well as telling the FBI that Julius Rosenberg had recruited him, he said that Ethel Rosenberg had known about her husband's activities and had helped him by typing up handwritten reports on the work being carried out at Los Alamos.

Unlike the others arrested, Julius and Ethel Rosenberg refused to talk. Both were indicted on charges of espionage, Ethel Rosenberg apparently charged more as a means of putting pressure on her husband to reveal details of his activities and those others who were involved rather than from an expectation that she would actually be tried. If that was the case, the ploy failed because both the Rosenbergs still refused to answer any questions and at their subsequent trial, which began in New York on

March 6, 1951, both cited the Fifth Amendment to the US Constitution, which gives people accused of crimes the right not to answer questions that might incriminate them, and taking the responsibility on themselves rather than incriminating anybody else.

The silence maintained by the Rosenbergs eventually led to the death sentence being imposed on them both. The members of the spy rings who had confessed were given long prison terms. There can be little doubt concerning the guilt of Julius Rosenberg, even if some of the evidence used to convict him was considered too sensitive to be made public at the time, leading to claims by his supporters that he had not received a fair trial. The existence of the VENONA intercepts, for instance, was not revealed until 1995, while the full transcript of the trial only came into the public domain in 2001. But since both have been made public it has become clear that he had engaged in spying for the Soviet Union. The question that remains over his conviction, then, does not concern his guilt but rather the severity of the sentence he received. America and the Soviet Union had been allies during most of the period when Rosenberg was spying, which largely occurred during the Second World War, and were at no point involved in a declared conflict during the Cold War. A conviction for espionage would only usually carry the death penalty during a time of war when secret information had been passed to an enemy, so it could be argued that Rosenberg had not committed a crime that carried the death penalty.

The guilt of Ethel Rosenberg is far less clear than that of her husband. The main evidence against her was the testimony of her brother and sister-in-law David and Ruth Greenglass, given in the knowledge that Ruth Greenglass had been given immunity from prosecution in exchange for the evidence the two of them had provided against the Rosenbergs. In 2001, David Greenglass, living under a false name in New York at that time, recanted the testimony he had made at the trial, saying that he had lied under oath in order to receive a lighter sentence for himself and to protect his wife. It was an extraordinary admission, casting himself as a person who was not only capable of committing treason against his country, but also of betraying his own sister. It would appear, then, that Ethel Rosenberg was the subject of a miscarriage of justice and that both of the Rosenbergs were victims of the hysteria over the threat posed by communism that had gripped America at that time.

MOTIVATION

Murder
Assassination
Treason
Espionage
Robbery
Hijacking
Fraud
Kidnapping

THE BLACK DAHLIA MURDER

ca. January 15, 1947

Location: America

Perpetrators: Unknown

Outcome: Still unsolved

She's Elizabeth Short. She's a ghost and a blank page to record our fears and desires. She was a flighty child–woman, a roamer, a sweet kid, and a liar. Her iconic noir status shrouds a key truth: She was her own blank page. She died before she grew up. Her life was her death transmogrified as a riddle. The real her only served to fuel speculation: What did she do to attract such devastation?

From James Ellroy's Foreword to
***The Black Dahlia Avenger* by Steve Hodel**

Not long after 10am on January 15, 1947, a woman walking with her young daughter along South Norton Street in the Leimert Park neighborhood of Los Angeles saw what she at first thought was a store window mannequin lying in the uncut grass of a vacant lot. She later described it as being of an ivory white color and, as it was split into two parts at the waist, it looked as if it had fallen off a truck and broken. As she got closer, she realized that it was not a mannequin, but the naked body of a woman. She called the police, who arrived shortly afterward. A reporter from the *Los Angeles Examiner* who had been monitoring the police radio beat them to it, arriving with a photographer who took pictures of the crime scene. As well as having been severed in two, the body had been extensively mutilated. Flesh had been removed, the legs had been slashed with a knife, and deep upward cuts made on either side of the mouth to give the

ELIZABETH SHORT
The 22-year-old aspiring actress was given the name of the Black Dahlia by the press after she was murdered in Los Angeles.

corpse a gruesome smile. The body had been drained of blood, explaining its whiteness, and the lack of blood at the scene clearly demonstrated that the woman had been murdered somewhere else and the body dumped on the lot, the two parts apparently arranged into a pose with the arms above the head and the legs spread apart.

MURDER IN LOS ANGELES

The policed identified the body as that of 22-year-old Elizabeth Short, and noted that her wrists and ankles had been tied when she died. Her death was caused by repeated blows to the head. Before the police had informed her mother, a reporter from the *Examiner* called her and said that her daughter had won a beauty contest, then pumped her for biographical details before finally telling her that, in reality, her daughter had been murdered. Even by the low standards of the tabloid press, it was a despicable thing to do and set the tone for the reporting of the case, which concentrated on salacious and lurid details, most of them invented, which cast Elizabeth Short as a femme fatale who lived a promiscuous lifestyle and, as a consequence, had brought her fate upon herself. They named the case the Black Dahlia for the Hollywood movie of that title starring Alan Ladd and Veronica Lake, which had been released the previous year, and also because the victim had her hair dyed black and usually wore black clothes.

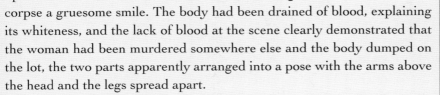

Elizabeth Short was born in Boston and grew up in Medford, Massachusetts, before living for periods in Florida and California. In August 1945 she became engaged to a major in the US Army Air Force, who was killed on active service shortly afterward, and a year later she moved to Los Angeles, working as a waitress and apparently dreaming of breaking into the movies. Ten days after her body was found a man claiming to be the murderer phoned the *Examiner* to say that he would send them a package containing some of her possessions. It arrived the next day and included her birth certificate, social security card, and an address book with the name Mark Hansen embossed on the cover. Police investigators interviewed Hansen, a well-known nightclub owner in Los Angeles, who had rented a room to Short for a period and said that the address book had been stolen some months before the murder had occurred. A number of witnesses said that they had seen several different men visit Short while she was staying in the room she rented from Hansen, who knew numerous people in the movie industry and was said to have connections to the Mob in LA, gossip that was never substantiated. The rumors led to speculation in the newspapers that Short had been a Hollywood call girl, but besides establishing that she had dated several men in her time in Los Angeles, the police found nothing to suggest that she had ever worked as a prostitute.

POLICE SEARCH
Two police officers examine blood-stained clothing found in a storm drain during the investigation into the murder.

At about the same time as the package turned up at the *Examiner*, the police received information that Short's purse and shoes had been spotted in a trash can about 20 blocks from where her body had been found. A search of the city dump began and the purse and shoes were recovered, identified by somebody who knew Short, but neither provided the police with any new leads. The investigation had established her movements up to January 9, but could not account for where she had been during the entire last week of her life. Several people who had known her described her as giving the impression that, in the weeks before she disappeared, she was afraid of somebody, possibly a boyfriend, without any of them being able to provide a name or description. The police received thousands of phone calls from people claiming to have information about the murder, and more than 50 people confessed to being the murderer, all of whom were proved to be lying. And so, despite one of the largest murder investigations ever mounted by the LAPD, after six months the police had hit a brick wall.

The Black Dahlia murder remains unsolved, which partly accounts for the enduring public fascination with the case; it allows for the sort of speculation that identifies suspects on the basis of little or no evidence. The salacious press coverage that the case attracted right from the beginning has also added to its notoriety, together with the unanswerable question of why the murderer mutilated and displayed the body in a way that suggested some sort of ritualistic aspect to the killing. But there is more to the case than it being another example of a true-life murder mystery that armchair detectives can attempt to solve. It involves the dark and seedy underbelly of Los Angeles, which contrasts so sharply with the wealthy and glamorous image that is more usually attached to the city. The fine line between these two extremes forms the backdrop to the novels of Raymond Chandler, who also wrote the screenplay for *The Black Dahlia*, in which his fictional private eye Philip Marlowe moves between these apparently separate worlds, exposing as he does so how closely the two are intertwined.

Numerous novels and non-fiction books have been written about the case over the years, some of which have blurred the distinction between the real and the imaginary. One of the best is James Ellroy's novel *The Black Dahlia*, the first of his LA Quartet, which is based on the case but does not pretend to be anything other than a work of fiction. In 1958, when Ellroy was 10 years old, his mother was murdered, a crime that remains unsolved, and he has written that this terrible event has fueled an obsession with the Black Dahlia case which led him in his novels to delve into the moral corruption and depravity he perceived to exist in society. He has cited *The Black Dahlia Avenger* by Steve Hodel, a former detective in the LAPD, as being the most convincing of the numerous non-fiction books that have attempted to solve the case. Hodel identifies the murderer as being his own father, Dr. George Hodel, who was a suspect in the original police investigation, but while he presents a better case than most of the other books on the subject, he cannot prove his father's guilt beyond doubt. Despite all the attention, the Black Dahlia has remained elusive for all these years and the case is as mysterious today as it has ever been.

MOTIVATION

Murder

Assassination

Treason

Espionage

Robbery

Hijacking

Fraud

Kidnapping

THE ASSASSINATION OF GANDHI

January 30, 1948

Location: Delhi

Perpetrator: Nathuram Godse

Outcome: The death of one of the great figures of the twentieth century

The light has gone out of our lives and there is darkness everywhere. I do not know what to tell you and how to say it. Our beloved leader, Bapu as we called him, the Father of the Nation, is no more. Perhaps I am wrong to say that. Nevertheless, we will never see him again as we have seen him for these many years. We will not run to him for advice and seek solace from him, and that is a terrible blow, not to me only, but to millions and millions in this country.

The beginning of a radio address made by Prime Minister Jawaharlal Nehru on the day of the assassination

In the early evening of January 30, 1948, Mahatma Gandhi was walking toward a platform with members of his family to address a crowd gathered for a prayer meeting being held in the garden of Birla House in New Delhi, where he was staying at the time, when he was shot three times in the chest and stomach at point blank range by Nathuram Godse, a 38-year-old Hindu nationalist from the city of Pune in Maharashtra. Godse then attempted to turn the gun on himself, but it was wrenched from his hand before he could do so and he was then rescued from being attacked by people in the crowd by police officers and arrested. Gandhi was carried back to the house and died there half an hour later, at about 5:40pm, from the injuries he had sustained. It was a terrible irony that the man who had dedicated his life to the cause of ending British rule in India through the use of nonviolent protest and campaigns of civil disobedience had been killed by an assassin's bullets less than six months after Indian independence had been achieved.

After his return to India from South Africa in 1915, Gandhi became the most prominent member of the independence movement. He would later write that his experiences of discrimination while in South Africa, both personally and against the Indian community in that country as a whole, shaped his way of thinking and political development. He cited a particular incident in which he had been thrown off a train after refusing to move from his seat in first class to the third class compartment despite having the correct ticket because a white man had objected to his presence. While waiting at the station for another train, he decided that he was no longer prepared to accept such injustice and began to develop what he described as *satyagraha*, literally "truth-force," which advocated the use of nonviolent protest against oppression based on the practice of active civil disobedience rather than passive resistance.

After gaining international attention for his campaigns in South Africa concerning the treatment of indentured Indian laborers, Gandhi adopted the same methods to protest against the injustices of the British colonial administration in India. The moral authority he gained by adhering to the principle of nonviolence meant that, while the British did not know how to deal with him, they could not ignore him either. Perhaps his most famous protest was what became known as the Salt March, a walk he set out on in March 1930 from the ashram were he lived in Ahmedabad

THE MAHATMA

SALT MARCH
Gandhi engaging in civil disobedience by picking up salt from the beach in Dandi. It was one of his most famous protests against British rule in India.

to the village of Dandi on the coast of Gujarat, a distance of about 250 miles (400km), in order to highlight the injustice of the tax on salt imposed by the British. Once at the coast, Gandhi intentionally broke the law by making salt himself, leading to his arrest and the arrest of tens of thousands of people all over India who had emulated him. The British did not abolish the salt tax, but Gandhi's protest had a unifying effect on the independence movement and demonstrated the potential impact of his methods of nonviolent civil disobedience.

More protests followed, including the Quit India movement during the Second World War, a campaign of civil disobedience demanding that Britain undertake to leave India immediately. It did not succeed in its immediate aims, and again resulted in Gandhi's arrest, along with thousands of others, but it made clear that British rule in India was becoming increasingly untenable. In the aftermath of the Second World War and with Britain almost bankrupt, it finally accepted the inevitable and announced its intention to leave India, initially stating that it would do so by the summer of 1948 but then bringing that forward by a year because of the threat of a civil war erupting between factions with different ambitions concerning the structure of the future independent state.

PARTITION

Gandhi had always envisaged a unified and pluralistic state replacing the British Indian Empire, in which people of all religions and castes were considered equal, but the differences between the political leaders of the various factions made this impossible. The predominantly Muslim provinces in the north were not prepared to join a unified state in which the future government would inevitably be controlled by the majority Hindus, presenting what appeared to be an intractable problem in the creation of a single independent state. The solution was the partition of British India into what would become the independent states of Pakistan and India, a border being drawn between the two that bisected the provinces of Bengal, Punjab, and Kashmir. After Pakistan became independent on August 14, 1947, and India followed suit the following day, a huge exchange of populations began in which more than 10 million Muslims and Hindus moved from one state to another in order to live in the newly formed country where people of their religion were in a majority. This was accompanied by outbreaks of serious civil unrest, rioting, and factional fighting in which it has been estimated that up to a million people died.

The fighting between Muslims and Hindus was exactly what Gandhi had been desperate to avoid. He may have been a devote Hindu himself, but he opposed injustice of whatever form, including when Muslims suffered at the hands of Hindus. On a number of occasions after independence he announced that he would embark on a fast, until death if necessary, in protest against what he considered to be unjust policies pursued by the Indian government. A few weeks before his death, he had begun one of these fasts in an attempt to force the government to transfer a share of the treasury of British India to Pakistan, as had been agreed in the partition settlement, but that had been withheld as a consequence of the military action taken by Pakistan in an attempt to take control of the Indian part of Kashmir. As they had done in the past when faced with a protest by Gandhi, the government quickly backed down and agreed to hand over the money, but it was seen by a small number of extreme Hindu nationalists as another example of many in which Gandhi had shown favoritism to Muslims over Hindus.

Nathuram Godse was one of these extreme nationalists and he would later say that he regarded Gandhi's conciliatory attitude to Muslims as a betrayal and held him personally responsible for the partition of British India because he had been prepared to negotiate with Muhammad Ali Jinnah, the leader of the Muslim League. Godse had been part of a group of seven men, all from Pune, who had previously mounted an unsuccessful attempt to assassinate Gandhi ten days before he died. On that occasion, one of the group named Madan Lal Pahwa planted a small incendiary bomb near to the platform where Gandhi gave his address to his prayer meeting with the intention of setting it off so that it would create panic in the grounds, giving another one of the group an opportunity to shoot Gandhi and then escape in the chaos. The plan came apart when the bomb went off but did not cause a panic in the crowd, leading to the arrest of Pahwa while the others aborted the assassination attempt and got away.

Pahwa provided the police with the names of the other conspirators, but, despite the clear threat to Gandhi's life, the security measures in place to protect him were not enhanced. It would later become one of the arguments employed by people who claimed that the conspiracy to kill him was much more extensive than the seven members of the assassination group and included high-ranking politicians who wanted him silenced because of the influence he could exert over the Indian people. No evidence has ever been produced in support of these allegations beside the fact that the seven were affiliated to a number of Hindu nationalist organizations, and the subject remains a controversial one in India today.

After the first attempt, Godse expected to be arrested at any moment, leading him to try again while he was still free. He came to New Delhi on his own the day before the second attempt so that he did not attract attention and, on the day, simply walked up to Gandhi and shot him. After

THE ASSASSIN
Nathuram Godse, on the left, with Narayan Apte at their trial. Both were found guilty and sentenced to death.

Godse was arrested, the remaining five members of the group were also arrested and stood trial together in the following year. Godse and one other, Narayan Apte, received death sentences after being found guilty and were both hanged on November 15, 1949, despite pleas for the sentences to be commuted to prison terms by, among others, two of Gandhi's sons and the Indian prime minister Jawaharlal Nehru, who all stated that they thought Gandhi would not have wanted his killers to be executed. The remaining defendants received long jail sentences for their parts in the conspiracy and most would be released in the mid-1960s without at any stage expressing remorse for what they had done.

In the aftermath of the assassination there was an enormous outpouring of grief across India and in many other parts of the world, bringing the nation together as perhaps no other event could have done. Gandhi has become known as the "Father of India" and his birthday, October 2, is now a public holiday in the country, while his life and work inspired countless others, including Martin Luther King Jr. and Nelson Mandela. Since independence, India has faced numerous problems, not least in disputes with Pakistan over the border regions created during Partition, but it remains a democracy and is at least nominally secular, even if tensions between different religious factions and other opposing groups can still lead to civil unrest.

ED GEIN: THE ORIGINAL PSYCHO

1950s

MOTIVATION

Murder
Assassination
Treason
Espionage
Robbery
Hijacking
Fraud
Kidnapping

Location: Plainfield, Wisconsin

Perpetrator: Ed Gein

Outcome: Gein spent the rest of his life in a mental institution

Madison, Wisconsin—Ed Gein has an Oedipus complex which drove him to murder two women who resembled his mother.

That was learned during the questioning of the confessed killer and self-admitted grave robber... Gein's complex was revealed by investigators who had been on the case since it broke last weekend with Gein's arrest and the finding of the mutilated body of Mrs. Bernice Worden.

From a report in the *Milwaukee Journal* on November 21, 1957

Late in the afternoon of November 16, 1957, Frank Worden returned to his home town of Plainfield, Wisconsin, after a day of deer hunting. He stopped by the hardware store run by his 58-year-old mother, Bernice Worden, to find that it was open, but she was nowhere to be seen. A trail of blood on the floor led to the back door, as if something had been dragged out, so Worden called the local sheriff's office. A sales receipt made out to Ed Gein, a local farmer and handyman, for half a gallon (1.9L) of antifreeze was found on the counter in the store—apparently the last transaction Mrs. Worden had made before she disappeared. Frank Worden told Sheriff Art Schley that Gein had been in the store the evening before and they had talked about his deer-hunting trip. Schley and one of his deputies drove to Gein's farm about 6 miles (10km) west of Plainfield to find out if he knew anything about the disappearance or had seen anything suspicious when he had been in the store.

HOUSE OF HORRORS

When they arrived at Gein's house, the sheriff and deputy uncovered a scene of unimaginable horror. In the summer kitchen, a shed attached to the house, they came across the headless body of a woman suspended by the ankles from the roof and eviscerated in a similar way to how deer and hogs are butchered. Inside the house, the scene was equally as gruesome. They found Bernice Worden's head in a sack in the kitchen, prepared as if it was going to be mounted on the wall as a trophy, and her heart was in a saucepan on the stove. It was only the beginning of what would prove to be a grisly collection of body parts and objects made out of them. Soup bowls had been fashioned out of the tops of skulls, lampshades and seat covers of tanned human skin, together with an apron, leggings, and a mask made from the corresponding parts of a woman's skin that looked as if they were intended to be worn as a ghoulish suit of clothes. Nine shrunken heads of women were found hanging on the wall, one of them belonging to Mary Hogan, a middle-aged woman who had gone missing from the nearby town of Pine Grove three years previously. The basement looked like a slaughterhouse, with decaying body parts and entrails scattered around, while, in complete contrast, the upstairs rooms did not look as if they had been lived in for years, it later emerging that Gein had preserved this part of the house in exactly the condition it had been in when his mother had died in 1945, giving the state investigators the sheriff had called to the scene the first clue as to what may motivated him to carry out such terrible crimes.

All together, the remains of at least 15 different women were found in the house. When confronted, Gein admitted that he had killed Bernice Worden and Mary Hogan, but claimed he had stolen all of the other body parts from the local cemetery. He said that from 1947 onward he regularly went there at night and would dig up the graves of women shortly after they had been buried, usually removing some body parts rather than the whole body and then covering over the graves again and taking whatever he had recovered home with him. After being assessed by psychiatrists, he was declared to be insane and unfit to be tried on the charges of murder that had been brought against him. He was sent to a secure mental hospital for the next ten years, to then be declared fit enough to stand trial for murder, whereby he was found guilty and sentenced to life imprisonment. He was sent to the Mendota Mental Health Institute in Madison, Wisconsin, where he remained for the rest of his life, being described by the staff there as a model patient, before dying in 1984 at the age of 77 from a heart attack.

KITCHEN HORROR
A police officer going through the littered kitchen of Ed Gein's house, where numerous human body parts were found.

A MOTHER FIXATION

Attempts to explain Gein's behavior have concentrated on his relationship with his mother, Augusta Gein. She is reputed to have been a domineering woman with deep religious convictions who had become convinced that the world was an evil place. She attempted to shield Ed and his older brother Henry from this perceived evil as much as she could; other than going to school, they rarely left the farm and had no friends, leading to Ed in particular becoming dependent on his mother. His father, George Gein, was a chronic alcoholic who could become physically abusive when drunk. He died of a heart attack in 1940, leaving the two brothers to run the farm.

In 1944 a fire the brothers had started on the farm to burn off brush got out of control. After the fire department had been called and had brought it under control, it was discovered that Henry Gein had died in the inferno. Despite being found with bruises on his face, his death was recorded as being caused by smoke asphyxiation. This didn't prevent speculation after Ed Gein was arrested in 1957 that he had killed his brother out of jealousy, which echoed the biblical story of Cain and Abel in which Cain murders his brother in a fit of jealousy after God appeared to favor Abel. Whatever the truth of the matter, the mother and son did not have long together. In 1945 Augusta Gein suffered a series of heart attacks before dying in December of that year, leaving Ed devastated and completely alone. It was at this point that he closed off the upper part of the house and not much more than a year later began to dig up bodies in the cemetery, perhaps in his mind attempting to bring his mother back or, by wearing the clothes he had fashioned out of skin, to actually transform himself into her.

After the details of Gein's crimes were revealed in 1957 and the speculation mounted concerning what had motivated him to behave in such a depraved way, he began to gain a reputation as the archetypal deranged and mother-fixated killer. The novel *Psycho* by Robert Block, on which Alfred Hitchcock's movie was based, was in part inspired by Ed Gein, in particular the idea that an individual committing such terrible acts could live within a small rural community like Plainfield, where everybody usually knows everybody else's business, without anybody realizing what their neighbor was capable of doing. Gein appears to have been regarded by those who knew him as being a little odd, a man who mostly kept himself to himself, but was nevertheless entirely harmless. Grief over his mother's death and the isolated life he must have led on the farm appear to have unhinged his mind, creating a split personality in which one part of him continued to live normally while the other part was prepared to do whatever it would take to assuage his sense of loss, causing him to commit acts of depravity. After he was caught and sent to a mental institution, he was no longer alone and this appears to have brought him some sort of relief.

ED GEIN
Gein, on the right, after his arrest, with Sheriff Art Schley on the left and Deputy Sheriff Leon Muryt in the center.

GREAT BRINK'S ROBBERY

January 17, 1950

MOTIVATION

Murder

Assassination

Treason

Espionage

Robbery

Hijacking

Fraud

Kidnapping

Location: Boston

Perpetrators: Joseph O'Keefe, Joseph McGinnis, Anthony Pino, Stanley Gusciora, and seven other Boston criminals

Outcome: An almost perfect crime

Biggest Bank Raid in US History.

Nine Robbers Steal $1,500,000. Leave Another Million at Brink's.

5 Armed Guards Bound, Gagged.

**Headline on the front page of the
Boston Herald on January 18, 1950**

We all have our benchmarks and for us the benchmark was the Brink's robbery in Boston in 1950, which was the largest robbery in the United States at that time. We wanted to do something as spectacular as that.

**Bruce Reynolds, the leader of
the Great Train Robbers**

BRINK'S BUILDING
The building where the robbery took place in the North End district of Boston, now used as a parking garage.

The building located on the corner of Commercial Street and Prince Street in the North End district of Boston is currently used as a parking garage. It was originally built in 1925 as a garage for the North Terminal Corporation and in 1997 was considered of sufficient architectural and historical interest to be listed on the National Register of Historic Places. In December 1948 the building attracted the attention of a gang of criminals from Boston, but not because of its architecture or history. At that time it was occupied by security company Brink's, who used it as a secure storage facility and a garage for the armored trucks they used to transport money and other valuables for their customers. The gang had been watching the Brink's operation in previous premises in Boston and continued to do so when Brink's moved to what became known as the Brink's building. Their purpose was to plan and prepare what, on January 17, 1950, would become the largest robbery carried out in America at that date, netting the gang about $2.8 million in total, including $1.2 million in cash and the rest in money orders, checks, and other securities.

Despite extensive investigations into the robbery, the police and FBI failed to make any arrests for six years and then only succeeded when one of the gang ratted on the others. Joseph O'Keefe had been one of the four original members of the gang, along with Joseph McGinnis, Anthony Pino, and Stanley Gusciora, who had cased the Brink's building before seven others, all associates from the Boston criminal underworld, had been brought in for the robbery itself, so he knew all about how it had gone down. After the robbery, the gang had agreed to hide the money for six years before spending any of it, by which time the statute of limitations would have run out and they could use the cash with impunity even if the authorities traced it back to the robbery.

O'KEEFE RATS

O'Keefe was arrested on a number of occasions after the robbery for other crimes, including burglary and the illegal possession of a firearm, and needed money for his defense. When that was not forthcoming from the gang, he became convinced that the others were attempting to take his share of the loot for themselves. In an effort to get hold of some of the money, he is said to have taken one of the other members of the gang, a man called Vincent Costa, hostage and demanded a ransom. A few thousand dollars were paid to release Costa, but the bad feeling created by O'Keefe, together with the suspicion that he was about to rat, led to three attempts on his life, the last of these allegedly involving a professional hitman hired by Anthony Pino. O'Keefe was shot by the hitman but survived, only to be sent to prison again not long after he recovered. FBI agents visited him on several occasions while he was inside, finally persuading him to talk on January 6, 1956, just 11 days before the statute of limitation on the robbery expired.

As well as giving the FBI the names of all members of the gang, O'Keefe described in detail how the robbery was planned and executed. After watching the Brink's operation over the course of months from the roofs of the surrounding buildings, the gang built up a detailed picture of the routines followed by the employees to determine the best time for the robbery. Late one night they then picked the lock of the external door on Prince Street, removed the cylinder of the lock and took it away so that a key could be made to fit it, replacing it with another lock while this was happening so that passersby would not become suspicious. Over the course of several more nights they entered the building again and again, taking the locks from internal doors to get keys made and getting acquainted with the internal layout of the building. They then conducted a number of trial runs with the full gang and established a getaway route, before deciding that the preparations were concluded.

At about 7pm on January 17, 1950, nine members of the gang pulled up outside the Prince Street entrance in a truck they had recently stolen. Seven of them, armed with handguns, entered using the key that had been made for the lock. They were all dressed in clothes similar to those worn by Brink's employees and were all wearing gloves, Captain Marvel masks to cover their faces, and chauffeur caps. Once inside, they made their way up to the second floor of the building, using the other keys they had made to open the necessary doors, which enabled them to enter the part of the building where five Brink's employees were going through their usual evening routine of checking and storing whatever money and valuables had come into the building during the day. The gang took the employees by surprise, tying them up and using adhesive tape to cover their mouths. They then began to stuff whatever they could find into sacks, interrupted

A PERFECT CRIME

only by an employee from the garage downstairs ringing the buzzer to be allowed into the secure part of the building. When nobody answered the buzzer he walked away, allowing the gang to continue with the robbery unimpeded. Once they had filled the sacks, they attempted to open a metal box containing the payroll of the General Electric Company, but failed because they had not brought any tools with them and decided to leave it, exiting the building at about 7:30pm, throwing the sacks of loot into the truck, and driving away.

PLAN OF BUILDING shows path taken by bandits in holdup of Brink's, Inc., in million-dollar Boston robbery.

THE PLAN
Diagram showing the route taken by the gang through the Brink's building. The handwritten numbers from one to six indicate locked doors.

The whole gang assembled at a house in the Roxbury neighborhood of Boston, a few miles to the south of the Brink's building, including the lookout, who had driven there separately, and Joseph McGinnis, who had been involved in the planning but had played no part in the robbery, instead making sure that he had an alibi by talking to a policeman in a liquor store while it was underway. They divided up the loot under the understanding that, except for some of the used bills they had stolen, nobody would spend their share for six years because most of the rest could be traced. They then split up and made efforts to be seen by other people to establish alibis for themselves, going, for instance, to bars they often frequented.

The robbery had gone like clockwork and, had O'Keefe not fallen out with other members of the gang and then talked to the FBI, they would have gotten away with it. All of the gang were rounded up and arrested with the exception of one who had died during the six years between the robbery and the arrests. Stanley Gusciora also died before the case came to trial, at which all but one of the eight surviving members of the gang received life sentences. O'Keefe, who had previously pleaded guilty, was given a reduced sentence of four years due to the help he had given to the FBI. Over the years only $58,000 of the $1.2 million cash that had been stolen has ever been recovered, an indication of how close the gang came to committing the perfect crime.

THE BOSTON STRANGLER

1962–1964

MOTIVATION

Murder

Assassination

Treason

Espionage

Robbery

Hijacking

Fraud

Kidnapping

Location: Boston

Perpetrator: Albert DeSalvo

Outcome: The identity of the killer was not confirmed until 2013

Woman Slain in Back Bay Home

Headline in the *Boston Globe* from June 15, 1962, on what would prove to be the first of the murders committed by the Boston Strangler

In "Boston Strangler" Case, Patience was Key

Headline in the *Boston Globe* from July 13, 2013, on the DNA test that linked Albert DeSalvo to the thirteenth and last murder

At some point in late February or early March 1965, Albert DeSalvo told George Nassar that he was the Boston Strangler, the man who had terrorized the city for 18 months between June 1962 and January 1964 by murdering 13 single women in their apartments. Both were inmates of Bridgewater State Hospital at the time, a secure mental institution in Massachusetts, Nassar as a convicted murderer and DeSalvo having been sent there for psychiatric assessment following his arrest for a sexual assault and his subsequent admission of committing a string of rapes and burglaries in four different states. Nassar contacted his attorney, F. Lee Bailey, who interviewed DeSalvo and then took on his case when he made a confession to the police in which he provided them with details of the murders that had not been made public.

At first sight, it appeared to provide a resolution to the extensive police investigation in Boston and the surrounding neighborhoods where the murders had occurred, which had, up until that point, experienced little success in tracking down the killer. But not everybody was convinced by DeSalvo's confession. Some people suspected that he had conspired with Nassar so that Nassar could claim the reward posted for information leading to the arrest of the murderer, which would then be split between them, DeSalvo's share going to support his wife and two children. According to this scenario, DeSalvo had decided that, since he was most probably going to receive a life sentence for the string of rapes he had admitted to committing, he could take the blame for the murders as well without risking the death penalty as long as he provided a confession. Some of the investigators also suspected that, even if DeSalvo was involved, the crimes were the work of more than one man and, as there were some inconsistencies in his confession and no physical evidence linking him to the crime scenes, in the end he was never charged with any of the murders attributed to the Boston Strangler. Many of his rape victims had positively identified him, leading to the apparent decision by prosecutors that, as he was certain to be convicted on those charges, not to take the risk of him being acquitted of the murders.

Allowing a potential serial killer, as we would now call DeSalvo, to avoid prosecution for 13 murders that he had confessed to having committed still appears to have been an extraordinary decision and one that would fuel intense speculation over his guilt or innocence. The apparent reluctance of the investigators to pursue the case after DeSalvo's confession has also led to some questions, not least because they had given the impression of wanting to close down the investigation as quickly as possible, perhaps, it has been alleged, to cover up its failings.

Whatever the truth of the matter, by that time the murders attributed to the Boston Strangler had become some of the most notorious committed in American history. The first attack occurred on June 14, 1962, when Anna Slesers, a 55-year-old woman who lived in Boston on her own, was raped in her apartment and then strangled with the belt of her dressing gown, which had then been tied into a bow around her neck. There was no sign that the killer had forced his way into the apartment, leading police to conclude that the victim had either known him or that he had talked his way in. Two weeks later a second woman, 68-year-old Nina Nicholls, was found dead in her apartment, attacked in much the same way except that she had been strangled with her nylon stockings. More victims followed and it quickly became clear that a serial killer was operating in the Boston area, causing a media frenzy and a wave of panic to sweep across the city and the surrounding towns.

THE STRANGLER STRIKES

CRIME SCENE
The building on Huntington Avenue in Boston's Back Bay neighborhood where the body of 20-year-old Sophie Clark was found.

The Boston Strangler, as he was named by the press, continued to find more victims, the attacks sometimes occurring only a matter of days apart and sometimes after several months had elapsed. He was apparently able to talk his way into the apartments of single women despite the huge amount of publicity the murders were attracting. In 1963, the strangler began to attack younger women using the same method, until, after the murder of 19-year-old Mary Sullivan on January 4, 1964, no more murders occurred. At that time, the police attributed 11 murders to the Boston Strangler, two more victims who had been stabbed rather than strangled later being added to the list after DeSalvo's confession. The investigation made little progress in identifying the perpetrator and, with witness descriptions of men seen in the area

of the crimes differing and the disparity in the ages of the victims, some of the investigators became convinced that more than one man was involved. The failure of the investigation attracted a great deal of criticism, particularly after a well-known psychic called Peter Hurkos, who regularly appeared on TV in the early 1960s, was brought in to help and gave a detailed description of a man that turned out to be a complete dead end.

On October 27, 1964, almost 11 months after the murder of Mary Sullivan, a man posing as a policeman talked his way into the apartment of a young married woman, tied her up and indecently assaulted her, then apologized and left. The woman gave the police a description of her attacker that matched that of Albert DeSalvo, who was known to them after being arrested on a number of occasions for burglary. He had also been identified a few years previously as the so-called Measuring Man, in which he had talked his way into the apartment of a number of young women by saying that he worked for a modeling agency and had been given their names as potential recruits. Once inside, he had taken the women's measurements and then left, saying that somebody from the agency would be in touch. After DeSalvo was caught during a burglary, he was identified as being the Measuring Man, but was considered as being a nuisance rather than a danger to women and was given a ten-month sentence for breaking and entering.

ALBERT DESALVO
A photograph taken of DeSalvo in Walpole State Prison shortly before he was killed by an unknown assailant.

After being arrested in October 1964, his picture was published in newspapers, prompting numerous women in Massachusetts and three other states to identify him as the man who had raped them. The police had caught a serial rapist who claimed to have committed over 300 assaults. While that was thought to be an exaggeration, a connection to the murders in Boston was not immediately made until DeSalvo made his confession four months later. At his subsequent trial on multiple charges of rape, his attorney F. Lee Bailey would attempt to employ the highly unusual strategy of introducing the murder confession as evidence for the defense in an effort to show that DeSalvo was insane. The trial judge ruled that the confession was inadmissible and, after DeSalvo was found guilty, sentenced him to life imprisonment, at which time he returned to Bridgewater Hospital.

In February 1967, DeSalvo escaped from Bridgewater, leaving a note to say that he had done so as a protest against the conditions there. He surrendered to his attorney the following day and was then sent to a maximum security prison near Walpole, Massachusetts, where he remained until he was stabbed to death during the night of November 27, 1973, by an unknown assailant. The day before his death he had contacted a psychiatrist named Dr. Ames Robey, who had been treating him, to say that his life was in danger and that he had something important to tell him, requesting that Robey bring a reporter with him. DeSalvo was moved to the infirmary, where it was thought he would be safe, but was nevertheless murdered there in what is thought to have been an argument over drug dealing in the prison and, Robey would later allege, with the involvement of prison guards, who had left the infirmary unlocked that night.

A CONFIRMED KILLER

Dr. Robey believed that DeSalvo was about to tell the truth about his involvement in the Boston Strangler murders and that his death prevented the case finally being resolved. In more recent years, the development of DNA testing has opened up new fields of enquiry, leading some to claim that the case is now closed. In 2013, semen that had been found on a blanket at the scene of the murder of Mary Sullivan was DNA tested and, when compared to a DNA sample from a living relative of DeSalvo, was found to be a close match. DeSalvo's body was then exhumed and an exact genetic match was established, proving beyond reasonable doubt that he could be placed at the scene of the murder. On announcing the conclusive results of the DNA, the Massachusetts Attorney General Martha Coakley went on to say that she was convinced that not only had DeSalvo murdered Sullivan, but that he had been responsible for the other murders as well. As no DNA samples were recoverable from whatever has been preserved of these other crime scenes, it remains impossible to say with absolute certainty that DeSalvo was responsible for all of the murders attributed to the Boston Strangler, but the combined evidence of the DNA test and his confession have finally convinced many people who had previously questioned his involvement of his guilt.

MOTIVATION

Murder

Assassination

Treason

Espionage

Robbery

Hijacking

Fraud

Kidnapping

THE GREAT TRAIN ROBBERY

August 8, 1963

Location: Buckinghamshire, UK

Perpetrators: A 15-man gang led by Bruce Reynolds, plus a number of other associates

Outcome: One of the most famous crimes ever committed in Britain

You're not going to believe this. They've stolen a train.

Radio message reportedly sent by one of the first policemen to reach the scene of the robbery

Let us clear out of the way any romantic notions of daredevilry. This is nothing less than a sordid crime of violence inspired by vast greed.

Judge Mr. Justice Edmund Davis in his summing up of the case at the trial of 11 of the robbers in 1964

Up until 2004, when the service was discontinued, the British Royal Mail operated night trains known as "traveling post offices" (TPOs) in which staff sorted mail in the carriages of the trains while they were in transit. In some of these trains, the first carriage behind the engine carried what were called "high value packages," or HVPs, including money as well as registered mail. At some point in 1962 a man with inside information on the Royal Mail approached a gang of armed robbers in London, England, led by Bruce Reynolds and known as the South West Gang, which also included Gordon Goody, Charlie Wilson, and Buster Edwards. The identity of this man has never been established and he has since become known as the Ulsterman. He was introduced to the gang by a solicitor's clerk, Brian Field, known to the gang after he had arranged their defenses during previous arrests. The Ulsterman said that he had contacts in the Royal Mail and could supply information concerning the transfer of money on TPOs in return for a cut of the loot from a successful robbery.

Once the connection between the Ulsterman and the gang had been established, Reynolds and Goody, acknowledged as the brains behind the operation, began to plan to rob a train. The information provided by the Ulsterman led them to identify the Glasgow-to-London TPO as being the highest-value target and the best time to raid it as being immediately after a public holiday, when it would be carrying money collected over the course of the weekend as well as the bank holiday itself. They also found the ideal place for the robbery: a quiet rural spot on the line shortly after the train left Leighton Buzzard, where there was a red light that could stop the train. Half a mile further along the track, there was also a road bridge where the loot could be unloaded once the engine and the first HVP carriage had been be moved after first being uncoupled from the other carriages so that the Royal Mail staff in them would not be aware that a robbery was taking place.

It may have been a straightforward plan, but Reynolds and Goody were faced with a number of problems before it could be carried out, primarily the need to recruit more robbers for a job of such size. They also needed to find a way of changing the signals to stop the train and somebody who could move the train from the red signal to the bridge so they did not have to rely on the train driver, who might refuse to cooperate. The first two of these problems were solved together when Reynolds joined forces

THE PLAN COMES TOGETHER

with another gang of armed robbers called the South Coast Raiders, which included a number of members who had experience of train robberies and a man named Roger Cordrey, who had already developed a method of rigging trackside signals to stop trains that simply involved connecting a battery to the amber signal that alerted the train driver to an upcoming red light, turning it on, and then covering over the green light of the next signal and attaching another battery to the red light. The problem of moving the train was then apparently solved by a man Reynolds had met in prison, Ronnie Biggs, who was not a member of either gang but knew a retired train driver who might be persuaded for the right amount of money to drive the train.

While details of the robbery itself were being worked out, the gang were also working on the getaway. They decided to find a place where they could hide out for a period afterward rather than risk returning to London straight away, reasoning that they would get an hour after the train had been stopped before the alarm was raised, giving them half an hour to conduct the robbery, but not enough time to drive back to London before the police began to look for suspicious vehicles. The solution came with the purchase of Leatherslade Farm, an isolated property then on the market 27 miles by road to the west of the site of the robbery. It was bought by Lennie Field, a client of the solicitor's office where Brian Field worked, although no relation to him, and, in what must be considered a huge oversight in such a carefully worked out plan, the farm was bought using Lennie Field's real name, meaning that, should the hide-out be discovered by the police, it could be connected to him and Brian Field and, from Field, to members of a known gang of armed robbers.

THIS IS IT The gang assembled at the farm on Tuesday August 7, 1963, the day after a bank holiday in Scotland, posing as decorators employed by the new owner. That evening they got word from the Ulsterman, via Brian Field, that the money was not on the TPO train that evening. They waited for the next train on Wednesday evening, apparently idling away the time playing Monopoly, before getting word that the money had been loaded into the HVP carriage of the train in Glasgow and that it had left on time at 6:50pm and was due at Leighton Buzzard shortly before 3:00am. The gang, made up of a total of 15 men, left the farm at about 1:00am that night, traveling in stolen ex-army vehicles, a truck, and two Land Rovers, and wearing military uniforms because the British army regularly used the streets in the area in the middle of the night. Once they arrived at the chosen site, they then put overalls on over the uniforms so that they now looked like railway workers.

At 3:00am the train came through Leighton Buzzard station and Bruce Reynolds, acting as lookout further up the track, radioed the gang that the robbery was on by repeating the phrase "This is it" three times. The signals were set, first the orange warning light and then the red stop light, prompting the train to stop at the expected spot. The fireman in the cab of the engine got out to use the trackside telephone, little knowing that the gang had cut all the telephone wires in the vicinity, and was grabbed, then three men climbed into the cab. A short scuffle occurred with the driver, named Jack Mills, who tried to stop them, and he was hit over the head with a metal bar by one of the three gang members who has never been identified. Mills was dazed but still conscious, and is said to have suffered health problems for the rest of his life as a consequence of the blow.

ROBBERY SITE
The railway bridge in Buckinghamshire, England, where the uncoupled engine and TPO carriage of the train were stopped and robbed.

Biggs and the driver he had brought along then climbed into the cab while the engine and HVP carriage were uncoupled from the rest of the train. The new driver attempted to get the train moving, but at some point the pressure in the breaking system had dropped, possibly as a result of the decoupling, and he could not release the brakes. After a few minutes Mills was persuaded to drive the train, but still had to wait for the pressure to rise to release the brakes. Eventually he got the engine moving for the short distance to the bridge. Once there, what the gang called the "assault team" broke into the HVP carriage and quickly overpowered the Royal Mail workers inside, who were tied up and gagged. The gang then formed a human chain, passing the sacks containing the money down to the truck parked on the street at the bottom of the railway embankment. After exactly half an hour Reynolds signaled that it was time to leave. The gang had moved 120 sacks and only eight remained, but rigorously stuck to the plan and left the rest behind. Before leaving, Mills and the fireman were warned

RONNIE BIGGS
A typical pose for the
press by Ronnie Biggs while
he was living in Rio de
Janeiro, out of the reach
of the British police.

not to move for 30 minutes, then the gang drove back to the farm having taken off their overalls so that they looked like soldiers again and, as Biggs would later say, singing along to songs like *The Good Life* by Tony Bennett on the radio.

By the time the police arrived on the scene almost an hour later, the gang were back at the farm counting the money. The 120 sacks have been estimated as weighing 2.5 tons and contained packets of used bills, mostly in small denominations. In total they had stolen about £2.6 million, equivalent to $68 million (£45 million) today. It was divided up into 15 shares for the gang members who had actually taken part in the robbery, plus shares for the Ulsterman, Brian Field, and Lennie Field, and smaller amounts known as "drinking money" for a number of other people who had helped the gang in one way or another. The scale of the robbery, together with the audacity of the gang, led to a media storm in which it was named "The Great Train Robbery," in the process becoming one of the most famous crimes ever committed in Britain. The gang listened to news reports on the radio while they were hiding out at the farm, realizing that they needed to leave after hearing that the police were searching isolated properties within a 30-mile (50km) radius of the robbery after being told by Jack Mills of the warning not to move for 30 minutes and assuming that this was the amount of time the gang had allowed to drive to their hide-out.

Before leaving the farm, the gang attempted to wipe it clean of fingerprints, but left numerous articles behind, including the sacks that had contained the money, various items of bedding and food, and the Monopoly set. They would later claim that they had paid a man known only as "Mark" to burn down the farmhouse, but he had pocketed the money and disappeared, so that when the police arrived a few days later after a tip-off from a local farmer, they recovered these items, finding fingerprints on a bottle of tomato ketchup and on the pieces of the Monopoly set. It represented a major breakthrough for the police investigation, which, by that time, was being led by Scotland Yard's Flying Squad under the command of Detective Chief Superintendent Tommy Butler, a dedicated and meticulous police officer sometimes known as "the Thieftaker."

In the press, the robbery was presented as being a challenge to the establishment and the robbers as being likeable rogues rather than dangerous criminals. The perceived failure of the police to catch the Great Train Robbers quickly resulted in a great deal of merriment at the expense of the government, but what the press and the public did not know was that the investigation was making steady progress. The Flying Squad had a good idea who was involved from the early stages, both from their knowledge of the criminal underworld in London and from the evidence obtained from the farm.

Over the fall and winter months of 1963, most of the gang were rounded up by the police, beginning with Roger Cordrey, who had been hiding out in a flat in Bournemouth, England, and was caught after using a bundle of 10 shilling notes to pay advanced rent on a garage. Brian Field and Lennie Field were arrested not long afterward and, as more arrests followed, Bruce Reynolds and Buster Edwards fled the country for Mexico, although both would later also be caught. After being found guilty at the subsequent trial, seven of the gang were given jail terms of 30 years, the rest receiving between 20 and 25 years, sentences widely perceived as excessive and reflecting the embarrassment the robbers had caused to the British authorities rather than the severity of their crimes. Ronnie Biggs would later become the best known of the gang, despite the relatively minor role he had played in the robbery, after escaping from prison and going on the run to Brazil, from where he would regularly be interviewed by British journalists, usually from a beachside bar in Rio de Janeiro. The sentences received by the robbers who had been caught were all later reduced, including that given to Bruce Reynolds after he returned to Britain in 1968, serving nine years of a 25-year term. Despite getting caught, Reynolds, like most of the other members of the gang, did not express regret for committing the crime, rather seeing it as the highlight of his career and perhaps also reflecting the fact that only about £350,000 of the £2.6 million stolen was ever recovered.

ROBBERS' REUNION
Seven of the gang at a book launch in 1979. Bruce Reynolds is in the center at the back, Buster Edwards on the far left.

MOTIVATION

Murder

Assassination

Treason

Espionage

Robbery

Hijacking

Fraud

Kidnapping

THE ASSASSINATION OF JOHN F. KENNEDY

November 22, 1963

Location: Dallas

Perpetrator: Lee Harvey Oswald, who either acted alone or as part of a conspiracy

Outcome: The death of a president and a turning point in American history

Any effort to explain what happened in Dallas must explain Lee Harvey Oswald, and Lee Harvey Oswald is a mystery wrapped up in an enigma, hidden behind a riddle. Your explanation of him tells me more about you than about the evidence about his life. He is not an easy man to explain.

From an interview conducted in 1993 for the PBS documentary *Who was Lee Harvey Oswald?* with G. Robert Blakey, chief counsel to the 1978 House Select Committee on Assassinations

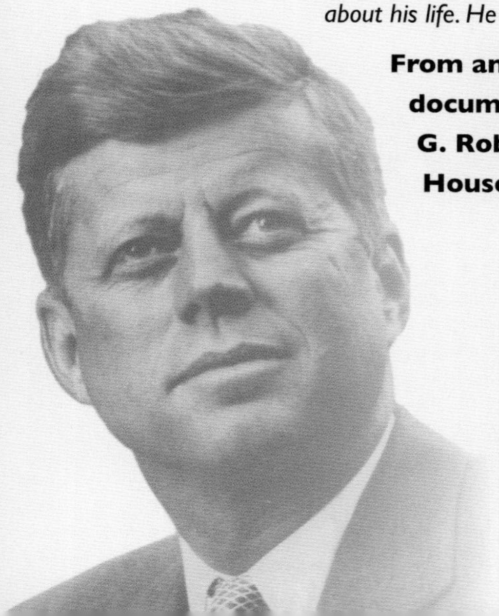

At about 1:15 in the afternoon of Friday November 22, 1963, Officer J. D. Tippit of the Dallas Police Department pulled up in his car alongside a man walking in the Oak Cliff district of the city, a few miles to the southwest of Dealey Plaza where, 45 minutes before, President John F. Kennedy and the Texas governor John Connally had both been shot. Witnesses had reported seeing a man at the sixth-floor window of the Texas Book Depository on Dealey Plaza

DALLAS MOTORCADE
Crowds line the street to catch a glimpse of JFK and Jackie Kennedy. Governor Connally and his wife are sitting in front of them.

with a gun and one of the employees, the 24-year-old Lee Harvey Oswald, known to have been in the building at the time of the shooting, had been reported as missing. The man on the sidewalk resembled the description of Oswald that had gone out over the police radio and, as Tippit got out of his car, the man walked toward him, pulled out a handgun, and shot him three times in the chest and then, while standing directly over him, once more in the head. A few minutes later a man was seen entering a nearby movie theater without buying a ticket and the police were informed. As an officer approached the man in the theater, he attempted to pull a gun, later shown to be the one used to kill Officer Tippit, but was overpowered and arrested.

The man arrested in the movie theater was Lee Harvey Oswald. He was taken to the Dallas Police Headquarters where he was first charged with the murder of Officer Tippit and then later that evening with the assassination of President Kennedy. Over the course of that evening he spoke to reporters gathered in the building on a number of occasions, describing himself as a patsy and saying that he had not shot anybody. During the interrogations that followed he repeatedly denied the charges and refused to say anything further in the absence of the lawyer he had requested. Shortly after 11am on Sunday November 24, Oswald was taken down to the basement of the police headquarters where a police van was waiting to take him to the county jail. The transfer was being broadcast live on TV and an audience of millions were watching when a man later identified as Jack Ruby, the manager of a seedy nightclub in Dallas who is reputed to have been connected to the Mafia, rushed at him and shot him once in the

OSWALD

LEE HARVEY OSWALD
Mugshot of Oswald taken after his arrest for the murder of Officer Tippit. He was later charged with the assassination of President Kennedy.

chest. Oswald was taken unconscious to the Parkland Memorial Hospital, where President Kennedy had been taken after he had been shot, and died there later that day.

The details of Oswald's bizarre life before the assassination have been raked over again and again in an effort to understand why, if he was the shooter rather than the patsy he claimed to be, he had assassinated Kennedy. In 1956, at the age of 17, Oswald joined the US Marine Corps and was trained as a radar operator and in aerial surveillance techniques. Like all Marine recruits, he also received training in the use of firearms and achieved above average scores in the rifle tests he took. After serving in Japan and the Philippines he was discharged from the Marines in September 1959 and, in the following month, defected to the Soviet Union, where he lived for almost three years, marrying a Russian woman, Marina Prusakova, and having a daughter. In May 1962, he returned to America with his wife and daughter, living at first in the Dallas area not far from his mother and brother, and then moving to New Orleans, where he had grown up.

On a number of occasions while in New Orleans, Oswald handed out leaflets on street corners in support of the Castro government in Cuba, claiming to represent a pro-Castro organization of which, in reality, he was the only member. In late September 1963, Oswald traveled to Mexico City, going to the Cuban embassy where he was granted a visa to visit the country. He also went to the embassy of the Soviet Union on two occasions and was interviewed by KGB officers, but was refused a visa to travel on from Cuba to Russia. He then returned to America, going to Dallas and finding a job in the book depository that began about five weeks before the assassination. A great deal has been made of these activities by different researchers into his life and he has variously been cast as a Soviet agent, as either a pro-Castro or anti-Castro Cuban agent, as a loyal American who was working for the CIA all the time, or as a fantasist who believed he was involved with one or possibly even all of them. An understanding of how this unusual background led to his involvement in the assassination, in whatever form, could provide the key to unraveling the full story behind it. However, the chance to do so was, in all likelihood, ended by his murder.

President Kennedy had arrived in Dallas at 11:25am that Friday morning along with his wife, Jackie Kennedy, and their entourage on board Air Force One, the presidential plane. They set off in a motorcade for the drive from Love Field airport to the city, the president and first lady sitting in the back seat of a specially adapted Lincoln Continental convertible with Governor Connally and his wife sitting in front of them. Kennedy had come to Dallas as part of an effort to boost his support in states that would be crucial for his bid to be elected president for a second term. He was well aware of the publicity he would enjoy by driving through crowd-lined streets in an open-topped car, the presence of Jackie Kennedy increasing that publicity even further because she was being treated by the media at the time as if she were a movie star. He also hoped to be able to smooth over serious differences that had emerged between different factions in the Democratic party in Texas, hoping that his visit would concentrate their minds on fighting against the Republicans in the forthcoming elections rather than with each other.

The route taken by the motorcade through Dallas had been published in newspapers so that people knew where to stand to get a good view of the president and his wife. When they reached Dealey Plaza, they turned right and then immediately left onto Elm Street, taking them past the Texas Book Depository on the corner of those two streets, heading for the Texas Trade Mart where Kennedy was due to make a lunchtime speech. As the cars approached a low bank on the right-hand side of Elm Street, now known as the grassy knoll, a loud bang rang out, initially taken to be a firecracker or a car backfiring by onlookers in the crowd. As the president's limousine drew level with the grassy knoll, at least two more bangs rang out, leaving nobody in any doubt that the sounds had been made by gunfire.

LOVE FIELD
The Kennedys arriving at Love Field Airport outside Dallas before setting off in a motorcade through the city.

The limousine sped away, heading toward the Parkland Memorial Hospital with one of the president's security detail clinging to the back of the car. In the ensuing chaos, and with the sound of the shots echoing off the building surrounding Dealey Plaza, some people who had been watching the motorcade had difficulty in determining where the shots had come from or how many there had been. A couple standing near the grassy knoll had thrown themselves to the ground thinking the shots had come from behind a wooden fence on top of it, while others near the book depository thought they had come from there, a few reporting that they had seen a man with a rifle at a corner window on the sixth floor. A man working on the fifth floor of the building said that, as well as the shots, he distinctly heard the bolt action of a rifle being worked and the sound of three spent cartridges hitting the floor above him. The cartridges were found by police officers by the window on the sixth floor and, in a subsequent search, an Italian-made Mannlicher-Carcano rifle fitted with telescopic sights was recovered, having apparently been stuffed into a gap between stacks of boxes on the other side of the room. The rifle was later shown to have been bought by Oswald by mail order six months previously and a photograph of him holding it, taken by his wife, also came to light.

In the subsequent investigation it was determined that the first of the three shots from the book depository most likely missed, and the bullet was never recovered. The second bullet hit Kennedy in the upper back and exited through his throat and then wounded Governor Connally, sitting directly in front of the president, in the back and right wrist. It was later found intact on the stretcher that had been used to carry Connally into the hospital and became known as the "magic bullet" by people who doubted that it could have caused all of the injuries attributed to it. The devastating impact of the third bullet was caught on film by Abraham Zapruder, who was standing on a concrete pillar next to the grassy knoll shooting footage of the motorcade with a home movie camera as it went past him.

The Zapruder film shows in graphic detail the moment when Kennedy was shot in the head, the bullet that hit him causing a gaping wound that would be given as the cause of his death by doctors in Parkland Hospital not long afterward. The footage must surely be the most analyzed film sequence ever taken and, from the movement of Kennedy's body after he was shot, it certainly appears to suggest that the bullet that killed him had been fired by a shooter positioned in front and to the right of him, from, in other words, the direction of the grassy knoll. If this is correct, then it demonstrates that a fourth shot was fired that day by somebody other than the man seen in the book depository, thereby providing evidence of a conspiracy to kill Kennedy.

The murder of Oswald, the only suspect in the assassination, meant that no trial would be held to determine his guilt or innocence. Lyndon Johnson, who had been sworn in as president within hours of Kennedy's death, appointed Chief Justice Earl Warren to chair a commission to investigate the circumstances of the assassination, which published a report in September 1964 stating that Lee Harvey Oswald had fired the two shots that had hit Kennedy and that he had acted alone. The commission was criticized by some commentators, who contended that the investigation had been rushed and that insufficient attention had been paid to the possibility of a conspiracy, alleging that the commission had been set up in the first place to come to the lone gunman conclusion because it would have caused the Johnson administration serious difficulties internationally and at home if any other countries, organizations, or individuals had been implicated.

Over the years, numerous conspiracy theories have been developed in an effort to explain the assassination and to implicate others in it. Among those accused of playing some part have been agents from the Soviet Union and Cuba, the American mafia, rogue elements in the CIA, President Johnson himself, alleged to have staged a secret coup against Kennedy, and a loosely defined entity known as the military-industrial complex. Many of these conspiracy theories have been highly speculative in nature, but even if they are wrong, they indicate a widespread unease with the official version of events, held by many to have told only part of the story. They also indicate doubts as to whether the security agencies involved on the day and in the subsequent investigation had revealed all that they knew.

OSWALD SHOT
Oswald was murdered by Jack Ruby while he was being transferred from Dallas police headquarters to jail.

More than 50 years after the event, numerous CIA files relating to the assassination remain classified, supposedly for reasons of national security, but suspicions have been expressed by more cynical observers that the actual reason why these files have not been released is either because they contain details of the agency's failure in their duty to protect the president or the identities of CIA agents who were more involved in the assassination than the agency would like to admit. These files are due to be released in 2017. Assuming this happens, more light may yet be shone onto one of the most studied and discussed crimes ever committed and one that for many people has come to be regarded as one of the defining moments of the twentieth century.

MOTIVATION

Murder
Assassination
Treason
Espionage
Robbery
Hijacking
Fraud
Kidnapping

THE MOORS MURDERS

July 1963–October 1965

Location: Manchester

Perpetrators: Ian Brady and Myra Hindley

Outcome: A crime that shocked Britain more than any other, before or since

There was utter silence as we listened to the little girl pleading. I had covered lots of big trials involving all sorts of killers but I had never seen grown men cry before as they did listening to Lesley. Policemen walked out of court because they could not bear it anymore. No one who heard that tape could ever escape from the memory.

Daily Mirror reporter Brian Crowther, writing in 2013, on the moment the tape of Lesley Ann Downey made by Ian Brady and Myra Hindley was played at their trial

The full extent of the crimes committed by Ian Brady and Myra Hindley, known as the Moors Murders, was confirmed in 1985, more than 20 years after the events, when Brady finally confessed to what the police had long suspected, that he had killed two other children who had gone missing in Manchester at around the same time as the three that he and Hindley were already known to have murdered. After their arrest in October 1965 and the terrible nature of the murders they had committed was reported in the media, a wave of revulsion swept across Britain, further compounded by the total lack of remorse they showed during the subsequent trial in April 1966, in which both appeared to adopt a disdainful attitude toward the proceedings. The trial judge described Brady and Hindley in his summing up as being "two sadistic killers of the utmost depravity," an opinion that encapsulates the public view of the couple who have become the two most reviled murderers in British criminal history.

Myra Hindley first met Ian Brady in 1961, when at the age of 18 she got a job as a typist at Millwards Merchandise in Manchester, England, a small chemical distribution company where he had worked for a number of years. She became infatuated with Brady, who was four years older than her and, after apparently initially ignoring her, eventually responded. Brady had experienced a difficult childhood and had been in trouble with the police on a number of occasions. He was sent to a borstal at the age of 17, an experience he would later claim had brutalized him and turned him against British society in general, and he had developed a morbid fascination with violence, and in particular with Adolf Hitler and the atrocities committed by the Nazi regime. At the start of the relationship Brady appears to have exerted a controlling influence over Hindley, but by the time he moved into the house she shared with her grandmother in Gorton in June 1963, she appears to have become less submissive, apparently encouraging his fantasies of violence and sadism.

Hindley would later claim that she had been completely under Brady's influence at the time when they committed their first crime and that he had often talked about his desire to commit the perfect murder. It would appear more likely that they were actually involved in the sort of relationship in which both encouraged the other to go further than either might have done on their own. Far from being the passive onlooker she claimed to be, it is probable that Hindley played an active role in the murders right from the

BRADY AND HINDLEY

start. In July they decided on a plan in which Hindley drove around the streets of Gorton in a hired minivan with Brady following behind on a motorbike looking for suitable victims to kidnap, their reasoning being that whoever they selected would be more likely to get into a van with a woman on her own than if there had been a man present.

At about 8pm on July 12 Brady and Hindley put their plan into action and, after a first abortive attempt, Brady selected a girl walking on her own along a street in Gorton and flashed the lights on his motorbike in a prearranged signal to Hindley. She stopped alongside the girl, who turned out to be Pauline Reade, the 16-year-old friend of Hindley's younger sister Maureen, and offered her a lift. Reade accepted the lift with a woman she knew and, once she was in the van, Hindley suggested that they take a detour out to Saddleworth Moor, a few miles outside Manchester, so that they could look for a glove Hindley said she had lost while walking there. Reade agreed and, once they had driven out to a spot on the moor, they were joined by Brady, who, Hindley said, had also come to help in the search for the glove. He then hit Reade over the head with a shovel, sexually assaulted her and murdered her by cutting her throat. Brady and Hindley buried the body in a shallow grave on the moor, where it would remain until 1987, when it was recovered after Hindley had led the police to its location.

The next two murders followed a similar pattern. The victims, two 12-year-old boys, were strangled with lengths of string. John Kilbride was murdered on November 23, 1963, and his body was found buried on the moor after the location had been determined from photographs taken of Brady and Hindley posing by the grave, which they apparently revisited on a number of occasions after the murder. The body of Keith Bennett, murdered on June 16, 1964, has never been found, despite intensive searches of the moor over the years. Brady has said that he knows where the body is buried but has refused to reveal the location, causing Keith Bennett's family great distress.

The fourth murder was different from the previous three. On Boxing Day, 1964, Brady and Hindley lured 10-year-old Lesley Ann Downey into their car after she became separated from her family at a fairground. They took her home, tortured her, and took indecent photographs, before strangling her and taking her body to Saddleworth Moor. While they were torturing their victim, they made a sound recording of her screaming and begging for her life that was so harrowing that it is reputed to have reduced some of the seasoned police officers who later listened to it to tears.

No further murders were committed by the pair until October 6, 1965, when Brady and Hindley attempted to get Hindley's 17-year-old brother-in-law David Smith involved in their crimes. Brady met Edward Evans, also 17, at Manchester railway station and persuaded him to come back to the house he and Hindley had recently moved to in Hattersley, a few miles from Gorton, while Hindley invited Smith over for a drink. Smith was in the kitchen when Evans began to scream in the living room and, on going in to find out what was happening, came across Brady hitting Evans over the head with a hand ax. Brady then handed the ax to the stunned Smith, strangled Evans to make sure he was dead, and then the two of them carried the body to a bedroom upstairs. Later that night, after Smith had gone home, he phoned the police and told them what had happened.

BRADY AND HINDLEY
Mugshots of Ian Brady and Myra Hindley taken after their arrest in October 1965.

The police arrested Brady the next morning after they had found Evans's body. They were led to the spot on Saddleworth Moor where John Kilbride and Lesley Ann Downey were buried after a young girl had told them that Brady and Hindley had taken her there without harming her. Hindley was not arrested for a further five days, not until the police had recovered a suitcase from the left luggage office of Manchester railway station that contained the tape and photographs of Lesley Ann Downey, from which it was clear that Hindley had been involved in that murder as well as Brady. The tape was played at the subsequent trial. Both were found guilty of the three murders for which the bodies had been recovered and were sentenced to life imprisonment. After many years of campaigning in an effort to secure her release, Hindley died in prison in 2002 at the age of 60, while Brady was transferred to a maximum security psychiatric hospital in 1985, where he remains to this day.

MOTIVATION

Murder

Assassination

Treason

Espionage

Robbery

Hijacking

Fraud

Kidnapping

THE THEFT OF THE STAR OF INDIA

October 29, 1964

Location: New York

Perpetrators: Allan Kuhn, Jack "Murph the Surf" Murphy, and Roger Clark

Outcome: The return of most of the stolen gems to the American Museum of Natural History in New York and an upgrade of the museum's security arrangements

It won't happen again, the American Museum of Natural History vowed today.

"Maximum security measures have been taken for the redisplay of the Star of India and its companion" said a spokesman for the old gray palace of culture in New York City. He would not go into details, but it is understood a 24-hour guard will be put around the jewels in the J. P. Morgan area of the museum.

From a report in the *Miami News* on January 6, 1965, the day the Star of India was recovered

In 1901 the hugely wealthy financier J. P. Morgan presented part of his collection of gemstones to the American Museum of Natural History in New York, an institution he had helped to found 30 years previously. The gems formed the basis of a permanent exhibition in a gallery of the museum named for Morgan and they included one of the most famous sapphires in the world, the Star of India, which, despite its name, is thought to have been found in Sri Lanka about 300 years ago. It is milky

J. P. MORGAN
The financier gave the Star of India to the American Museum of Natural History, where it was displayed in a gallery named after him.

gray-blue in color and exhibits the phenomenon of asterism, caused by the presence of the mineral impurity rutile within the molecular structure of the sapphire, which produces the effect of a six-pointed star on its surface. At 563.35 carats, it is the second-largest star sapphire in the world, behind the 733-carat Black Star of Queensland, and it has been cut in a style known as *en cabochon*, shaped and polished to have a convex surface most suited to displaying the asterism. On October 29, 1964, it achieved new heights of celebrity when it was stolen from the museum along with 21 other gemstones in what was the largest jewel heist in American history.

A NIGHT AT THE MUSEUM

In Hollywood movies, jewel heists are usually depicted as being highly elaborate affairs in which burglars have to contend with all manner of alarms, motion sensors, noise detectors, and more often than not an array of lasers that they have to negotiate their way past without breaking the beams. The reality of the theft from the American Museum of Natural History was rather different. At the time of the robbery, the museum's antiquated alarm system had broken down, the door to the gem gallery was not kept locked at night and, after the museum was closed in the evening, only one security guard patrolled the first floor where it was situated. In the gem gallery itself, a single rail separated the public from the glass cases where the gems were displayed and only the display case containing the Star of India had its own dedicated alarm, powered by a battery that, on the night of the robbery, was flat.

Two young men from Miami accepted the invitation. Allan Kuhn and Jack Murphy, both in their mid-20s, led playboy lifestyles funded by the money they made from burglarizing houses belonging to wealthy Miami residents. Murphy was the kind of person who gives the impression of being effortlessly good at everything. Before moving to Miami, he had been a tennis professional and had played the violin in a concert orchestra and, after he had arrived, he fitted easily into the beach life of the city, becoming well known when he won a surfing championship and acquiring the name of "Murph the Surf." Allan Kuhn was another beach boy and he was responsible for introducing Murph to a life of crime, first getting him to drive the speedboat used to get away from robberies of beachfront properties and then persuading him to join in with the break-ins as well.

In late October 1964, Kuhn and Murphy arrived in New York looking to make a bigger score than they had so far managed to achieve in Miami. They took a suite in a hotel across the street from the museum where they held parties at which they were happy to discuss their intentions with their guests. After casing the gem gallery in the museum and finding it almost completely unprotected, even talking to a security guard about his job on one occasion, they appear to have decided that it was too good an

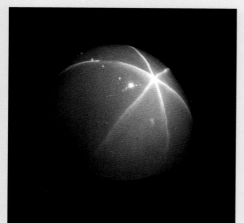

STAR OF INDIA
The six-pointed star on the surface of the sapphire is caused by the presence of a mineral impurity within its molecular structure.

opportunity to turn down. Shortly before the museum closed in the evening on October 29, one of them unlocked a window in a bathroom on the second floor, leaving it so that it could be opened from the outside. That night they scaled the outside of the building while a New York friend named Roger Clark kept watch outside, climbed in through the open window, went down to the gem gallery on the floor below, making sure they avoided the lone security guard, and helped themselves to the gems in the display cases.

Kuhn and Murphy pocketed 22 gems in total. As well as the Star of India, they took the 116-carat Midnight Star sapphire, the 100-carat DeLong Star ruby, and the 10-carat Eagle Diamond, together with other smaller but nevertheless highly valuable stones. Kuhn and Murphy went straight back to Miami with the gems after the heist, while Clark stayed in New York. They were then faced with the problem of how to dispose of such well-known items. The smaller stones could be fenced and the Eagle Diamond disguised by cutting it into a number of smaller stones, but the two star sapphires and the star ruby were far too famous to sell as they were and cutting them down would ruin the asterism, rendering them almost worthless. They appear to have decided to offer these stones back to the museum for a ransom, but before they got very far with this plan, the police received an anonymous tip-off and Kuhn, Murphy, and Clark were all arrested.

The police may have gotten the burglars, but they did not find any of the stolen goods. All were charged and then released on bail, then what appears to have happened is that a gang of Miami criminals stole the gems from Kuhn and Murphy, who then entered into a deal with the police to receive a reduced

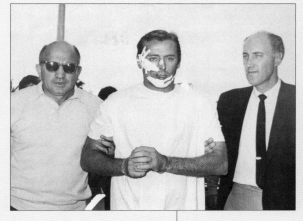

"MURPH THE SURF"
Jack Murphy being arrested in a Miami hospital in 1968 after being treated for injuries sustained during a failed robbery.

sentence for the original robbery in return for their help in recovering the gems. In early January 1965, Kuhn was with New York detectives when a deal with the people in possession of the stones appears to have been under negotiation. Another anonymous phone call was made to tell the police that the stolen items were in a locker in a Miami bus station. The Star of India and the Midnight Star were both found in the locker, along with a number of the other stones, and returned to the museum, where rather more elaborate security measures were put in place. A ransom of $25,000 was paid for the return of the DeLong Star a few months later and it was recovered after being left in a designated drop-site, a phone booth in Miami, but the Eagle Diamond has never been found.

Kuhn, Murphy, and Clark all received extremely lenient jail sentences of three years for the robbery and were released on parole in 1967. Kuhn and Clark appear to have learned from their experiences, going straight after being released from jail, or, at least, not getting caught again. Murphy, on the other hand, became involved in more violent criminal activity and would serve almost 20 years in prison after being convicted of murder. He became a born-again Christian in prison and after being paroled began work with a program to rehabilitate prisoners, which he still does today.

MOTIVATION

Murder

Assassination

Treason

Espionage

Robbery

Hijacking

Fraud

Kidnapping

THE ASSASSINATION OF MARTIN LUTHER KING JR.

April 4, 1968

Location: Memphis

Perpetrator: James Earl Ray

Outcome: The death of the man who led the Civil Rights movement

Well, I don't know what will happen now. We've got some difficult days ahead. But it doesn't matter with me now. Because I've been to the mountaintop. And I don't mind. Like anybody, I would like to live a long life. Longevity has its place. But I'm not concerned about that now. I just want to do God's will. And He's allowed me to go up to the mountain. And I've looked over. And I've seen the promised land. I may not get there with you. But I want you to know tonight, that we, as a people, will get to the promised land. So I'm happy, tonight. I'm not worried about anything. I'm not fearing any man. Mine eyes have seen the glory of the coming of the Lord.

From the speech delivered by Martin Luther King Jr. on April 3, 1968, the day before he was assassinated

On April 3, 1968, Martin Luther King Jr. flew in to Memphis from Atlanta to support protests by black sanitation workers in the city who had been on strike since February over the discriminatory working conditions that had been imposed on them by the newly elected mayor, Henry Loeb. Not only were they paid less than white workers for doing the same job, but were expected to work no matter what the weather when their white colleagues were not. King had been to Memphis several times since the strike had broken out, always staying in Room 306 of the Lorraine Motel on Mulberry Street. On this occasion he had endured a difficult flight, his plane being delayed in Atlanta by both bad weather and a bomb threat. That evening he addressed a gathering at the Mason Temple in the city, delivering a speech that would later come to be regarded as one of his finest. Much of the speech concerned the sanitation strike and the civil rights movement in general, but as he was bringing it to a conclusion he referred to the flight and to vague rumors then circulating in Memphis that an attempt to assassinate him would be made in the city. His words, quoted at the beginning of this chapter, now have an eerie prescience. At 6pm the following day, he was shot in the throat as he stood on the balcony of his motel room and was pronounced dead in hospital an hour later.

MARTIN LUTHER KING
King making a speech on April 15, 1967, at an anti-Vietnam War demonstration in New York.

The shot that killed King appeared to have been fired from Bessie Brewers Rooming House on the other side of Mulberry Street from the motel. A number of witnesses reported a man to the police who they had seen leaving the rooming house immediately after the shooting. He had dumped a large package in the doorway of the building next door and had then driven away in a white Ford Mustang. The police put out a description of the car and recovered the bundle, which turned out to be a rifle, binoculars, clothes, and several other items wrapped in a blanket. One of the other items was a Memphis newspaper in which the location of the motel where King was staying was given. The staff of the rooming house identified the man in the white Mustang as John Willard, who had arrived that afternoon and, after being given a room at the back, asked to move to the front. He had taken room 5B, which had a clear view across the street to the Lorraine Motel.

IDENTIFYING THE SHOOTER

LORRAINE MOTEL
King was shot while he was standing on the second-floor balcony of the motel, now part of the National Civil Rights Museum in Memphis.

JAMES EARL RAY

By that evening the FBI had taken over the investigation from the Memphis police. Over the next few days they traced the rifle to a gunstore in Birmingham, Alabama, where the receipt for it had been signed for by a man calling himself Harvey Lowmeyer. Laundry tags on some of the clothes found in the discarded bundle led them to a laundry service in Los Angeles, where a man named Eric S. Galt had asked for them to be cleaned. The FBI initially concluded that three men had been involved in the assassination of King, but after the Mustang was found in Atlanta and its movements tracked to both Birmingham and LA, they also considered the possibility that it could have been committed by one man using three different aliases. This was confirmed when only one set of fingerprints was found in apartments rented in all three locations. A comparison of these prints with the entire fingerprint archive held by the FBI began, a huge undertaking, but one that paid off when a match was found on April 19 with James Earl Ray, a 40-year-old man with a long criminal history who was at that time on the run after escaping from a prison in Missouri, where he had been serving a 20-year sentence for armed robbery.

By the time he had been identified by the FBI, Ray was no longer in America. After the shooting he had first driven to Atlanta, where he had been living immediately beforehand, collected some clothes, and had taken a Greyhound bus to Detroit. From there he had traveled by taxi across the Canadian border to Toronto, where he applied for a Canadian passport in the name of George Sneyd. The passport came through on April 25, five days after the FBI had discovered his real identity and released a photograph to the media in America. He immediately bought a plane ticket to London with the apparent intention of traveling on from there to Rhodesia, as Zimbabwe was then called, because no extradition treaty existed between Rhodesia and America and in the apparent belief that the white minority government then in power in that country would welcome him as a fellow white supremacist.

From London, Ray flew on to Lisbon in Portugal and attempted to find a passage on a ship going to the African continent. After ten days without success, he returned to London in an effort to find a different route to

Rhodesia and attempted to commit two robberies while he was there because he was running out of money, first of a jewelry store and then a bank, getting nothing from the store and only a small amount of cash from the bank. In the meantime, the Canadian police had matched a photograph of him provided by the FBI to the passport issued in the name of George Sneyd and then traced his movements to London, Lisbon, and back to London again. On June 8, he bought a plane ticket to Brussels. When he attempted to board the flight at Heathrow Airport, the name on his passport was identified on an international watch list by an immigration officer and he was arrested.

JAMES EARL RAY
Mugshot of Ray aged 27, taken while he was serving three years for theft and fraud in Leavenworth State Penitentiary in Kansas.

The extradition process, normally a long and drawn-out affair, was completed in a matter of a few weeks and, on July 19, he was sent back to Memphis to face the charge of murder. After reviewing the evidence against him, Ray's defense attorney advised him to plead guilty. In the knowledge that, if the case was heard before a jury, he could face the death penalty, Ray confessed and received a 99-year prison sentence. Almost immediately afterward, he attempted to retract the confession, claiming that he had been forced to make it in order to avoid the death penalty and saying that he had only acted as the getaway driver during the shooting and that a man he named only as "Raoul," who he had claimed to have first met in Canada, had been the actual assassin.

Ray remained in prison up until his death in 1993 at the age of 70 and continued to maintain his innocence, coming up with a number of different conspiracy theories in which he was always cast as the fall guy, set up by others to look guilty while the real culprits escaped justice. The overwhelming nature of the evidence against him and the fact that he clearly had a plan of escape worked out beforehand indicate that he must surely have been involved in some capacity, and the most likely scenario is that he really did shoot Martin Luther King. There are nevertheless some grounds for supposing that the full story has yet to emerge. Chief among these has been the attitude of the FBI, which has insisted on keeping many of the files it holds on the assassination and on King in general secret, leading to accusations that the agency was in some way involved itself or has been protecting others who were.

CONSPIRACY THEORIES

The extensive surveillance operation carried out on King on the personal orders of the FBI director, J. Edgar Hoover, which became public knowledge in 1975, has, at least according to conspiracy theorists, added fuel to the fire. Hoover appears to have developed a strong personal dislike for King, describing him as a great threat to America and accusing him of having links to the American Communist party. However, the surveillance failed to uncover anything incriminating against King beyond his numerous extramarital affairs, which may not have been very fitting for an ordained minister of the Baptist church but hardly represented a threat to national security.

On the day of the assassination both the FBI and Memphis police department were watching King's motel room in an effort to provide security to such a high-profile public figure. The fact that they do not appear to have checked the rooming house across the street from the motel and the relatively slow police response after the shooting have also been cited by conspiracy theorists as evidence of their involvement in the assassination, but could equally as well be explained as either incompetence or indifference. In 1993 a man named Loyd Jowers, who ran a restaurant near the motel at the time of the assassination, claimed to have been part of a conspiracy to kill King and named a Memphis police officer as the assassin.

An investigation by the US Department of Justice found the story told by Jowers not to be credible, so no charges were brought against him. Members of King's family, some of whom have always maintained that Ray did not act alone, brought a civil case against Jowers in 1998 that found in their favor, citing him as being part of a conspiracy that included Memphis police officers. The judgment was reached on the basis of statements made by Jowers rather than the existence of evidence linking him, or anybody else other than Ray, to the scene of the assassination. Unless further information comes to light, in truth we will get no closer to knowing for certain if anybody other than James Earl Ray was involved in King's death.

THE KILLER INSTINCT OF JACQUES MESRINE

1960s and '70s

MOTIVATION

Murder

Assassination

Treason

Espionage

Robbery

Hijacking

Fraud

Kidnapping

Location: France

Perpetrator: Jacques Mesrine

Outcome: The death of a French icon or a dangerous criminal, depending on your point of view

Some people like golf or skiing. My relaxation is armed robbery.

Jacques Mesrine, *L'Instinct de Mort* (1977)

I will never surrender. Now, it is war.

From an interview with Jacques Mesrine published in *Paris Match* on August 4, 1978, after his escape from La Santé prison

At the time of his death on November 2, 1979, Jacques Mesrine had been a thorn in the side of the French authorities for more than ten years. Despite the violent nature of many of the crimes he had committed, which included murder, he had become something of a folk hero in some sections of French society, in part because of his ability to make fools of the police and embarrass the government, but also because of the public image he managed to maintain despite being a fugitive, in which he came across as being witty and charming. At the end of October 1979, the police had finally tracked him down after he had escaped from the supposedly escape-proof La Santé maximum security prison in May of the previous year. With typical audacity, Mesrine had been living under a false name with his girlfriend Sylvia Jeanjacquot in her apartment in Paris, disguising his appearance so that, despite being one of the most famous people in France at that time, he had not been recognized. But the police had finally found him after Jeanjacquot's car, a distinctive gold BMW, was spotted in Paris and traced to the apartment.

A surveillance operation began until the identity of the man living in the apartment had been confirmed by a police officer who had encountered Mesrine in the past. On Friday November 2, Mesrine and Jeanjacquot were driving out of Paris, apparently intending to spend the weekend in the country, when the car was boxed in by police vehicles as it pulled up at an intersection at Porte de Clignancourt on the outskirts of the city. What happened next remains controversial in France. According to the police officers involved, they issued a warning before opening fire on Mesrine, but eyewitnesses claimed that those police officers who were in the back of a truck that had pulled up in front of the BMW started firing immediately, hitting him 15 times, and then one of them shot him in the head at point blank range in what amounted to an execution. At the time of his death, he was armed with a pistol and two hand grenades and, in an interview with *Paris Match* given after he had escaped from La Santé prison, he had declared war on the French state and said that he would rather die than be taken alive again, so it was understandable for the police to exercise extreme caution when approaching him. No charges have ever been brought against any of the officers involved in the shooting, but it must be said that the witness statements are rather more convincing than the official account, leading to the conclusion that an extrajudicial killing had taken place. The French authorities, it would appear, were not about to give Mesrine another opportunity to make fools of them.

In the autobiography Mesrine wrote while in La Santé prison, titled *L'Instinct de Mort* (*The Killer Instinct*), he claimed to have murdered 39 people and identified the three years he spent in the French army in his early 20s as being the turning point that led him into a life of crime. He served in the Algerian War and is thought to have been a member of one of the counter-insurgency units formed by the French army that were involved in the torture and execution of prisoners. After leaving the army in 1959, he failed to settle down into civilian life and in 1961 became involved with the OAS (*Organisation de l'armée secrète*), which began a violent campaign of bombings and assassinations in 1961 after President Charles de Gaulle's decision to withdraw from Algeria. The OAS funded its campaign through robberies and other illegal activities, introducing Mesrine to the life of crime he would continue to pursue after the OAS campaign effectively came to an end over the summer of 1962, when most of its leaders were either captured or killed.

Over the next few years Mesrine became a well-known figure in the Parisian criminal underworld, staging a number of robberies and serving the first of what would be a number of prison terms. He also made a number of efforts to go straight, taking regular jobs and running a restaurant in the Canary Islands, but always returned to crime, apparently addicted to the buzz and the lure of easy money. The crimes became more serious after he left France for Canada in 1968 with his then girlfriend, Jeanne Schneider, kidnapping the wealthy industrialist Georges Deslauriers who had employed them when they first arrived in the country. The kidnapping did not go to plan and the couple were caught in 1969 after going on the run to America. Mesrine ended up in the maximum security wing of Saint-Vincent-de-Paul prison near Montreal, regarded as the most secure prison in Quebec. In August 1972, he, along with

PUBLIC ENEMY

MASTER OF DISGUISE
Over the course of his criminal career Mesrine adopted numerous different disguises, a selection of which are shown here.

the convicted murderer Jean-Paul Mercier and four others, escaped by cutting through three layers of wire fencing surrounding the exercise yard with pliers stolen from a workshop in the prison.

After the escape, Mesrine and Mercier went on a crime spree, robbing banks in Montreal, including two on the same day. They then attempted to stage a mass break-out at the maximum security wing of the prison, driving up to the exercise yard armed with sawn-off shotguns with the intention of throwing guns and wire cutters over the fences to convicts in the yard, but were prevented from doing so by prison guards, who opened fire on them and forced them to abandon the attempt. A week later they shot and killed two forest rangers who came across them engaged in target practice in what they thought was a remote part of a forest. The murders led to an intensification of the manhunt for Mesrine in Canada. By that time he had become the most notorious criminal in the country as a consequence of the murders, bank robberies, prison escape, and attempted prison break-out, and had also become a regular feature on the front pages of the newspapers in France.

Mesrine returned to France toward the end of 1972 and continued the crime spree he had begun in Canada by robbing yet more banks. In March 1973 he was caught after he assaulted a police officer called to a café after he had got into an argument with the cashier and had pulled a gun. At the time of his arrest he bragged that he would escape in less than three months and, true to his word, on June 6, he took the judge hostage in the courtroom where his trial was being heard, using a gun he had retrieved from behind the cistern of a toilet in a bathroom, where it had been hidden by an accomplice. He then used the judge as a shield to escape from the courthouse and was driven away in a car that was waiting outside for him.

Mesrine's name was on the front pages of the newspapers in France again and he appeared to enjoy the attention he received, but his freedom would be short-lived. In September 1973 he was tracked down to an apartment by the police thanks to a tip-off from an informer and, after barricading himself inside, negotiated his surrender. With typical bravado, he then opened the door to the apartment and offered his arresting officer a glass of champagne. It made for great copy in the newspapers, increasing his fame as an antiestablishment figure who had managed to upstage the authorities even at the moment of his recapture. In an effort to prevent him from causing any more embarrassment, he was sent straight to La Santé prison where he would remain until his trial, this time held under conditions of the strictest security, at which he was sentenced to 20 years to be served in the maximum-security prison.

The authorities may have thought they had finally rid themselves of Mesrine, but he wrote letters protesting about the harsh conditions in the prison and gave interviews to the press in which he claimed that his crime wave had been directed against symbols of the wealthy elites in France so that, rather than solely being about enriching himself, he had been campaigning for social justice. He also said on numerous occasions that he would escape from La Santé, claims that were not considered credible by anybody until he actually did it. The circumstances of what would become his third successful escape are not entirely clear, but, at about 10am on May 8, 1978, Mesrine and two other convicts used a gun that had been somehow smuggled into the prison to capture three prison guards. They then used keys they had taken from the guards to let themselves out into the prison yard and then a length of rope and a grappling hook, together with a ladder they got from workmen who were in the yard repairing the bars to a window, to scale the 50 feet (10m) high outside wall of the prison. Mesrine and one of the other escapees, François Besse, got away in a car they hijacked, while the third was shot dead in the street by police.

Once on the outside again, Mesrine embarked on yet another crime spree, robbing the casino in the town of Deauville and carrying out a number of successful kidnappings. In September 1979 he lured the journalist Jacques Tillier to a meeting with the promise of an interview but then shot him three times. Tillier, who had written disparaging articles about Mesrine, survived and was able to provide the police with information about the car he had used, the gold BMW belonging to Sylvia Jeanjacquot. It has been alleged that the subsequent police operation in which Mesrine died was authorized at a very high level in the French government, possibly by the president, Valéry Giscard d'Estaing, who, after the event, personally congratulated the police officers involved. An intense public debate began concerning the circumstances of Mesrine's death and the lack of a police investigation into it, demonstrating that, even from beyond the grave, he was still causing trouble for the government.

THE THIRD ESCAPE

MOTIVATION

Murder

Assassination

Treason

Espionage

Robbery

Hijacking

Fraud

Kidnapping

THE HIJACKING OF FLIGHT 305

November 24, 1971

Location: Between Portland, Oregon, and Seattle, Washington

Perpetrator: An unidentified man known by the press as D. B. Cooper

Outcome: The mystery remains

I think it's a great mystery. What happened to this guy? The last thing we knew is he had $200,000 and bailed out of the back of a 727 on November 24, 1971, and then from there we don't know.

FBI Special Agent Larry Carr

On February 19, 1980, an 8-year-old boy found three packets of money on the banks of the Columbia River in Washington State at a location known as Tena Bar, about 20 miles (32km) southwest of the community of Ariel. Two of the packets each contained 100 $20 bills and the third one contained 90, amounting to $5800 in total. From the serial numbers of the bills, it was established that the money had been part of the ransom paid in November 1971 to a hijacker who, despite being given the name of D. B. Cooper by the media, had never been positively identified by the police and FBI. The incident is the only unsolved case of air piracy in American history. Apart from an instruction board from a Boeing 727 on how to lower the rear stairs of the plane, which was found in Washington State the previous year and could possibly have come from the hijacked plane, the money was the only evidence of the hijack ever found after the event itself was over. At the time, the recovery of the money was viewed as an important breakthrough in a case that had had everybody stumped up to then, but, in the end, it only added a new layer to the mystery. It could not even be established with any degree of certainty how the money had gotten to the location on the Columbia River where it had been found, whether it had been deliberately buried there or had washed down in the river and been deposited on the bank. In the end, it has provided no help in identifying the man responsible for the hijacking or cast any light on what happened to him afterward.

DAN COOPER

On November 24, 1971, a man in Portland International Airport paid $20 for a ticket on Northwest Orient Airlines Flight 305 for the 30-minute flight to Seattle. He gave his name as Dan Cooper, which was later confused by news reporters after the police interviewed a resident of Oregon by the name of D. B. Cooper, whose first name was not Dan and who proved to have nothing whatsoever to do with the case they were investigating, but whose name has been attached to it ever since. The Dan Cooper who boarded the plane in Portland was described as being in his mid-40s, of medium build, between 5 feet 10 inches to 6 feet tall (1.78m–1.83m) with dark brown or black hair and wearing a raincoat over a dark suit and white shirt with a black tie. The only luggage he had with him was a black briefcase, which was not inspected by any security officials before he carried it onto the plane. Once on board, he took a seat toward the back and, after the plane took off from Portland at 2:50pm, he lit up what would prove to be the first of a number of Rayleigh cigarettes and ordered a bourbon and soda from the stewardess. According to those witnesses who spoke to him, he remained calm and polite for the entire time he remained on the plane.

Shortly after the plane took off, Cooper gave one of the stewardesses a note that she put into her purse without reading, assuming that it was his telephone number. After seeing her do this, he suggested that she read the note because he had a bomb in his briefcase. He would later retrieve the note from the stewardess, who remembered it as saying words to the effect that he was hijacking the plane and wanted her to sit down next to him. When she complied, he opened the case to show her that it contained some red cylinders connected to a battery by wires and then told her that, when the plane arrived in Seattle, he wanted it to be refueled. He also wanted a ransom of $200,000 in what he described as "negotiable American currency," together with four parachutes, at which point he would release all of the other 36 passengers. Once his demands had been communicated to the ground by the captain of the plane, he ordered another bourbon and soda, paid the stewardess the tab for his drinks, including a tip, and pointed out a few landmarks on the ground as the plane flew over Washington State, suggesting that he was familiar with the region.

SKYJACKER
Two FBI sketches of the unidentified man known by the press as D. B. Cooper who parachuted out of Flight 305 over Washington State.

The plane remained in the air for about two hours while the ransom money was put together and then landed at Seattle-Tecoma Airport, where it was refueled and the money and parachutes delivered to the plane. Cooper kept his part of the bargain, allowing the passengers and two of the three

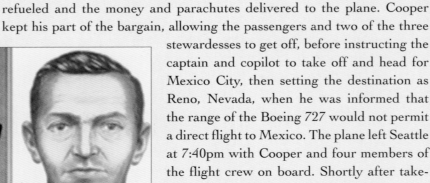

stewardesses to get off, before instructing the captain and copilot to take off and head for Mexico City, then setting the destination as Reno, Nevada, when he was informed that the range of the Boeing 727 would not permit a direct flight to Mexico. The plane left Seattle at 7:40pm with Cooper and four members of the flight crew on board. Shortly after take-off, he asked the one remaining stewardess to join the captain, copilot, and engineer in the cockpit. Then, shortly after 8pm, he parachuted out of the plane through the rear door after deploying the stairs, the crew noticing the change in pressure in the cabin and the pilot having to compensate the plane when the stairs were activated. Once the plane had landed in Reno, it was established that Cooper, two of the parachutes, and the money were not on board. The only sign of him left was the black tie he had been wearing, together with a mother-of-pearl tie pin attached to it, which he appears to have taken off before jumping.

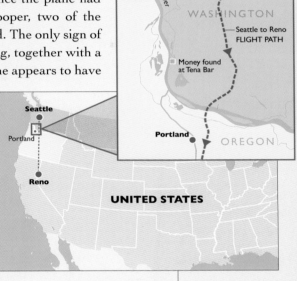

Flight 305 had been tracked by US Air Force jets after taking off from Seattle and, from the pilot's flight plan and the amount of time the plane had been in the air when Cooper jumped, it was possible to get a rough idea of where he had left the plane, but he had jumped in darkness so it was difficult to know for sure other than it was over the southern part of Washington State. The next morning searches by air and on land began, concentrating on the region in the southwest of the state where it was thought he had most likely landed, a wilderness area in the foothills of Mount St. Helens not far from Ariel. One of the largest searches ever mounted in America ensued, but no sign of him or the parachute was found, and, despite an intensive investigation, no definite trace of him or the money came to light until the three packets of $20 bills were found on the banks of the Columbia River more than eight years later. The FBI put out a description and composite picture, which showed Cooper to be a very ordinary-looking man. The serial numbers of the bills he had been given were circulated and a reward put up for any that were found, but aside from what turned out to be a scam when fake $20 bills with the correct serial numbers were handed into a newspaper in an effort to claim the reward, nothing else has come to light, even after the statute of limitations on the hijacking had run out.

The FBI came to the conclusion that Cooper had most likely died in the jump, landing in a remote part of Washington State where his body was never recovered. He certainly attempted a difficult feat, jumping from a fast-moving plane at night and onto unknown terrain, and the weather

LANDING ZONE
Although police could calculate an approximate area in which they believed Cooper to have landed, difficult terrain and a lack of physical evidence on the ground meant that their search was in vain.

DEATH OR GLORY?

that night had not been good so, even if he survived the drop, he could well have found himself in the middle of an extensive forest, many miles from anywhere. But, in the absence of any evidence concerning what happened to him, the FBI file remains open. The mystery of his identity and the audacious nature of his crime has led to numerous attempts by amateur detectives to solve the case, but most of these have been highly speculative in nature.

One of the more convincing of the amateur attempts to solve the case was made by Lyle Christiansen and set out in the book he co-wrote in 2010 with the private detective Skipp Porteous called *Into the Blast* in which he identified his brother, Kenneth Christiansen, as being Cooper. Kenneth Christiansen had trained as a paratrooper toward the end of the Second World War and, although he had never made a combat jump, continued to parachute after the war was over. In 1954 he had joined Northwest Orient Airlines, working as a mechanic and then a flight attendant based in Seattle, giving him knowledge of planes and the routes flown by the airline. According to his brother, he appeared to have come into some money in the early 1970s and, shortly before he died in 1994, apparently said that he had a secret that he did not divulge. But, as with all the other speculative identifications of Cooper, there are a number of problems, not least that the only evidence to connect Christiansen to the hijack is entirely circumstantial and, as the FBI have pointed out, he does not match the description provided by eyewitnesses, many of whom, such as the stewardesses on the plane, got a good view of Cooper. The truth is that, more than 40 years after the event, the case appears to be no nearer to being resolved today than it has ever been.

THE WATERGATE BURGLARY

June 17, 1972

MOTIVATION

Murder

Assassination

Treason

Espionage

Robbery

Hijacking

Fraud

Kidnapping

Location: Washington, D.C.

Perpetrators: John McCourt, Virgilio González, Frank Sturges, Bernard Barker, Eugenio Martínez, and members of the White House staff, all the way up to President Richard Nixon

Outcome: The resignation of a US president

I gave them a sword, and they stuck it in and they twisted it with relish. And I guess if I had been in their position, I'd have done the same thing.

From an interview with Richard Nixon conducted by David Frost and broadcast in May 1977

At about 7:30 in the evening of September 19, 2012, the British member of parliament Andrew Mitchell, Chief Whip of the government at the time, left his office in 9 Downing Street, next door to the residence of the prime minister, to cycle home. One of the police officers providing security at the gates at the end of Downing Street refused to open the main gate, telling him to go through the side gate next to it. For some reason Mitchell took exception to this, swore at the police officers, and is alleged to have called them "plebs," a pejorative term for the lower classes in Britain. The insult was politically damaging because the government had regularly been accused of being elitist and out of touch with ordinary people. Almost immediately, the political scandal was named "Plebgate" by the British media, an allusion to Watergate, the mother of all political scandals, which, since it came to light in the mid-1970s, has provided a reference point for all manner of questionable dealings, political or otherwise.

Plebgate has proved to be rather different from most other political scandals in that, as well as actually involving a gate, the politician at the center of the scandal has since been proved innocent of the accusations made against him. The same cannot be said of the Watergate scandal, which began with the arrest of five burglars on June 17, 1972, and spiraled from there to include numerous employees of the American government. Finally, on August 9, 1974, it resulted in the resignation of President Richard Nixon, the first and only American president to resign his office, a course of action he was forced to take because, had he not done so, then he would almost certainly have been impeached by the US Senate and House of Representatives. A total of 43 people were successfully prosecuted on a variety of charges arising out of the scandal, but Nixon was not one of them, having been granted a pardon by his successor, President Gerald Ford. But his reputation was completely destroyed and, overall, the scandal had confirmed what many people in America and around the world had long suspected, that politicians could not be trusted and would go to almost any lengths to achieve their ambitions.

NIXON'S TAPES
President Nixon announcing the release of edited transcripts of the Whitehouse tapes in April 1974. He resigned in August of that year.

The Watergate Complex is composed of five buildings near the Potomac River in the Foggy Bottom district of Washington D.C., a little over a mile to the west of the White House. In 1972, the governing body of the Democratic party, the Democratic National Committee (DNC), was using offices on the sixth floor of the Watergate Hotel and Office Building for their headquarters. Shortly after midnight on June 17, a security man in the building noticed that tape had been placed over the latches of the locks on a number of doors leading to the DNC offices so that each could be closed without being locked. It may have aroused his suspicion at the time, but he initially did nothing about it other than to remove the tape. But when he returned an hour later to find that somebody had replaced the tape, he called the police.

Five men were discovered in the DNC offices by the police, named as John McCourt, Virgilio González, Frank Sturges, Bernard Barker, and Eugenio Martínez, who had been engaged in photographing documents and installing wire taps on telephones. All five refused to say anything at the time of their arrests, but it quickly became clear that the burglars had connections to the Republican party. Two of the burglars were also found to have the contact details of two former CIA agents, F. Gordon Liddy and Howard Hunt, who worked in the White House and were members of a group informally known as the White House Plumbers, which had initially been formed in an effort to improve security by preventing leaks, but had then apparently widened its remit to include a dirty tricks campaign against the Democrats aimed at gathering damaging information against them, using such illegal methods as tapping telephones and, it would appear, breaking and entering. Questions remained as to who was responsible for authorizing these activities and how far up the chain in the White House the responsibility went.

A blizzard of denials, evasions, half-truths, and outright lies came out of the White House amid allegations that extensive document shredding had occurred in an effort to cover up the full extent of the scandal. Both Liddy and Hunt were on the Committee for the Re-Election of the President (CRP), as was one of the burglars, John McCourt, and the committee was chaired by John Mitchell, a close associate and personal friend of President Nixon, who, before chairing the committee, had been the attorney general

THE WHITEHOUSE PLUMBERS

THE WATERGATE COMPLEX
A view of the complex from the south. The Watergate Hotel and Office Building is second from the left.

in the Nixon administration. But that in itself did not prove that anybody else from the CPR was involved, even if it certainly looked that way. What was required was evidence of connections between the CPR and the burglary and, as is often the case, the way in which this was eventually achieved was by following the money trail.

WOODWARD AND BERNSTEIN

With the FBI investigation apparently failing to find any evidence of connections to the White House, much of the detail was uncovered by investigative journalists, in particular Bob Woodward and Carl Bernstein of the *Washington Post*. In a series of articles published from 1972 to 1974 they gradually pieced together the conspiracy behind the burglaries and the subsequent cover-up, relying on information gathered from their contacts in the government and security agencies. The most famous of these was known as Deep Throat, who is said to have regularly met Woodward in secret in a parking garage to pass on information or to corroborate what Woodward already knew. The identity of this informant was not revealed until 2005, when Mark Felt admitted that it was him. Felt was the associate director of the FBI when the burglary occurred until he retired a year later and had access to all of the files of the investigation. He did not make clear what motivated him to pass on information to Woodward, which may have been because he was outraged when he discovered that the FBI had been involved in the cover-up or possibly because Nixon had overlooked him for the post of director of the FBI.

WOODWARD AND BERNSTEIN
Bob Woodward, on the left, and Carl Bernstein, who uncovered the link between the Watergate burglary and the Whitehouse.

Woodward and Bernstein used the information they had received to connect money paid out by the CRP to Bernard Barker, one of the burglars, who had received the money from Gordon Liddy and attempted to hide it by banking it offshore. It was then found that the CPR had access to a secret slush fund to finance the dirty tricks campaign. As well as paying the burglars to break into the Watergate Hotel, the CPR had paid for

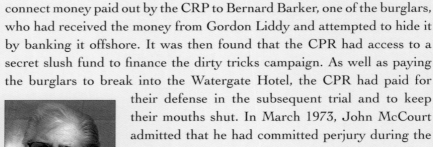

their defense in the subsequent trial and to keep their mouths shut. In March 1973, John McCourt admitted that he had committed perjury during the trial for the burglary and named John Mitchell as being among the senior White House staff involved, together with the White House Consul John Dean and two of President Nixon's closest advisors, Bob Haldeman and John Ehrlichman.

The scandal had gradually been getting closer and closer to President Nixon himself, who nevertheless attempted to bluff it out. He was finally implicated after an investigation was begun by the US Senate. The Select Committee on Presidential Campaign Activities, or the Watergate Committee, as it is commonly known, convened in public session from February 1973. By July of that year they had been made aware of the existence of private tape recordings of White House meetings that the president had made for his personal files. By that time John Dean had agreed to cooperate with the Watergate Committee in the belief that the others involved in the scandal were attempting to make him a scapegoat. Dean's testimony had implicated Mitchell, Haldeman, and Ehrlichman, and the committee members decided to obtain the tapes in order to confirm what Dean had told them.

The committee issued Nixon with a subpoena in an effort to compel him to hand over the relevant tapes and a long legal battle ensued when he refused to comply, citing "executive privilege" and "national security" as his reasons for withholding them. In July of the following year a Supreme Court ruling found in favor of the committee, forcing Nixon's hand. At that moment, he must have known that the game was up because the conversations he had recorded contained abundant evidence of his involvement in the cover-up that followed the burglary, even if there was nothing on them that implicated him in any of the original decisions taken by the CRP to engage in dirty tricks in the first place.

The most damning tape, known as the "smoking gun," was made by Nixon six days after the break-in. He is heard discussing an option of covering it up by asking Vernon Walters, the director of the CIA, to approach FBI director Patrick Gray to request that the investigation be stopped because it represented a threat to national security. It was not only evidence that Nixon was involved in the cover-up, but also that he was attempting to obstruct a federal investigation. It was enough on its own for the committee to begin the process of impeachment, but other tapes also clearly showed that Nixon had known about the cover-up right from the beginning, had been kept informed about it, and had authorized the payment of hush money and bribes whenever it was thought necessary. The contents of the tapes were made public on August 5, 1974. With his position now made completely untenable, Nixon announced his resignation four days later.

NIXON'S TAPES

MOTIVATION

Murder

Assassination

Treason

Espionage

Robbery

Hijacking

Fraud

Kidnapping

THE KIDNAPPING OF PATTY HEARST

February 4, 1974

Location: California

Perpetrators: The Symbionese Liberation Army

Outcome: Patty Hearst survived, most of the Symbionese Liberation Army did not

Death to the fascist insect that preys on the life of the people.

Slogan of the Symbionese Liberation Army

At about 10am on April 14, 1974, security cameras in a branch of the Hibernia Bank in the Sunset District of San Francisco caught a robbery as it was in progress. It was strange enough to attract attention in the first place because four of the five robbers were women, but the jerky black and white pictures made headline news around the world because one of them was clearly recognizable as Patty Hearst, the granddaughter of the newspaper tycoon William Randolph Hearst who had been kidnapped ten weeks previously by a group calling themselves the Symbionese Liberation Army, or SLA. In messages that she had sent to her family through the kidnappers before the robbery, she had said that she was renouncing her former life and joining the group, but it was widely assumed that she had been forced to make these statements. Now the security camera pictures showed her brandishing a semi-automatic M1 carbine in the bank and apparently barking orders to the people caught up in the robbery, with no sign that she was being coerced in any way. It prompted a debate over the recently described phenomenon of Stockholm syndrome, a psychological condition in which some people who have been taken hostage begin to sympathize with their captors. On TV screens around the world, Hearst appeared to be providing a textbook example.

THE S.L.A.

Despite the name, the Symbionese Liberation Army was made up entirely of American citizens, mostly white middle-class college dropouts. It had emerged out of the radical fringes of the counter-culture movement of San Francisco in the late 1960s, combined with elements of the anti-Vietnam war and civil rights protests. The members appear to have adopted a mix of hippy philosophy and left-wing revolutionary ambitions of the sort expressed by Mao Tse-tung and Che Guevara, but would most likely have remained entirely obscure had they not been joined by Donald DeFreeze, who had escaped from prison in March 1973, where he had been serving a sentence for mugging a prostitute. He had been radicalized while in prison by a number of groups advocating a black uprising in America and, after joining the group, and despite the fact that he was the only black member, he galvanized them into action to follow this agenda.

The first action taken by the SLA came in November 1973, when members of the group murdered a well-known black educator, Dr. Marcus Forster, who was the superintendent of a school in Oakland, California, shooting him with bullets that had been laced with cyanide. It was a senseless killing, which the group attempted to justify by claiming that he was a "fascist" because he was attempting to introduce identity cards into the school in an effort to reduce violence. It cost the group any support they may have enjoyed among the radical counter-culture of the Bay Area, together with much of their membership, which had probably never exceeded 20 and was now reduced to a core of eight or nine. In January 1974 two SLA members, Joseph Remiro and Russell Little, were apprehended by the police and were both sentenced to life in jail.

The SLA's response was to plan a kidnapping with the apparent intention of exchanging their victim for Remiro and Little, although it is not clear that they ever issued a demand to that effect. They chose the 19-year-old Patty Hearst as a target because of the wealth and renown of her family, which would ensure high levels of publicity, but also because she was at that time living in a house with her fiancé, Stephen Weed, near the campus of the University of California in Berkeley, where she was a student. At about 10pm on February 4, 1974, three members of the gang raided Hearst's house, assaulted Weed when he opened the door to them and then snatched Hearst, before firing warning shots into the air and bundling her into a car.

A huge police and FBI investigation began, together with a media frenzy in which Hearst was always described as being an "heiress." The identity of the group was immediately apparent after unused bullets laced with cyanide were found at the scene of the kidnapping, confirmed when the SLA sent a number of communications demanding that Patty's father, Randolph Hearst, organize a program in which everybody in California who was in receipt of state benefits be given $70 worth of food. Hearst calculated that this would cost $400 million and, after some negotiating, agreed instead to distribute $6 million worth of food to poor people in the Bay Area. The program began toward the end of February and, despite chaotic scenes at some of the distribution points and accusations that the food was of low quality, was considered a success, gaining the SLA some sympathy for their actions, but they nevertheless refused to release their captive.

On April 4 another message was sent by the SLA, arriving at a radio station in Berkeley and accompanied by a photograph showing Patty Hearst posing with a machine gun in front of the symbol used by the group, a cobra with seven heads. This was the message telling her parents that she had joined the SLA, in which she also branded them as being evil and said that she had adopted a *nom de guerre* of Tania, naming herself after a woman who had fought in Cuba alongside Che Guevara. The bank robbery followed two weeks later, after which DeFreeze decided to move the center of the SLA operation to Los Angeles due to the huge police and FBI presence in San Francisco.

In the middle of May 1974, the SLA were traced to a house in South Central LA and a huge police operation began in which the house was surrounded. A large gun battle erupted, said to have been the largest ever fought by the Los Angeles police, in which two SLA members were shot as they were coming out of the house, which then caught fire, possibly as a result of a smoke grenade thrown into the house by the police. Those remaining in the house all died in the subsequent inferno, a coroner later establishing that DeFreeze had committed suicide by shooting himself in the head. Once the identities of all six people who died were known, it became clear that Patty Hearst had not been in the house at the time and, afterward, she and two other surviving members of the group returned to San Francisco.

STOCKHOLM SYNDROME
The photograph of Patty Hearst posing with a machine gun in front of the symbol of the Symbionese Liberation Army.

Hearst remained on the run for more than a year, until she was finally caught in September 1975, and charged with bank robbery. At her trial, beginning in January 1976, she claimed that she had been brainwashed by DeFreeze, held blindfolded in a closet after she was kidnapped and subjected to physical and sexual abuse, and that she had been drugged with LSD before taking part in the robbery. She was found guilty in March 1976 and sentenced to 35 years in prison, later commuted by President Jimmy Carter so that she actually served a total of 22 months. Since her release, she has talked of her experiences in a number of TV interviews, but, for the most part, appears to have preferred to live a quiet life out of the public eye. In 2001 she was granted a full pardon by President Bill Clinton on the last day of his presidency, perhaps finally allowing her to bring some sort of closure to such a traumatic experience.

MOTIVATION

Murder

Assassination

Treason

Espionage

Robbery

Hijacking

Fraud

Kidnapping

THE LUFTHANSA HEIST

December 11, 1978

Location: New York

Perpetrators: Jimmy Burke, Henry Hill, and other wiseguys from New York

Outcome: The wiseguys didn't win in the end

Marty was bound to be next. He was breaking Jimmy's balls. He was breaking my balls. He was crying that he needed his money to pay the loan sharks. He wanted to know why he had to pay the interest every week. I told him to take it easy. I told him he'd get the money. But Marty didn't want to pay the interest. By this time it was already January and he was hanging around Robert's Lounge every day. You couldn't get rid of the guy. He was getting worse and worse. He was where he wasn't supposed to be.

Henry Hill, quoted in *Wiseguy* by Nicholas Pileggi, discussing the reasons why Marty Krugman was murdered

Anybody who is familiar with the movie *Goodfellas*, directed by Martin Scorsese, will have a good idea of how the Lufthansa heist went down. Unlike many Hollywood movies, it is a reasonably accurate adaptation of the book on which it is based, the true-crime *Wiseguy* by the journalist Nicholas Pileggi, who collaborated with Scorsese on the screenplay for the movie. In the book, Pileggi charts the career of New York mobster Henry Hill, played in the movie by Ray Liotta, who after a 25-year criminal career in the Mafia associated with the Lucchese family, became a police informant and entered the witness protection scheme. The details he provided of his life of crime led to the prosecution of more than 50 people and also included details of the Lufthansa heist, which he had been involved in from the earliest planning stages, together with the subsequent murders of many of the other men who had taken part.

According to Hill, about two months after he had been released from prison in July 1978 after serving four and a half years of a ten-year sentence for extortion, his bookmaker Marty Krugman told him about the huge quantity of dollar bills that were regularly stored in the Lufthansa cargo terminal at New York's Kennedy Airport. One of Krugman's clients, who had run up a large gambling debt, worked in the terminal and had explained that once a month dollar bills, which had been exchanged in the American military bases in Germany, together with other cash collected from tourist transactions from around the country, was brought back to Kennedy Airport by Lufthansa, where it was stored in a vault in the cargo terminal before being dispatched to a bank. The Lufthansa employee had also said that he and a number of his colleagues at the airline would be prepared to act as inside men if a robbery was organized.

THE JOB

Hill took the information to Jimmy Burke, another associate of the Lucchese family, who recognized it as a potentially straightforward opportunity to steal a large amount of money. Burke put together a team of six men, including his son Frank, but not Hill himself, which was later enlarged by the inclusion of an associate of the Gambino family, another New York Mafia family, because they controlled part of the territory where the airport was situated and had been promised a share of the loot. On December 11, 1978, once the gang had been informed that a shipment of money from the Commerzbank in Frankfurt had arrived and was being held in the Lufthansa vault before being forwarded to Chase Manhattan Bank in New York, the robbery began.

At about 3am a van containing the gang and a car driven by Frank Burke drove up to the front entrance of the cargo terminal and dropped two of them off. While Burke waited in the parking lot, the rest of the gang drove round to the loading bays at the rear, cutting the lock off a gate in the security fencing on the way, and three of them went into the building through the back. They rounded up the employees and forced one of them to disable the alarm systems protecting the building and the vault, then simply backed the van up to a loading bay, emptied the vault and threw everything they got into the back of the van.

Once they had loaded up the van, the robbers drove away, having instructed the Lufthansa employees not to move for 15 minutes, enough time for them to get clear of the airport, and they were followed by Frank Burke in the car, whose role in the robbery was to provide cover for the van should it be discovered by the police. As it turned out, the "crash car," as they called it, proved not to be necessary and the robbers arrived at the meeting place arranged with Jimmy Burke without incident. The loot was transferred to the car he was driving and, together with his son, he drove to a safe house to count the takings while everybody else went home and another man called Stacks Edwards, who had not participated in the actual robbery, was supposed to drive the van to a breakers' yard to be crushed. Once the money had been counted, it added up to about $6 million, made up of about $5 million in cash and the rest in jewels, making it at the time the largest cash robbery ever committed in America.

THE AFTERMATH Rather than drive straight to the breakers' yard, Stacks Edwards stopped off at his girlfriend's house on the way, leaving the van in a no parking zone. The next morning, before he had retrieved the van, it had been picked up by the police, who found incriminating evidence in the back of it, including the ski masks the robbers had worn in the cargo terminal. Fingerprints were also found on the steering wheel that matched those of Edwards and, as he was known to frequent Robert's Lounge, a bar owned by Burke in Queens, not far from the cargo terminal, the connection was quickly made by the police. A huge surveillance operation began in an effort to prove that Burke had been involved and this appears to have led him to conclude that too many people knew about the heist and that some of them were bound to talk. He had also agreed with the members of the gang who carried out the robbery to pay them a fixed amount of money rather than a share of the loot and, at least according to Hill, became paranoid that some of them would come after him once they found out they had stolen a great deal more than had been expected.

A week after the robbery, Edwards was found murdered in his apartment, most likely shot by Burke or one of his associates in the first part of his clean-up exercise. Krugman, the bookmaker, was next, who, according to Hill, had demanded $500,000 and then disappeared at the beginning of January 1979, his body reputed to have been dismembered and buried by Burke. At least six more murders occurred which can be connected to the heist, leaving only those members of the gang with direct associations to the Lucchese family left alive, presumably because they were the only ones Burke trusted. After Hill was arrested in April 1980 on drugs trafficking charges, he became convinced that Burke, who he had known for more than 30 years by that time, was planning to kill him as well. It was one of the motivating factors behind him becoming an informer. Despite the information supplied by Hill, Burke was not charged with either the robbery or any of the murders associated with the Lufthansa heist, instead being convicted of a separate murder of a drugs dealer. Only one person has ever been charged with anything to do with the heist, one of the employees of Lufthansa who supplied inside information, who cooperated with the police and received a relatively light sentence. None of the money or jewelry stolen has ever been recovered.

GOODFELLA
Jimmy Burke, center, with his attorney and witnesses waiting for the FBI to turn up to begin a search.

MOTIVATION

Murder

Assassination

Treason

Espionage

Robbery

Hijacking

Fraud

Kidnapping

THE PERTH MINT SWINDLE

June 22, 1982

Location: Perth, Western Australia

Perpetrators: Unknown

Outcome: The police stitch-up of the Mickelberg brothers finally came to light

*I gave evidence at the trial and at numerous appeals. All that evidence
in relation to the [brothers'] so-called confessions was false.*

**Tony Lewandowski, a detective involved
in the stitch-up of the Mickelberg brothers**

The Perth Mint opened in 1901 as an outlet for the gold mined in Western Australia, as it still is today, providing miners with a facility for refining and minting gold into coins and bullion. The nature of its business required the original building to be designed to be impregnable, so that anybody who was foolish enough to attempt a robbery was sure to come unstuck. In 1982 somebody came up with a scheme to stage a robbery without actually breaking into the building, which effectively involved no more than asking the mint for some gold bars and walking away with them. The beauty of the Perth Mint Swindle, or Great Mint Swindle, as it is sometimes called, was in its simplicity, in which the robbers employed other people to carry out most of the necessary work without them realizing they were involved in anything illegal.

THE SCAM

The first stage of the swindle involved stealing some bank checks from a branch of the Western Australian Building Society in Perth and then starting a fire in it in order to cover up the theft. That part of the operation would be the only time the robbers got their hands dirty. After that, all they did was make some phone calls and then wait for the gold to be delivered to them. They hired an office on a short-term let in the Subiaco suburb of western Perth, dealing with the agent on the phone, arranging to have the office key delivered to a mail box in a post office and paying in advance with a bank check sent by post. A receptionist was also hired from an agency to work in the office and, when she arrived at work on June 22, 1982, she found three sealed envelopes, each of which contained a check, and was given instructions over the phone to get them delivered separately to the Perth Mint by couriers from a security company. She was also told to ask the couriers to take some tool boxes that were in the office with them so they would have something to carry the gold in.

In the months beforehand, two men had phoned the mint on a number of occasions, giving their names as Fryer and Blackwood, both enquiring about the price of gold and saying that they were thinking of placing a large order. On the day, they both phoned again, making a total of three orders between them for a substantial amount of gold and arranging to pay for it with bank checks drawn on the Western Australian Building Society. As each courier arrived, they handed over the envelopes, which, as the sales staff were expecting, contained bank checks. These were accepted as being genuine without anybody apparently thinking to ring the building society to make sure and, as bank checks are guaranteed by the bank that issues them, the relevant quantities of gold were released to each courier straight away. Altogether, they picked up 49 gold bars from the mint, weighing 150 pounds (68kg) and valued at A$653,000. The couriers put the bars into the tool boxes, as they had been instructed to do, and took the boxes back to the office in Subiaco. A different courier was then engaged by phone and instructed to pick up the boxes, which they were told contained mineral samples for the mining industry, and deliver them to Jandakot Airport in the south of the city. By the time the swindle had been discovered, the boxes and whoever had received them at the airport were long gone.

THE STITCH-UP

The loss of such a large amount of gold from the Perth Mint was a major embarrassment for the authorities in Western Australia, particularly considering that the perpetrators did not even set foot in the building. The police came under considerable pressure to solve the case as quickly as possible and, despite an almost complete lack of evidence, they managed to identify some suspects. One of the few leads they had turned up was the report of a Ford Falcon car being seen by a witness outside the Subiaco office, driven by a man who may have been trying to hide his appearance by wearing a wig and dark glasses. It led the police to the 22-year-old Peter Mickelberg, who was alleged to have bought a second-hand Falcon using a false name shortly before the robbery took place. The police could not prove that Mickelberg had bought a Falcon or that he was the man seen outside the office, but nevertheless came to the conclusion that he had committed the robbery along with his two older brothers, Ray and Brian Mickelberg.

During a search of Ray Mickelberg's house, gold was found hidden under the floorboards. Ray produced receipts showing that he had bought the gold from the Perth Mint, but it emerged that he had done so using a bank account he had opened under a false name. Further investigation showed that, two years previously, the Mickelberg brothers had sold a huge gold nugget named the Yellow Rose of Texas, which they said had been found in the Kalgoorlie goldfields, for A$350,000 to the high-profile Perth businessman Alan Bond. The police found photographs in Ray Mickelberg's house that showed him making the nugget in his workshop, presumably using gold he had bought from the mint, proving that the nugget was a fake, worth less than half of what Bond had paid for it.

The police were now convinced they had the right suspects, men who were familiar with the way in which the Perth Mint did business and had previously committed fraud with gold bought from it in an illegal way. What they did not have was direct evidence of their involvement in the Perth Mint Swindle. Don Hancock, the lead detective on the case, decided to put pressure on the Mickelbergs to see if he could make them talk. Ray was considered to be the ringleader, but he had served in the Australian Special Air Service during the Vietnam War and it was thought that he was unlikely to crack under interrogation, so Hancock had Peter arrested. He was held in an interview room in a police station, where Hancock and one of his junior colleagues, Tony Lewandowski, obtained a full confession that implicated Ray and Brian. At about the same time, forensic analysis of one of the bank checks used in the swindle turned up a fingerprint that provided a match for Ray. The police, it appeared, had got their men.

All three Mickelberg brothers protested their innocence, Peter claiming that the confession had been beaten out of him, but at their trial they were found guilty and sent to prison. Ray served eight years of a 20-year sentence, Peter did seven years of 14, while Brian was released after being acquitted on appeal and then, shortly afterward, was killed when the light plane he was piloting crashed. Ray and Peter continued to protest their innocence throughout their time in prison and after they were released, having had a total of seven appeals against their convictions turned down. The full story did not come out until 2002, a year after Don Hancock had died. During the eighth appeal, Tony Lewandowski finally admitted that he and Hancock had beaten Peter Mickelberg while he was in custody and had falsified his confession, going on to say that the fingerprint on the bank check had also been planted by Hancock. It was now clear that the Mickelbergs had been stitched up by the police. Their convictions were quashed and substantial damages were later awarded, bringing their ordeal at the hands of the police to an end after 20 years of trying. But one question about the swindle remains: If the Mickelbergs didn't do it, then who did?

GOLD BARS
Whoever robbed the Perth Mint got away with 49 gold bars like these without even setting foot in the building.

MOTIVATION

Murder

Assassination

Treason

Espionage

Robbery

Hijacking

Fraud

Kidnapping

THE BCCI SCANDAL

1991

Location: Pakistan, Britain, Luxemburg, and worldwide

Perpetrators: Agha Hasan Abedi and senior BCCI staff, together with dictators, terrorists, drug traffickers, corrupt politicians, and who knows who else

Outcome: The bank was eventually forced into liquidation

BCCI's criminality included fraud by BCCI and BCCI customers involving billions of dollars; money laundering in Europe, Africa, Asia, and the Americas; BCCI's bribery of officials in most of those locations; support of terrorism, arms trafficking, and the sale of nuclear technologies; management of prostitution; the commission and facilitation of income tax evasion, smuggling, and illegal immigration; illicit purchases of banks and real estate; and a panoply of financial crimes limited only by the imagination of its officers and customers.

Excerpt from the Executive summary US Senate Foreign Relations Committee report on the BCCI Affair by Senator John Kerry and Senator Hank Brown, published in 1992

These days banking scandals are such a regular occurrence that it can be hard to remember the time when banks were thought of as being trustworthy and bankers considered to be pillars of the community. Much of the attention on the banking industry has occurred as a consequence of the 2008 financial crisis, largely caused by the irresponsible behavior of banks and financial institutions, and this led to the discovery of all kinds of shady dealing, including fraud, insider dealing, and the manipulation of money markets. But the revelations that have emerged since 2008, shocking as they may be, pale in comparison to what is arguably the greatest banking scandal of them all, perpetrated over the course of two decades by the Bank of Credit and Commerce International before its activities finally came to light in 1991, at which point it collapsed in a blaze of publicity with debts estimated to have been $16 billion and leaving one million depositors out of pocket.

The bank was founded in 1972 by the well-known and, at the time, highly respected Pakistani banker Agha Hasan Abedi after the Pakistani government had nationalized the banks in the country. The new bank was registered in Luxemburg with headquarters in London. At first it was a very small operation, but Abedi had made numerous contacts in the oil-rich states of the Middle East and as a result of the increasing volume of business he did through these contacts, the bank expanded quickly. Almost all of the board of directors and senior management were made up of people from Pakistan with whom Abedi had worked in the past and, even though there is no evidence of any illegal activity in the banks he had been involved with previously, BCCI appears to have been set up deliberately right from the beginning as a means of committing financial crime. As it expanded, it developed a labyrinthine structure of subsidiaries and holding companies, splitting its business dealings between numerous countries, including offshore tax havens where the nature of its dealings were rarely questioned. It made the task of regulating the bank extremely difficult because it was impossible to keep track of the money flowing through it and because it was regulated by institutions in many different countries.

Concerns about the bank were often raised by regulators in Britain and America and allegations surfaced as early as the mid-1970s that it was using money from its deposits to fund its day-to-day activity rather than investing the money on behalf of its clients, as legitimate banks would do,

THE SHADY BANK

BCCI BRANCH
Before it was forced
to close in 1991, BCCI
had more than 400
branches and operated
in 70 countries
around the world.

which would imply that it was either insolvent or that some form of fraud was occurring. Despite this, little was done to curtail its activity, however suspicious it may have appeared. It continued to expand, opening branches around the world so that, at its height, it was one of the largest privately owned banks in the world, employing something like 20,000 staff on five continents.

The bank maintained a front of legitimacy, apparently continuing with the normal business of banking, taking deposits, making loans, and investing money. When things began to unravel in the late 1980s, however, the scale of the criminal activity became clear. One principal activity was money laundering—moving huge sums of money obtained illegally by its clients through various subsidiaries in different parts of the world, most of which had been set up in a way that disguised the fact that they were owned by BCCI. Once the money trail had become sufficiently complex, conventional investments could be made in legitimate financial institutions that would then be available to the original clients as clean money. In this way, BCCI became the bank of choice for dictators and autocratic regimes around the world, including Saddam Hussein in Iraq and Manuel Noriega in Panama, as well as for criminal organizations such as the Medellin Cartel of Colombia, which over the course of the 1980s developed into one of the largest drug trafficking networks in the world, said to handle deals worth billions of dollars a year.

As well as avoiding regulation through its complexity, the bank also protected itself by operating a vast system of bribes and kickbacks in many of the countries in which it operated. The US Senate report already quoted at the beginning of this chapter had this to say:

> The result was that BCCI had relationships that ranged from the questionable, to the improper, to the fully corrupt with officials from countries all over the world, including Argentina, Bangladesh, Botswana, Brazil, Cameroon, China, Colombia, the Congo, Ghana, Guatemala, the Ivory Coast, India, Jamaica, Kuwait, Lebanon, Mauritius, Morocco, Nigeria, Pakistan, Panama, Peru, Saudi Arabia, Senegal, Sri Lanka, Sudan, Suriname, Tunisia, the United Arab Emirates, the United States, Zambia, and Zimbabwe.

As the report makes clear, this list was by no means complete. BCCI operated in more than 70 countries and employed much the same techniques in most of them. The remarkable thing is that, after the bank collapsed and details of its dealings began to emerge, hardly any charges were brought against senior employees of the bank or officials in any of these countries.

THE CENTRAL BANK OF TERRORISM

As if all this were not enough, the bank was involved in financing international terrorism, both by providing a means for funds to be supplied to the terrorist organizations and also supplying banking services to the terrorists themselves. Abu Nidal, for instance, one of the most notorious and active terrorists of the 1970s and '80s, is reputed to have had an account at the BCCI branch in Sloane Square, Central London, while, before he came to the attention of the world, Osama bin Laden was another client of the bank and is thought to have modeled his later financial dealings on it. Bin Laden could also have been one of the beneficiaries of money channeled through the bank by the CIA to fund the Mujahideen in Afghanistan in their war with the occupying forces of the Soviet Union, and these Afghan fighters also used the bank to launder the money they made through the heroin trade. The CIA held numerous accounts with the bank, using it to fund covert operations around the world, some of which would prove to be highly controversial once details became known. One of these was the Iran-Contra affair, in which the money from illegal arms sales to Iran was channeled through the bank to fund right-wing rebels fighting against the government of Nicaragua.

It could be argued that, by the late 1980s, the bank had become so successful that it could no longer be ignored by regulators. By that time, some details of the bank's dealings were beginning to appear in the media and, in July 1991, the authorities in America, Britain, and several other countries closed the bank down and forced it into liquidation. Abedi was indicted on fraud and money laundering charges in America, along with a number of the senior staff of the bank, but Pakistan refused applications for their extradition. The full extent of the criminal activity will probably never be known because of the complexity of the bank, and perhaps also because many people in positions of power would prefer that some of the bank's dealings were not exposed, leaving the only people to pay a price for its crimes as its depositors at the time of its liquidation, most of whom, no doubt, were not involved in anything illegal.

MOTIVATION

Murder
Assassination
Treason
Espionage
Robbery
Hijacking
Fraud
Kidnapping

THE BACKPACKER MURDERS

1990s

Location: New South Wales, Australia

Perpetrator: Ivan Milat

Outcome: Milat is serving seven consecutive life sentences

The things I can tell you are much worse than what Ivan's meant to have done.
Everywhere he's worked, people have disappeared. I know where he's been.

**Remark made by Boris Milat, Ivan Milat's brother,
to a journalist in 2005**

The Belanglo State Forest is in the Southern Highlands of New South Wales, about an hour and a half's drive from Sydney along the Hume Highway, one of the main arterial roads of Australia, which continues to Canberra and then on to Melbourne. It was originally a commercial forest, planted with non-native pine trees in 1919, and is still managed for timber today, even if it is now more valued as a recreational space. Since the early 1990s it has also become associated with the Backpacker Murders, some of the most notorious crimes ever committed in Australia, after the bodies of all seven known victims were found in the forest.

THE VICTIMS

On Saturday September 19, 1992, two men who were taking part in an orienteering run through the forest stopped near an overhanging rocky outcrop just off the trail and could not help but notice a terrible smell. At first they thought that a kangaroo or some other animal must have died in the vicinity, but then one of them saw a boot protruding from underneath a pile of sticks and leaves, together with a bone and some clothing. It was clear that they had discovered a decomposing human body, so they alerted the police in the nearby town of Bowral as quickly as they could. Once the police had uncovered the body, they were able to determine that it was a young woman who had been stabbed multiple times in the neck and chest. The following morning the body of another young woman was found not far away, also concealed under sticks and leaves. She had been stabbed and then shot in the head ten times from close range. A pile of cartridges from a .22 Ruger rifle was found 10 feet (3m) from the body and, from the nature of the wounds and from the bullets that were recovered at the scene, it appeared that the shooter had moved the body three times while taking shots, as if using it for target practice.

Once the bodies had been removed from the forest it was determined that the two women had been sexually assaulted. Dental records established their identities as being Joanne Walters and Caroline Clarke, two 22-year-old British backpackers who had last been seen together in April in the King's Cross district of Sydney, saying that they were thinking of heading south to look for work. They had been reported missing shortly afterward by members of their family in Britain, but there had been no further sign of them until their bodies were found. Over the following year, the police investigation made little progress in determining what had happened. It was speculated that more than one person was involved in their murders because of the difficulty a single person would have encountered in attempting to kidnap two people at the same time, but no evidence has ever been found to confirm such a conclusion. The police thought that the perpetrator was familiar with the Belanglo State Forest and that the attack had been preplanned rather than opportunist, but after an intensive search turned up nothing further, they announced that it had been an isolated incident.

In October 1993, a man found a human skull and thigh bone in a remote part of the forest and a police search of the area then uncovered the remains of two bodies who, it was later determined, had been murdered in much the same way as the first two. Cartridges from a .22 Ruger rifle were found near the bodies and they had been covered over with sticks and leaves. These bodies proved to be two 19-year-old Australians, Deborah Everist and James Gibson, who were from Frankston in Victoria and had been reported missing in 1989 after leaving Frankston to hitchhike to Sydney. Gibson's backpack had been found not long after the couple had gone missing by the side of a road in Galston Gorge on the outskirts of Sydney. Over the next few days three more bodies were discovered in the vicinity, first of the 20-year-old German backpacker Simone Schmidl, missing since January 1991, and then a young couple, also from Germany, Gabor Neugebauer, 21, and Anja Habschied, 20, who had not been seen since December 1991. Schmidl and Neugebauer had both been stabbed and shot in the head multiple times from close range, but it was not possible to say for certain if Habschied had died in exactly the same way because her head was missing, apparently severed with a sword or some similar sharp blade. All three had been in Sydney immediately before they had disappeared, enabling the police to say that a serial killer, or killers, was on the loose and was targeting backpackers traveling along the Hume Highway.

At that time the New South Wales police had more than 800 names on their missing persons file, some of whom were young backpackers, but no further bodies were found. A public appeal for information drew a huge response and the name of one family, the Milats, who lived in the area, came up on a number of occasions and, in particular, of Ivan Milat, who was said to be obsessed with guns. He was interviewed by the police, along with two of his brothers and numerous other suspects, but, other than local rumor, nothing appeared to connect him to the crime. What the police did not realize until almost six months later was that a key witness had already called the hotline they had set up, but then the information he had provided had got lost in the overwhelming response.

In November 1993 Paul Onions was at home in the UK when he heard reports about bodies being found in the Belanglo State Forest. He phoned the police hotline in Australia immediately to tell them about an incident that had occurred in January 1990 when he had been backpacking in Australia. He had hitchhiked out of Sydney along the Hume Highway and had been picked up by a man calling himself Bill in a four-wheel-drive vehicle. After he had got in the vehicle, the man had pulled a gun. Onions managed to escape and flag down a passing car, driven by a woman who, it would turn out, had also contacted the hotline. Onions had reported the incident at the time to the police and had then heard nothing further about it. In April 1994, a detective going through the notes taken down from callers to the hotline came across the information provided by Onions and recognized its significance.

Onions was flown over to New South Wales and picked Ivan Milat out from photographs shown to him. It led to a search warrant being issued for Milat's house, where a Ruger .22 rifle was found hidden in the roof of the garage which proved to be the one used in the killings. Clothing and camping equipment later shown to have belonged to some of the victims were also recovered from the house. Milat was arrested and claimed that he was being framed by other members of his family. He was charged with the seven murders and the attempted murder of Onions and, after being found guilty on all charges at his trial, he was sentenced to seven consecutive life sentences without the possibility of parole. He has been held in the maximum security prison in Goulburn, New South Wales, ever since and continues to protest his innocence. In truth, the only two questions that remain unanswered concern the possibility of other people being involved in the murders and whether or not he killed more people whose bodies have never been discovered.

THE KILLER

BACKPACKER MURDERER
Ivan Milat in 1997, smiling for the press cameras after making one of his numerous court appearances.

MOTIVATION

Murder
Assassination
Treason
Espionage
Robbery
Hijacking
Fraud
Kidnapping

THE COLUMBINE MASSACRE

April 20, 1999

Location: Jefferson County, Colorado

Perpetrators: Eric Harris and Dylan Klebold

Outcome: The murder of 12 children and one teacher, followed by the suicides of the two perpetrators

When it comes down to who's to blame for the high school murders in Littleton, Colorado [the nearest town to Columbine], throw a rock and you'll hit someone who's guilty. We're the people who sit back and tolerate children owning guns, and we're the ones who tune in and watch the up-to-the-minute details of what they do with them.

Marilyn Manson, writing in *Rolling Stone* magazine in May 1999

HOPE COLUMBINE
MEMORIAL LIBRARY

School shootings are by no means an exclusive phenomenon to America, but TV news pictures shot from helicopters showing armed police surrounding another US school or college campus have become a depressingly familiar sight and, in truth, these days only the most extreme incidents receive anything more than local coverage. On December 12, 2012, for instance, a 20-year-old man named Adam Lanza began shooting in an elementary school in Newport, Connecticut, killing 20 children aged between six and seven along with six adults before committing suicide. In the investigation that followed, it emerged that Lanza had been diagnosed with a number of relatively minor mental health issues and, it was subsequently suggested, these may have masked more serious problems such as schizophrenia. He was also shown to have become obsessed in the months before the shooting with the Columbine High School, which has come to epitomize the senseless loss of young lives that such massacres cause.

THE MASSACRE

Columbine is an unincorporated community in Jefferson County, Colorado, of about 24,000 people, which, if its name were not now associated with the massacre in its high school, would otherwise be unremarkable. The normalcy of the place served only to heighten the shock felt in America and around the world over the events of April 20, 1999, demonstrating that if something so shocking and unprovoked could happen there, it could happen anywhere. At about 11:00am on that day, 18-year-old Eric Harris arrived at Columbine High School alone in his car, having missed the classes he was supposed to have attended in the morning, followed shortly afterward by his friend Dylan Klebold, who was 17 at the time. They had with them two bags, each containing explosive devices made from propane canisters fitted with simple fuses and timed to go off at 11:17am. They carried the bags into the cafeteria and left them among the bags of the early lunch sitting, which had already begun. They then returned to their cars, apparently with the intention of waiting for the bombs to go off and then shooting students running from the blasts with the weapons they had brought with them.

Before arriving at the school, Harris and Klebold had planted another bomb in a field a few miles away, timed to go off at 11:14am and intended as a diversion to draw police officers and the fire services away from the school. It exploded on time, but to little effect, and the two bombs in the cafeteria did not go off at all. Once they realized that their plan had gone wrong, they walked back toward the school with their weapons concealed under the coats they were wearing. Harris had a pump-action shotgun and a 9mm carbine with him, while Klebold was carrying a sawn-off double-barreled shotgun and a TEC-9 semi-automatic handgun. They were also

carrying a considerable amount of ammunition and some homemade pipe bombs. As they approached the entrance to the school, they opened fire on a group of 17-year-old students eating their lunch on the grass outside, killing one of them and hitting another eight times.

From that point onward they began a shooting spree, firing at anybody they saw, as well as throwing the pipe bombs, most of which failed to detonate. A teacher came out of the nearby library, thinking that some

HARRIS AND KLEBOLD
A security camera in the school cafeteria recorded Harris, on the left, and Klebold, who is holding his TEC-9 semi-automatic handgun.

sort of student prank was going on, but was then hit by flying glass from a shattered window. She ran back into the library, shouted to the students in there to take cover and phoned the police. An officer arrived on the scene within minutes and was fired on by Harris and Klebold. He returned fire and they both ducked into the school building, walking through the corridors shooting and throwing bombs, and then entering the library, where 52 students and four staff were hiding under desks and any other cover they could find. Harris and Klebold walked between the tables and shot some of the students they found, while letting others go, apparently selecting anybody who was involved in the school's sports teams as victims.

At 11:36am Harris and Klebold left the library and, while a huge number of police officers gathered outside, including a SWAT team, they walked through the corridors of the school randomly shooting and letting off bombs. After almost half an hour they returned to the library, now empty except for two badly wounded students and the bodies of those they had killed. At 12:08pm, Harris used his shotgun to shoot himself in the mouth and Klebold shot himself in the temple with his TEC-9. The SWAT team entered the library about an hour later to find their dead bodies. Over the course of their rampage, which had lasted for about 50 minutes, they had killed 12 students and one teacher and wounded a further 24, some of them receiving multiple injuries.

As well as a deep sense of shock that swept over America in the aftermath of the massacre, the inevitable questions were asked concerning what had led Harris and Klebold to such extreme violence. During the police investigation, it emerged that the tragedy was anything but a spontaneous event triggered by a single specific event. Both boys had kept journals for more than a year beforehand that showed that they had planned what they were going to do over the course of many months and had talked people they knew who were over the age of 18 into buying the guns they needed for them. Without easy answers to the question of why they did it, a debate began in the media concerning what else was involved. Harris and Klebold were depicted as being part of the Goth movement and suggestions were made that they had been influenced by the music of Marilyn Manson, who proved to be much more eloquent and engaged with the problem than the journalists who were pointing the finger at him when he suggested that it was much easier to find a scapegoat than to address the real issues.

It would later become clear that neither of the boys were goths or listened to Marilyn Manson's music very much, preferring German industrial rock instead. Questions about their preference for playing violent video games did not take the debate very much further, particularly when people who knew Dylan Klebold said that his favorite game was the entirely harmless Super Mario Brothers. And the discussion of how easily they had managed to get hold of guns descended into what has now become the standard response after a school shooting. In the face of outrage from people demanding that something be done to increase gun control in America, members of the gun lobby waited for the initial shock to die down and then asserted their constitutional right to arm themselves to the teeth if they chose to do so without concern for anybody else. What none of this achieved was any kind of explanation for what had happened at Columbine, a situation probably best expressed by Marilyn Manson in his observation that all who lived in the same society as the boys who committed the murders bore some responsibility for what happened.

THE AFTERMATH

MOTIVATION

Murder

Assassination

Treason

Espionage

Robbery

Hijacking

Fraud

Kidnapping

THE ENRON SCANDAL

2001

Location: Houston, Texas

Perpetrators: Kenneth Lay, Jeffrey Skilling, Andrew Fastow, and other executives at Enron Corporation

Outcome: The exposure of enormous fraud in one of the world's largest companies

Former Enron executives Ken Lay and Jeffrey Skilling were found guilty of bankrupting the company and its employees. Both are facing over 100 years in prison. This makes them the only two Enron employees who don't have to worry about paying for retirement.

Comment by talk show host Conan O'Brien after Kenneth Lay and Jeffrey Skilling were found guilty of fraud in May 2006

At one point in its 16 years of trading, the Enron Corporation, based in Houston, Texas, was one of the largest companies in America. In 2000, it claimed to have revenues totaling $100 billion, having branched out from its original core trade in natural gas and electricity generation into a wide range of other activities, beginning in the wholesale energy markets and then encompassing other commodity markets, manufacturing, and services around the world. Kenneth Lay, its founder and chief executive officer, was one of the highest paid business leaders in America and one of the best connected. He was a business associate and personal friend of both President George H.W. Bush and President George W. Bush and, at the time, was considered a rising star of the Republican party.

THE ENRON COMPLEX
The lavish headquarters of the company in downtown Houston. After Enron collapsed it was sold, renamed, and is now occupied by Chevron.

Rumors that Enron might not be as healthy as it appeared on the surface had circulated in the financial press and concerns had been regularly expressed over the company's accounting practices, but these had been aggressively countered, particularly by Jeffrey Skilling, the company's chief operating officer, and its share price continued to rise, hitting in mid-2000 $90 a share. Eighteen months later, on December 2, 2001, Enron, with its shares trading at less than $1, went bust. At the time it was the largest corporate bankruptcy in American history. It would subsequently become clear that the company was rotten to the core, its fraudulent financial dealings hidden by opaque accounting procedures, and that both Lay and Skilling had sold off their shares shortly before the price crashed, making multi-million-dollar profits while regular investors lost almost everything and the company's pension scheme for its employees, based on shares, disappeared. In the fallout from the bankruptcy, one of the world's largest accountancy firms, Arthur Anderson, which had been responsible for auditing Enron, also folded and charges of fraud, insider trading, and a range of other financial crimes were brought against Lay and Skilling, together with a number of Enron's other executives.

SPEs   The complicated corporate structure of Enron and its convoluted accounting procedures are what made the fraud possible, but also meant that it has proved almost impossible to get a full picture of what its executives were doing. But at the center of its criminal activity was the extensive use of financial instruments known as special purpose entities (SPEs), a legal means of moving a company's assets offshore by transferring them to a separate company set up for that purpose and usually registered in a tax haven. When Enron began a rapid program of expansion in the early 1990s following the deregulation of energy markets in America and numerous other countries around the world, SPEs were used to shift any of its assets that were making a loss offshore, removing them from the company's books. This enabled the debts incurred in these loss-making ventures to be hidden so that, in the company accounts, it appeared to remain highly profitable, thereby protecting its share price on the stock markets. With the company apparently going from strength to strength, it could then use its high stock market valuation to take on more debt as it expanded even further, thereby continuing to hide losses by setting up further SPEs.

Over the course of the 1990s Enron's accounts showed that its profits had increased by more than 10% each year when other companies operating in the deregulated energy markets were considered to be highly successful if they achieved 2% growth. Questions asked about how it could keep up such remarkable progress were largely drowned out in the stampede to invest in its shares and by the accolades it was awarded, being named, for instance, as number 5 in the Fortune 500 list of global corporations ranked by revenue. It also benefited from hiring Arthur Anderson as its auditor, a highly respected company that, it was thought, could not afford to associate itself with anything irregular because of the need to protect its reputation.

JEFFREY SKILLING
Mugshot of the former CEO of Enron, who received a 24-year prison sentence for his part in the scandal, later reduced to 14 years on appeal.

Skilling became CEO of the company in place of Lay at the start of 2001 and then dramatically resigned in August 2001, having, in the three months beforehand, sold more than $33 million worth of the shares he held in the company. By that time the questions about Enron's accounting procedures had grown stronger and some financial analysts were beginning to question if its shares were overpriced because it was not apparent from its books where the extraordinary profits it posted had been made. The combination of the loss of its CEO and doubts about its accounting practices caused a sudden decline in confidence in its investors and a corresponding drop in its share value. Lay returned as CEO and released numerous statements intended to restore confidence in the company, among others, encouraging Enron employees to invest in shares after the price had fallen because, he assured them, it was sure to bounce back again in the very near future and they would all make healthy profits. It would later emerge that, at the same time as he was boosting the shares to his staff and other investors, he had been selling off his own shares in blocks small enough so as not to attract undue attention.

Despite Lay's best efforts, the share price continued to decline, particularly after profit statements for the previous few years were amended downward by over $600 million, after which shares were trading for $20. An investigation by the US Securities and Exchange Commission, the federal regulator of the stock market, followed and the shares went into freefall. The scale of the crisis finally became clear after a further $600 million was wiped off its profit statements and two of the SPEs that had lost hundreds of millions of dollars were brought to light. In November, a rival energy company from Houston, Dynergy, made a bid to buy Enron for $8 billion, less than a tenth of its value in the previous year. That, however, failed because it proved impossible to value the company's assets. The only other option was for the company to be declared bankrupt.

FRAUD EXPOSED

The complexity of the fraud charges brought against Lay and Skilling meant that it took more than four years for the case to come to trial. When it did, in January 2006, one of the witnesses for the prosecution was Andrew Fastow, an Enron executive who had been hired by Skilling to set up SPEs and who had previously pleaded guilty to fraud. His testimony regarding systematic and extensive fraud committed over the course of more than a decade guaranteed that Lay and Skilling would be found guilty. Skilling was given a 24-year prison term, later reduced on appeal to 14, but Kenneth Lay suffered a heart attack after being found guilty and died on July 5, 2006, before he had been sentenced. Had he lived, it is almost certain that he would have received a similar sentence to that of Skilling because, even though Skilling had been responsible for initiating much of the fraudulent practice, as CEO the buck stopped with Lay.

MOTIVATION

Murder

Assassination

Treason

Espionage

Robbery

Hijacking

Fraud

Kidnapping

THE ANTWERP DIAMOND HEIST

February 15–16, 2003

Location: Antwerp, Belgium

Perpetrators: Leonardo Notarbartolo and the School of Turin

Outcome: One of the largest and most ingenious diamond heists ever perpetrated

Antwerp is where all the key elements in the industry are concentrated: home to all the major mining companies that unearth these treasures, to over 1,800 individual diamond dealers originating from all over the world, to the dedicated diamond banks and insurance brokers, the forwarders that are equipped to send the precious parcels to every corner of the world, the best polishers in the world and high-tech researchers that get the best out of each and every rough stone.

From the Mission Statement put out by the Antwerp World Diamond Center, which gives an idea of why Leonardo Notarbartolo planned a diamond heist in the city

Over the weekend of Saturday, February 15, and Sunday 16, 2003, the attention of the Belgian city of Antwerp was focused on the Proximus Diamond Games, a women's tennis tournament in which the nation's two favorite daughters, Kim Clijsters and Justine Henin-Hardenne, were competing alongside Venus Williams of America for a valuable first prize: a diamond-encrusted tennis

DIAMOND QUARTER
The Antwerp World Diamond Center is a relatively nondescript modern building on the main street of the Diamond Quarter.

racket worth a million dollars. It was a fitting prize for the tournament played in the city at the heart of the world's diamond trade and where, in its Diamond Quarter, billions of dollars changes hands ever year. That weekend the Diamond Quarter was quiet, the offices and stores closed, not because everybody wanted to watch the tennis, but because a large proportion of the dealers and other workers in the trade were Jewish and were observing the Sabbath. On the Thursday beforehand, the monthly delivery of rough diamonds from De Beers had arrived as usual under the tightest security, filling up the safety deposit boxes in the vault of the Antwerp World Diamond Center while deals for them were struck.

The World Diamond Center is a 14-story building on Hoveniersstraat, the main street in the Diamond Quarter, and is one of the most secure buildings in one of the most heavily protected areas of the world. On that Sunday afternoon, Venus Williams disappointed the home crowd by beating Kim Clijsters in the final of the tennis, but that would prove to be a minor shock compared to the one that awaited the staff of the diamond center when they descended to the second floor basement of the building on Monday morning. Over the weekend somebody had opened the supposedly impregnable vault, drilled out the locks of more than 100 of the 160 safety deposit boxes inside and stolen as much of the contents as they could carry, leaving those diamonds, jewels, gold bars, and money that had proved too heavy behind on the floor, scattered in with the debris of the robbery. They had also taken the videotape from the security cameras in the building with them and left no clues to their identities behind. It proved to be the largest diamond heist ever committed, with the combined total of what had been stolen estimated

AN ALMOST PERFECT ROBBERY

at $100 million. In its planning and execution, it appeared to have been almost the perfect crime. Unfortunately for the robbers, the getaway did not go quite so smoothly.

That same day, Monday, February 17, a man who owned a small patch of woodland alongside the E19 motorway to the north of Brussels phoned the police to complain about illegal dumping of waste material on his land. Somebody had thrown a black trash bag into the woodland that had split open, scattering litter all over the place. When he mentioned that, among other things, the litter was composed of numerous envelopes with the name World Diamond Center printed on the front, the police suddenly became a great deal more interested than they had previously been, sending over officers straight away to collect as much of the litter as they could.

The rubbish was taken to the Diamond Squad in Antwerp, a division of the Belgium police set up in the city specifically to work in the Diamond Quarter. As well as the envelopes, the detectives in the squad now had an abundance of evidence, including a pile of videotape that had been pulled out of a cassette and a half-eaten salami sandwich. There was also a business card in the name of Elio D'Onorio, an electrical engineer from Turin, and a torn-up receipt for some video surveillance equipment made out in the name of Leonardo Notarbartolo, also from Turin. On the Friday after the robbery, the detectives were amazed when they got a call from a security guard at the diamond center to say that a man named Leonardo Notarbartolo had just entered the building using a security pass, which he had in his possession entirely legitimately because he was a diamond dealer who had occupied a rented office there for the past few years.

Once the police had arrested Notarbartolo, they searched his apartment in Antwerp, where they found a SIM card from a cell phone that led them to the third member of the Turin gang, Pietro Tavano, and a receipt for the same sort of salami that was in the sandwich. It had been bought from a nearby delicatessen and when the police checked the footage from a security camera in the store, they identified the man who had bought it as yet another man from Turin called Ferdinando Finotto. DNA evidence obtained from the salami sandwich and from adhesive tape that had been used in the vault during the robbery provided conclusive proof that the Diamond Squad had the right men and, as well as Notarbartolo, the other three were then arrested. The DNA recovered in the vault also showed that a fifth man who has never been identified was involved in the robbery and, at least according to Notarbartolo, who might not be entirely reliable, an Antwerp diamond dealer who he refused to name originally came up with the idea and then financed the planning stages.

Leonardo Notarbartolo is originally from Sicily and it has been alleged that he and other members of his family have links to the Mafia, which he has always denied. In 2000 he was living in Turin, in his early 50s and with a wife and adult children. He had been a career criminal for more than two decades, specializing in jewel theft and, by that time, had put together a crack team of robbers known as the School of Turin. Each member of the team had an expertise in a particular field needed in the robbery trade and included a locksmith who could make replica keys and an electronics expert to deal with alarm systems. As a means of disposing of the stolen goods, Notarbartolo had also become a smalltime diamond dealer himself, traveling to Antwerp regularly to do business, buying and selling legally obtained diamonds, as well as fencing those that had been stolen. In order to facilitate his business, and no doubt to give the impression that it was respectable, he rented the office in the World Diamond Center where he could meet other diamond dealers. It also gave him access to the building, with a pass card to get him through the automatic barriers at the entrance, and a safety deposit box in the vault, which he visited regularly in the company of a security guard.

Over the course of an 18-month period, Notarbartolo used the access he had gained to the diamond center to examine the security procedures employed within the building. The vault door was made of steel a foot (30cm) thick, was opened by a combination lock and a key, and was protected by a seismic sensor in case anybody tried to drill through it. On a number of occasions he wore a hidden camera on his visits to his safety deposit box, recoding the combination of the vault door as it was being opened and getting a clear picture of the key so that his locksmith would be able to replicate it. He also took the opportunity to film the alarm system and all the other security measures employed inside and outside the vault, which included heat, motion, and light sensors as well as video cameras, and then used the information he had gathered to reconstruct an identical setup in a warehouse so that the School of Turin could get to work figuring out how to disable or bypass them.

THE SCHOOL OF TURIN

CUT DIAMONDS
Antwerp is the largest diamond trading center in the world.

Notarbartolo took down details of the building's overall alarm system and watched the security guards to establish their routine. Once the diamond center was closed in the evening and the vault locked, the guards turned out all the lights and relied on the various electronic security devices to prevent anybody from breaking in, apparently confident that the technology employed could not be overcome. As the building was closed for the entire weekend, this meant that a Saturday night after the regular monthly De Beers delivery would be the perfect moment for the School of Turin to put the plan they had worked out into action.

Shortly before the building closed on Friday, February 14, 2003, Notarbartolo visited his safety deposit box in the vault and, taking the chance of being seen on the security cameras, used a can of hair spray to coat the heat sensors inside with a film of the spray which, the team had worked out, would provide enough insulation to give them time to disable the security devices, which were connected to a control panel on the wall of the vault. The next night, while Notarbartolo kept watch from a car parked in the street, the four-member team broke into the building by climbing up to a balcony on the second floor at the back of the building, used a piece of polystyrene to insulate themselves from the heat sensors installed there, and disabled the alarm on the window lock. Once they were in the building, they made their way down to the basement, using black plastic bags to cover the security cameras, and went through the procedure they had worked out in the warehouse, opening the vault using the key and the combination and then disabling all the security systems before the heat of their bodies got too much for the insulation provided by the hair spray on the heat sensors.

Once the security system had been overcome, the locksmith used a drill to break into the safety deposit boxes, taking a few minutes to open each one so that another member of the team could empty the contents into one of the bags they had brought with them. To save time, they did not check the leather pouches containing the diamonds that they put into the bags, but made sure to take the certificates of authenticity that proved the diamonds had been mined legally so it would be easier to sell them. After about three hours, they had filled their bags with as much as they could carry and made their way out of the building the same way as they had come in, going back to Notarbartolo's apartment with the loot.

Notarbartolo would later claim that many of the leather pouches the team had stolen were empty and that the estimate of the diamonds they had stolen being worth $100 million was about five times too high. According to this version of the story, the Antwerp diamond dealer had pulled an insurance scam, claiming money back on diamonds that had not been stolen, but there is no way of knowing if this is what actually happened. Whatever the truth of the matter, on the following Sunday evening, the five robbers set out for Turin in two cars, arranging to meet in the city the next day.

Notarbartolo traveled with Pietro Tavano and they took with them the black bag containing the debris of the robbery that would later lead to their arrest. As they were approaching Brussels they decided to burn the bag in case the robbery had already been discovered and they were stopped by the police, pulling over when they came to the woodland near the E19. In the dark, the bag somehow split open before they could burn it, tipping the contents into the undergrowth, and they decided to leave it rather than risk being seen in the time it would take to gather everything up. It proved to be the wrong decision, one that would result in Notarbartolo receiving a ten-year prison sentence and the other three robbers who were caught getting five years each. Considering the size of the robbery, the sentences were relatively lenient, reflecting the fact that nobody was harmed, or even threatened, while it was being carried out. In 2010 Notarbartolo was the last of the robbers to be released from prison and, as only a tiny fraction of the diamonds has ever been recovered, he is now presumably enjoying the fruits of his own ingenuity.

MOTIVATION

Murder

Assassination

Treason

Espionage

Robbery

Hijacking

Fraud

Kidnapping

THE HIJACKING
OF THE *SIRIUS STAR*

November 15, 2008

Location: Eastern Indian Ocean and the town of Harardhere in Somalia

Perpetrators: Mohamed Abdi Hassan and a band of Somali pirates

Outcome: A ransom was paid and the ship and its crew released

Our presence in the region is helping deter and disrupt criminal attacks off the Somali coast, but the situation with the Sirius Star clearly indicates the pirates' ability to adapt their tactics and methods of attack. Piracy is an international crime that threatens global commerce. Shipping companies have to understand that naval forces can not be everywhere. Self-protection measures are the best way to protect their vessels, their crews, and their cargo.

US Vice Admiral Bill Gortney, commander of combined naval force attempting to prevent piracy, quoted on November 18, 2008, in a report by CNN

SIRIUS STAR

By any standards the MV *Sirius Star* is a very big ship, classified by the shipping industry as a VLCC (Very Large Crude Carrier) and called a supertanker by the rest of us. It is slightly over 1000 feet (300m) long and can hold two million barrels of crude oil. At about 10am on February 15, 2008, it was fully loaded with oil from Saudi Arabia and heading south in the Indian Ocean, 450 nautical miles (830km) off the coast of Kenya, when it was boarded by Somali pirates. The Polish captain, Marek Nishk, and his 24-man crew, made up of 19 Filipinos, two Britons, and one each from Poland, Croatia, and Saudi Arabia, had no option other than to surrender once the pirates had boarded the ship because they were faced with men armed with automatic weapons, most likely Kalashnikov rifles, the gun of choice in Somalia at the time.

The captain and crew were forced to turn the ship around at gunpoint and head for the small fishing port of Harardhere, about 180 miles (300km) north of the Somali capital Mogadishu, where the pirates had most likely departed from three or four days previously. The ship arrived there on February 17 and it was anchored off shore. Armed guards were left on board and, once the pirates had moved their captives to an unknown location on land, they contacted the owners of the ship, Vela International Marine, a subsidiary of the Saudi state oil company, to demand a ransom. It was the most daring raid yet staged by Somali pirates, who had traveled further than they had ever done before to capture the *Sirius Star*, the largest ship ever hijacked. The ship itself was valued at $150 million and its cargo at a further $100 million, enabling the pirates to demand a substantial ransom. The details of the negotiations between them and the owners have never been made public, but by that time numerous other ships had been ransomed and something of a standard price for the return of ships and crews had emerged, so it is reasonable to assume that this group of pirates would have asked for something in the region of $5 million, perhaps opening negotiations with a higher figure.

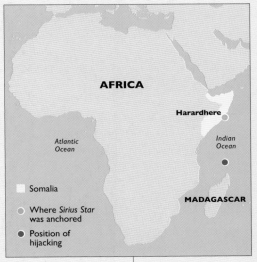

AFRICA

Harardhere

Atlantic
Ocean

Indian
Ocean

MADAGASCAR

☐ Somalia

◯ Where *Sirius Star*
was anchored

● Position of
hijacking

THE HIJACKING
The *Sirius Star*, boarded by pirates some 450 nautical miles from the Kenyan coast, was the largest vessel ever to be hijacked.

PIRACY IN SOMALIA

The hijacking of the *Sirius Star* was only the most prominent of more than 100 incidents of piracy that occurred off the coast of Somalia in 2008, demonstrating that the hijacking of ships for ransom had become an epidemic since it had begun a few years earlier. The Norwegian academic Stig Jarle Hansen is one of the few Westerners to have studied the phenomenon in the region where it has occurred, a considerable achievement considering the dangers involved. In his published work he has discussed the development of piracy since the late 1990s and the reasons behind it, which he has described as being more complicated than the explanations put forward in the Western media, which usually regard it as being the consequence of a combination of extreme poverty in the region and the failure of the Somali state in 1991, which left the country without a government or any sort of law enforcement.

The collapse of the government in 1991 left Somalia without any means of protecting its territorial waters, leading to the encroachment of foreign fishing vessels and a corresponding crash in fish stocks due to overfishing. Some unscrupulous international companies also made use of the undefended waters to dump toxic waste, further damaging the fish stocks and the health of the Somali people living in the regions affected. It is thought that some Somali fishermen began to take the law into their own hands, banding together in an attempt to drive off the foreign fishing vessels and waste dumpers in an effort to protect their livelihoods and this then evolved into more straightforward acts of piracy motivated by profit. The large amounts of profit to be made from the ransoming of ships then attracted people from Mogadishu and other parts of Somalia to the regions where the piracy was occurring, which had previously had little connection to the war that was being fought in the capital and elsewhere. One of these was Mohamed Abdi Hassan, who is commonly known as Afweyne, or Big Mouth, who arrived in Harardhere in around 2004 and is thought to have then started to recruit pirates, including the ones who hijacked the *Sirius Star*.

On January 9, 2009, Vela International delivered a $3 million ransom to the *Sirius Star*, reportedly parachuted onto the deck from a light plane. The pirates then returned the crew to the ship and allowed them to leave, the ship sailing to Fujairah in the United Arab Emirates. The pirates had apparently settled for a lower ransom than they might have initially wanted because they were coming under pressure from two fronts. A combined naval force made up of ships from America, China, Britain, and a number of other countries had been increased in response to the escalation of pirate activity and their apparent ability to hijack ships further from the base in Somalia than had previously been thought possible. There was also concern regarding Islamic fundamentalist groups then beginning to develop in Somalia. Such groups have committed many acts of terrorism in Somalia and the surrounding countries, but they were in fact responsible for cracking down on the illegal activity of the pirates.

THE PAYOFF
On January 9, 2007, the US Navy photographed a plane dropping a canister thought to contain a ransom onto the deck of the *Sirius Star*.

Some commentators have suggested that the presence of Islamic fundamentalists has been one of the reasons for the reduction in the incidence of piracy off the coast of Somalia since 2009 and argue that they could be drawn into becoming part of the solution to the lack of law enforcement in the region. The increased security measures taken by ship owners, which has seen armed guards on ships, together with the presence of a larger naval force in the waters off the coast of Somalia have no doubt also contributed. In January 2013 Mohamed Abdi Hassan announced that he was retiring from the piracy business and was encouraging others in the same line of work to do the same, most likely because the increased security had made it less profitable.

In October 2013 Hassan was arrested by Belgium police and charged over the hijacking of a Belgian ship in 2009 after apparently being lured to that country in a sting operation in which he was told that he would be interviewed for a TV documentary on piracy. But, retired or in prison, the fact that he is no longer involved in piracy is another reason for its decline off the coast of Somalia. Toward the end of 2013, a spokesman for US naval intelligence announced that there had been only nine reported incidents of attempted piracy over the course of that year and none of them had been successful, indicating that, while the problem may not have been completely solved, the eastern Indian Ocean is a great deal safer now than it was only a few years ago.

MOTIVATION

Murder

Assassination

Treason

Espionage

Robbery

Hijacking

Fraud

Kidnapping

THE MADOFF INVESTMENT SCANDAL

December 11, 2008

Location: New York

Perpetrator: Bernie Madoff

Outcome: The largest financial fraud in US history

Where's my money?

Question put to Bernie Madoff's son Andrew by a client shortly after Madoff's arrest

It's all just one big lie... basically, a giant Ponzi scheme.

Quote attributed to Madoff at the time of his arrest

If the arrest of Bernie Madoff had occurred a year earlier, it may well have caused a great deal more shock than it actually did. But after two FBI agents showed up at his Manhattan apartment at 8:30am on December 11, 2008, to arrest him for committing the largest financial fraud in American history, it became yet another news story in the catalog of greed, ineptitude, and criminal behavior that had become a feature of the global financial crisis that was then enveloping markets across the world. Before his arrest, Madoff had been one of the best-known dealers on Wall Street, the public face of the brokerage firm that he had founded in 1960 and that bore his name, Bernard L. Madoff Investment Securities LLC, and the fact that he had been exposed as a crook who had defrauded his clients of an estimated £65 billion was taken by many outside the financial world as being a further sign of the corruption and double-dealing of Wall Street.

WALL STREET
Street sign outside the New York Stock Exchange. Before being exposed as a fraudster Madoff was a big player on Wall Street.

The fraud Madoff was accused of committing had occurred in a branch of his business involved in wealth management for his clients, which included a long list of wealthy and famous individuals as well as other financial companies and public and charitable institutions. Over the course of the previous four decades, he had built up a reputation for being able to provide a consistent rate of return of around 10% a year on the money he managed no matter what the overall financial climate was like. It may not have been as spectacular as some of the returns achieved by other Wall Street financiers on short-term investments, but these were usually much more risky. Madoff offered stability and security rather than uncertainty and the possibility of making a loss as well as the opportunity to turn a profit. There was also a certain exclusivity about Madoff's firm, in which wealthy individuals were invited to invest with him rather than choose him as their investment broker. Many of his clients probably had no idea how he invested their money, but his reputation and the high profile he enjoyed in New York society, together with the returns they were getting on their money, meant that few bothered to ask any questions until after the fraud had been exposed, by which time many of them had lost all their money.

The detail of the fraud committed by Madoff is complicated and difficult to describe without becoming bogged down in the jargon of Wall Street and the financial world in general, but, at the heart of the affair, it was actually quite simple: Madoff had constructed a giant Ponzi scheme. When a client invested their money with him, he simply put it in a regular bank account and left it there rather than investing it in any of the financial instruments available on Wall Street, such as stocks and shares or the commodities and futures markets. He then fabricated a paper trail of trading reports to show that he was acting as a broker, giving the appearance that he was investing money for his clients when he was not, and then paid the interest due on the client's investment out of money he had received from other clients. As long as clients kept investing, there would be funds to keep paying the interest, together with the fees he charged for the management services he claimed to be providing. Many of his clients simply left their money with him anyway, happy to let their investment keep growing by 10% a year rather than take the money out and risk not being invited to rejoin the scheme at a later date.

A HOUSE OF CARDS

The trouble began for Madoff when the amount of new money coming in began to decline with the onset of the financial crisis. Other financial institutions, which accounted for almost half of the money he managed, were in trouble themselves and wanted to make withdrawals rather than continue to invest. In the past, he may have been able to ride out the storm by borrowing money from banks to cover the interest payments, but in 2008 sources of credit had almost completely dried up. As more and more people wanted their money back from him, it became increasingly clear that he didn't actually have it. Rather than being the financial wizard he purported to be, when he had actually invested money on Wall Street, he had, over the 40 years he had been in business, actually incurred staggering losses, estimated to have been in the region of $50 billion. Once the money had run out, he was left with no way of hiding the fact that he did not have most of the money from the original investments placed with him by his clients, never mind be able to continue paying interest on the money.

Signs that all was not as it appeared to be at Bernard L. Madoff Investment Securities had been detected some years before 2008 and reported to the Securities and Exchange Commission, the federal body charged with regulating financial markets in America. The financial analyst Harry

Markopolos was among a number of people within the industry who had studied Madoff's dealings and come to the conclusion that the sums did not add up and that he must be committing some sort of fraud to achieve the results he was getting. If the SEC did anything at all about the information they were receiving, it was to make an announcement that the allegations against Madoff had no basis. He had enjoyed a distinguished career on Wall Street over the course of four decades and had become a prominent member of the Jewish community, supporting many Jewish organizations and charities, apparently leading the SEC to conclude that a man who had attained such a position could not have done so fraudulently.

BERNIE MADOFF
A US Department of Justice mugshot of Madoff taken in March 2009, shortly after he was sentenced to 150 years in prison.

Once the nature and scale of Madoff's activities became known, the SEC had no other choice than to act, beginning a belated investigation along with the FBI that led to his arrest. Many of the people who lost money in the fraud were not rich and famous, even if media reports of the affair concentrated on people whose names would be recognized. Madoff had made use of his contacts in the Jewish community to develop his client base when he was starting out in business and many of these people had stuck with him over the years. They may have been reasonably well off, but were by no means part of any wealthy elite, and some of them lost everything they had as a consequence of the fraud.

After pleading guilty to the charges brought against him, the 70-year-old Madoff was given a prison term of 150 years, the severity of the sentence reflecting the almost total lack of cooperation he had given to the investigation. He appears to have been attempting to take the entire blame for the fraud on himself to protect others, including his brother and two sons, who all worked for his company, but it has also meant the exact nature and extent of his fraudulent activities may never be known in full. One thing the affair does illustrate is that the old saying that, if a deal looks too good to be true then it probably is too good to be true, still applies today as much as it ever did, although this probably does not provide much of a consolation to the thousands of people who lost their life savings thanks to Madoff.

MOTIVATION

Murder

Assassination

Treason

Espionage

Robbery

Hijacking

Fraud

Kidnapping

THE CARLTON CANNES ROBBERY

July 28, 2013

Location: Cannes

Perpetrator: One man, identity unknown

Outcome: One of the biggest and easiest jewel heists ever committed

A Lone Bandit and the Mystery of France's Greatest Diamond Heist.

A gunman stole $136 million of jewelry from an exhibition at the Intercontinental Carlton Cannes hotel in July. Investigators and gem experts are still wondering how it happened.

Beginning of an article by Ryan Jacobs about the robbery in *The Atlantic* magazine of September 5, 2013

The Carlton Cannes is the most prestigious hotel in the city of Cannes, the place were the A-list movie stars stay when they are attending the movie festival. It stands on the Promenade de la Croisette, overlooking the Mediterranean Sea and, for an additional charge, patrons can use its private beach across the street from the hotel. In 1955, Alfred Hitchcock filmed a number of scenes for his movie *To Catch a Thief* in and around the hotel. It starred Cary Grant as a retired cat burglar who sets out to catch the person responsible for committing a series of jewel thefts on the French Riviera in order to prove that he has not returned to his old ways. The female lead in the movie was Grace Kelly, who first met her future husband, Prince Rainier of Monaco, in the hotel, where she was staying while attending the movie festival to promote *To Catch a Thief*. Back in the real world, the hotel has been the scene of two actual jewel thefts, both of which give the impression of having more in common with the bungling Inspector Clouseau than with Cary Grant and Grace Kelly.

On August 11, 1994, three men wielding automatic weapons burst into the jewelry store in the hotel shortly before it was due to close, fired into the air with what later turned out to be blanks, and grabbed everything they could lay their hands on and made a run for it. The identity of the robbers has never been determined and the loot, valued at $63 million, has never been recovered. It was the sort of event, you might think, that would prompt the hotel to improve security for all future exhibitions, such as that of the gems and jewelry belonging to the Israeli billionaire Lev Leviev that opened in the summer of 2013. This is particularly true given the spate of jewelry thefts that occurred along the French Riviera at that time, including two in Cannes and one from a hotel down the street from the Carlton. It is, of course, easy to be wise after the event but, even so, the almost complete absence of any security measures at all beggars belief. As one of the insurance agents involved in the case commented, the hotel had gone to the trouble of hanging huge banners on its front to advertise the exhibition but had then left the jewels effectively unprotected, almost as if they were advertising for a thief to commit a robbery.

A ROBBER'S PARADISE

LEV LEVIEV
The Israeli businessman is a noted dealer and collector of high-quality diamonds. He owned the diamonds stolen from the Carlton Cannes.

Lev Leviev has been a major player in the diamond market for several decades and the collection of jewels he had put together included a number of high-carat flawless white diamonds as well as numerous other highly valuable gems. Shortly before lunchtime on Sunday, July 28, 2013, while the exhibition was in the process of being installed in a ground floor room of the hotel, a man walked in through a set of French windows, which appear to have been left unlocked, brandishing a gun. A security camera video, available to view on YouTube, shows the man wearing a baseball cap and a scarf over his face, dressed in black shorts that come down to below his knees and a black shirt, and, as he enters the room, he points the gun at the five or six staff who have previously been seen milling about, engaged in preparing the exhibition. Most of them get down on the floor, except one woman at the desk in the corner who remains standing, almost motionless in apparent terror, with her hands over her face. The robber goes up to the desk and picks up a black holdall from by the side of it. He appears to be about to leave when something catches his eye and he turns back to the desk and picks up what looks like an open briefcase, which he closes as he walks away and out of view of the camera.

The robber then apparently left the way he had come in, stumbling once he had got outside and spilling a few of the jewels, some of which he picked up, then, leaving the rest, he walked away with the loot and has never been seen since. The bag and the briefcase he stole contained most of the high-value jewels, including the flawless white diamonds, which had yet to be installed in display cases for the opening of the exhibition. The ease with which he got into the room, through an unlocked door, and the timing of the raid to coincide with a moment when the jewels were all together in the bag and briefcase just waiting for him to steal, has led to suggestions that he had inside information about the hotel and the exhibition, or perhaps even had an accomplice on the staff, but no evidence of any such complicity, or in fact, anything at all to do with the robbery has come

CANNES POLICE
By the time the police arrived at the hotel, the thief and the diamonds were long gone. No trace of either has been found.

to light. The man simply walked away with gems and jewelry worth an estimated $136 million, making it one of the biggest jewel heists of all time, and insurance investigators do not expect any of the loot to be recovered, speculating that the larger diamonds will have been cut and polished to make them unrecognizable.

In the aftermath of the robbery it was suggested that a well-known gang of jewel thieves based in Serbia and known as the Pink Panthers were responsible, specifically a man called Milan Poparić, one of the leading figures in the gang. Three days before the raid in the Carlton Cannes, Poparić had broken out of a prison in Switzerland, where he had been serving a six-year sentence for the robbery of a jewelry store in the Swiss city of Neuchatel. The Pink Panthers first came to light in 1993 and were given that name after hiding a diamond in a tub of face cream during a robbery in London that was reminiscent of a scene in the Peter Sellars movie *The Return of the Pink Panther*. They have certainly committed many robberies over the course of their criminal careers in many different locations around the world, but the way they operate does not match with the Carlton Cannes heist, particularly in the fact that they have never been known to send a single person on a job. Another theory suggests that a more local criminal gang on the French Riviera had got wind of the lax security in the hotel and decided it was too good a chance to miss, but, in truth, it is equally as likely that the raid was carried out by an opportunist robber who got lucky and probably had the shock of his life when he examined what he had stolen when he got home.

A PINK PANTHER?

FURTHER READING

Cain and Abel

Armstrong, Karen. *In the Beginning: A New Reading of the Book of Genesis*. London: Harper Collins, 1997.

Byron, John. *Cain and Abel in Text and Tradition: Jewish and Christian Interpretations of the First Sibling Rivalry*. Leiden: Brill, 2011.

Julius Caesar

Goldsworthy, Adrian. *Caesar: Life of a Colossus*. London: Weidenfeld and Nicolson, 2006.

Patenti, Michael. *The Assassination of Julius Caesar: A People's History of Rome*. New York: New Press, 2003.

Julia Drusilla

Winterling, Aloys. *Caligula: A Biography*. Berkeley: University of California Press, 2011.

The Thugs

Dash, Mike. *Thug: The True Story of India's Murderous Cult*. London: Granta Books, 2005.

Woerkens, Martine van. *The Strangled Traveller: Colonial Imaginings and the Thugs of India*. Chicago: University of Chicago Press, 2002.

Elizabeth Báthory

Thorne, Tony. *Countess Dracula: The Life and Times of the Blood Countess, Elisabeth Báthory*. London: Bloomsbury, 1997.

The Babington Plot

Alford, Stephen. *The Watchers: A Secret History of the Reign of Elizabeth I*. London: Allen Lane, 2012.

Cooper, John. *The Queen's Agent:. Francis Walsingham at the Court of Elizabeth I*. London: Faber and Faber, 2011.

Dunn, Jane. *Elizabeth and Mary: Cousins, Rivals, Queens*. London: Harper Collins, 2003.

Guy, John. *My Heart is My Own: The Life of Mary Queen of Scots*. London: Fourth Estate, 2004.

John Newcomen

Bunker, Nick. *Making Haste from Babylon: The Mayflower Pilgrims and Their World: A New History*. London: Bodley Head, 2010.

Philbrick, Nathaniel. *Mayflower: A Voyage to War*. London: Harper Press, 2006.

Captain Kidd

Zacks, Richard. *The Pirate Hunter: The True Story of Captain Kidd*. London: Review Books, 2003.

Dick Turpin

Brandon, David. *Stand and Deliver! A History of Highway Robbery*. Stroud: Sutton Publishing, 2001.

Sharpe, James. *Dick Turpin: The Myth of the English Highwayman*. London: Profile Books, 2004.

The Poyais Fraud

Sinclair, David. *Sir Gregor MacGregor and the Land that Never Was: The Extraordinary Story of the Most Audacious Fraud in History*. London: Review Books, 2003.

Burke and Hare

Knight, Alanna. *Burke & Hare*. Richmond: The National Archives, 2007.

Rosner, Lisa. *The Anatomy Murders: Being the True and Spectacular History of Edinburgh's Notorious Burke and Hare and of the Man of Science Who Abetted Them in the Commission of Their Most Heinous Crime*. Philadelphia: University of Pennsylvania Press, 2010.

The Lincoln Assassination

Goodwin, Doris Kearns. *Team of Rivals: The Political Genius of Abraham Lincoln*. New York: Simon and Schuster, 2005.

Kauffman, Michael W. *American Brutus: John Wilkes Booth and the Lincoln Conspiracies*. New York: Random House, 2004.

Ned Kelly

Brown, Max. *Australian Son: The Story of Ned Kelly*. Melbourne: Georgian House, 1948.

Osbourne, Charles. *Ned Kelly*. London: Anthony Blond, 1970.

The Jerilderie Letter at the State Library of Victoria, www.slv.vic.gov.au/our-collections/treasures-curios/jerilderie-letter

Jesse James

Stiles, T. J. *Jesse James: Last Rebel of the Civil War*. New York: Alfred A. Knopf, 2002.

Yeatman, Ted P. *Frank and Jesse James: The Story Behind the Legend*. Nashville: Cumberland House, 2003.

Details of a PBS documentary on James, www.pbs.org/wgbh/americanexperience/films/james/

The Union Pacific Big Springs Robbery

Miller, Rick. *Sam Bass and Gang*. Austin, Texas: State House Press, 1999.

The Whitechapel Murders

Begg, Paul. *Jack the Ripper: The Definitive History*. London: Longman, 2003.

The Dreyfus Affair

Bredin, Jean-Denis. *The Affair: The Case of Alfred Dreyfus*. New York: George Braziller, 1986.

Harris, Ruth. *The Man on Devil's Island: Alfred Dreyfus and the Affair that Divided France*. London: Allen Lane, 2010.

Franz Ferdinand

Clark, Christopher. *The Sleepwalkers: How Europe Went to War in 1914*. London: Allen Lane, 2012.

Fischer, Fritz. *Germany's Aims in the First World War*. London: Chatto and Windus, 1967.

The Black Sox Scandal

Asinof, Eliot. *Eight Men Out: The Black Sox and the 1919 World Series*. New York: Holt, Rinehart and Winston, 1963.

Recently rediscovered Pathé News footage from the 1919 World Series, thought to be the only film of the games to have survived, www.youtube.com/watch?v=0mPHqbJXDQI

The Man Who Sold the Eiffel Tower

Johnson, James and Floyd, Miller. *The Man Who Sold the Eiffel Tower*. New York: Doubleday, 1961.

St. Valentine's Day Massacre

Helmer, William J., and Arthur J. Bilek. *The St. Valentine's Day Massacre: The Untold Story of the Gangland Bloodbath That Brought Down Al Capone*. Nashville: Cumberland House Publishing, 2004.

The Papin Sisters

Edwards, Rachel, and Keith Reader. *The Papin Sisters*. Oxford: OUP, 2001.

The Lindbergh Kidnapping

Berg, Scott A. *Lindbergh*. New York: G.P. Putnam's, 1998.

John Dillinger

Burrough, Bryan. *Public Enemies: The True Story of America's Greatest Crime Wave*.

Gorn, Eliot J. *Dillinger's Wild Ride: The Year That Made America's Public Enemy Number One*. New York: OUP USA, 2009.

FBI webpage on Dillinger, www.fbi.gov/about-us/history/famous-cases/john-dillinger/famous-cases-john-dillinger

The Cambridge Spies

Andrew, Christopher. *The Defence of the Realm: The Authorised History of MI5*. London: Allen Lane, 2009.

Carter, Miranda. *Anthony Blunt: His Lives*. London: Pan, 2001.

Macintyre, Ben. *A Spy Among Friends: Kim Philby and the Great Betrayal*. London: Bloomsbury, 2014.

The Rosenbergs

Scheir, Walter. *Final Verdict: What Really Happened in the Rosenberg Case*. New York: Melville House Publishing, 2010.

The Black Dahlia

Ellroy, James. *The Black Dahlia*. New York: The Mysterious Press, 1987.

Hodel, Steve. *The Black Dahlia Avenger: A Genius for Murder*. New York: Arcade Press, 2003.

The Assassination of Gandhi

Fischer, Louis. *The Life Of Mahatma Gandhi*. London: Cape, 1951.

Khan, Yasmin. *The Great Partition: The Making of India and Pakistan*. New Haven: Yale University Press, 2007.

Malgonkar, Manohar. *The Men Who Killed Gandhi*. New Delhi: Roli Books, 2007.

Ed Gein

Schechter, Henry. *Deviant: The True Story of Ed Gein, the Original "Psycho."* New York: Pocket Books, 1999.

The Great Brink's Robbery

FBI page on the robbery, www.fbi.gov/about-us/history/famous-cases/brink's-robbery

The Boston Strangler

Frank, Gerold. *The Boston Strangler*. New York: New American Library, 1966.

Kelly, Susan. *The Boston Stranglers: Updated Edition*. New York: Pinnacle Books, 2013.

The Great Train Robbery

Reynolds, Bruce. *The Autobiography of a Thief*. London: Bantam Press, 1995.

Russell-Pavier, Nick, and Stewart Richards. *The Great Train Robbery: The Crime of the Century*. London: Weidenfeld and Nicholson, 2012.

JFK

Bugliosi, Vincent. *Four Days in November: The Assassination of President John F. Kennedy*. New York: W.W. Norton and Company, 2007.

Kaiser, David. *The Road to Dallas: The Assassination of John F. Kennedy*. Cambridge, Massachusetts: Harvard University Press, 2008.

Summers, Anthony. *Not in Your Lifetime: The Assassination of JFK*. London: Headline, 2013.

Text of the PBS interview with G. Robert Blakey, www.pbs.org/wgbh/pages/frontline/biographies/oswald/interview-g-robert-blakey/

The Moors Murderers

Goodman, Jonathan. *The Moors Murders: The Trial of Myra Hindley and Ian Brady*. London: David and Charles, 1986.

The Theft of the Star of India

Sofianides, Anna E., and George E. Harlow. *Gems and Crystals from the American Museum of Natural History*. New York: Simon and Schuster, 1990.

Martin Luther King Jr.

Branch, Taylor. *At Canaan's Edge: America in the King Years, 1965–68*. New York: Simon and Schuster, 2006.

King, Martin Luther, Jr. *The Autobiography of Martin Luther King Jr*. New York: Warner Books, 1998.

Sides, Hampton. *Hellhound on His Trail: The Stalking of Martin Luther King Jr. and the International Hunt for His Assassin*. New York: Doubleday, 2010.

Jacques Mesrine

Mesrine, Jacques. *L'Instinct de Mort*. Paris: Editions Lattes, 1977 (in French).

Scofield, Carey. *Mesrine: The Life and Death of a Supercrook*. London: Penguin Books, 1980.

The Hijacking of Flight 305

Porteous, Skipp, and Robert Blevins. *Into the Blast: The True Story of D. B. Cooper* (Revised Edition). Seattle: Adventure Books of Seattle, 2010.

Website of the Cooper Research Team, www.citizensleuths.com

Watergate

Bernstein, Carl, and Bob Woodward. *All the President's Men.* New York: Simon and Schuster, 1974.

Emery, Fred. *Watergate: The Corruption of American Politics and the Fall of Richard Nixon.* New York: Touchstone, 1994.

Patty Hearst

Graebner, William. *Patty's Got a Gun: Patricia Hearst in 1970s America.* Chicago: University of Chicago Press, 2008.

The Lufthansa Heist

Pileggi, Nicholas. *Wiseguy: Life in a Mafia Family.* New York: Simon & Schuster, 1985.

Volkman, Ernest, and John Cummings. *The Heist: How a Gang Stole $8,000,000 at Kennedy Airport and Lived to Regret It.* New York: Franklin Watts, 1986.

The Perth Mint Swindle

Lovell, Avon. *The Mickelberg Stitch.* Perth: Creative Research, 1985.

BCCI Scandal

Beatty, James. *The Outlaw Bank: A Wild Ride into the Secret Heart of BCCI.* New York: Random House, 1993.

Text of the US Senate report on the BCCI scandal, www.fas.org/irp/congress/1992_rpt/bcci/

The Backpacker Murders

Small, Clive. *Milat: Inside Australia's Biggest Manhunt.* Sydney: Unwin and Allen, 2014.

Whittaker, Mark, and Les Kennedy. *Sins of the Brother: The Definitive Story of Ivan Milat and the Backpacker Murders.* Sydney: Pan MacMillan Australia, 1998.

Columbine Massacre

Kass, Jeff. *Columbine: A True Crime Story.* Denver: Ghost Road Press, 2009.

The Marilyn Manson article from *Rolling Stone* magazine, www.rollingstone.com/culture/news/columbine-whose-fault-is-it-19990624

Enron Scandal

McLean, Bethany, and Peter Elkind. *The Smartest Guys in the Room: The Amazing Rise and Scandalous Fall of Enron.* New York: Viking, 2003.

The Antwerp Diamond Heist

Selby, Scott Andrew, and Greg Campbell. *Flawless: Inside the Largest Diamond Heist in History.* New York: Union Square Press, 2010.

Article by Joshua Davies from the March 2009 issue of *Wired* magazine that includes an interview with Leonardo Notarbartolo, archive.wired.com/politics/law/magazine/17-04/ff_diamonds

The Hijacking of the *Sirius Star*

Website of Somalia Report, which publishes regular updates on piracy in the East Indian Ocean, www.somaliareport.com

A report on the causes of Somali piracy by the Norwegian academic Stig Jarle Hansen, www.nibr.no/filer/2009-29-ny.pdf

The Madoff Investment Scandal

Henriques, Diana B. *The Wizard of Lies: Bernie Madoff and the Death of Trust.* New York: Henry Holt, 2011.

Markopolos, Harry. *No One Would Listen: A True Financial Thriller.* New York: Wiley, 2010.

The Carlton Cannes Heist

Article on the heist from September 2013 issue of *The Atlantic* magazine, www.theatlantic.com/international/archive/2013/09/a-lone-bandit-and-the-mystery-of-frances-greatest-diamond-heist/278969/

Security camera footage of the robbery, www.youtube.com/watch?v=Upr2USXiN4Y

IMAGE CREDITS